Arnold Wesker

Arnold Wesker

Fragments and Visions

EDITED BY

Anne Etienne and Graham Saunders

intellect

Bristol, UK / Chicago, USA

First published in the UK in 2021 by
Intellect, The Mill, Parnall Road, Fishponds, Bristol, BS16 3JG, UK

First published in the USA in 2021 by
Intellect, The University of Chicago Press, 1427 E. 60th Street,
Chicago, IL 60637, USA

A catalogue record for this book is available from the British Library.

Copy editor: Newgen KnowledgeWorks
Cover designer: Aleksandra Szumlas
Cover photo: Arnold Wesker in Wales in 1979, looking like 'a Spanish courtier'.
Photograph by Dusty Wesker
Production manager: Laura Christopher
Typesetter: Newgen KnowledgeWorks

Print ISBN 9781789383645
ePDF ISBN 9781789383652
ePUB ISBN 9781789383669

Printed and bound by CPI.

To find out about all our publications, please visit our website.
There you can subscribe to our e-newsletter, browse or download our current
catalogue, and buy any titles that are in print.
www.intellectbooks.com

This is a peer-reviewed publication.

Contents

Introduction

Anne Etienne and Graham Saunders

As we write this introduction, Jack Thorne's new play *The End of History* makes its premiere on the main stage of the Royal Court Theatre (RCT). *The End of History* is Thorne's first original play for the Royal Court (having previously adapted in 2013 the film/novel *Let the Right One In*) and has garnered mainly positive reviews. Amongst them, the veteran critic Michael Billington draws attention to its structure – in which over the course of the play we witness the fortunes of a single family in 1997, 2007 and 2017 – and similarities to Arnold Wesker's Royal Court debut, *Chicken Soup with Barley* (1958). However, the analogies with Wesker go far deeper than this insofar as the family in Thorne's play are classic Weskerian idealists, naming their three children Polly, Carl and Tom, after the political radicals Polly Hill, Karl Marx and Tom Paine. In this respect, they are highly reminiscent of characters such as Sarah and Ronnie Kahn in the aforementioned *Chicken Soup*, Beatie Bryant in *Roots* (1959) and Dave and Ada Simmonds in *I'm Talking about Jerusalem* (1960).[1] The relationship between the parents to their children also carries with it similarities to *Chicken Soup*, where Ronnie increasingly rejects his mother's staunch faith in communism, or vice versa in *Roots* where Beatie battles to try to get her parents to embrace the social and political ideals she has learnt in London. Yet, like many of Wesker's characters who seek to make real their utopian visions – characters such as Andrew Cobham in *Their Very Own and Golden City* (1965) and Shylock in the eponymous play (1976), *The End of History* concludes in an atmosphere of defeat. David's wife Sal has died of cancer and their three children who have gathered for the funeral have not followed the ideals that inspired their parents as young people growing up in the 1960s. However, the play ends on a note of hope when David announces that, rather than spend his final years in retirement, he will be selling the family home and moving to Eritrea for five years to work as an engineer on a sewer project (Thorne 2019: 91). A similar resilience is shown by other characters in Wesker's work – though increasingly more in his female roles – from the rebellious spirit of *Chips with Everything* (1962) to the uplifting meeting of two characters who had given up in *Groupie* (2001). Just over sixty years since the Royal Court staged his first play, something of Wesker's spirit lives on in the work and concerns of a significant contemporary British dramatist.

When he died in 2016, Arnold Wesker had written more than 40 plays – with the recent Oberon thematic editions still in print – as well as two novels (one erotic), short stories, poetry and essays. Part of a generation 'who helped change the face of British theatre' his importance in theatre historiography, and in British culture through Centre 42 (C42), cannot be denied (Billington 2016). Yet, he suffered from estrangement for most of his career, and references abound that define his position as marginal, from Ronald Bryden's assessment of him as 'the unique outsider in the British theatre' in his 1966 review of *Their Very Own and Golden City* to Billington's view of Wesker as a 'congenital outsider' in his review of *Denial* (2000: n.pag.). Certainly, a process has taken place whereby a young Jewish working-class pastry chef and aspiring film director at one point found himself in the spotlight between 1958 and 1970 and then gradually relegated to the margins of British theatre. One may therefore ask 'whatever happened to Arnold Wesker', as does Wesker to his female alter ego Lady Betty Lemon, 'née Rivkind from Dalston Junction' (Wesker 2001: 91) in *Whatever Happened to Betty Lemon?* (1986). The question implies either that once 'in the public eye [he] has now slipped from view' or that 'longer processes of time and environmental influences' have transformed the once hopeful, socially committed young writer into an allegedly curmudgeonly, angry old man (Wilcher 1991: 140).

In the case of Wesker, the situation is rather more complex. Undoubtedly, his sudden fame and central involvement in both British artistic and political life through C42 shifted perceptions; additionally, he seemed to attract publicity through his frequent expostulations and even news about his personal life regularly made the headlines. Wesker had become unavoidable in the 1960s. But 'when a society invites one of its rebels inside, a society without whose support serious stage plays and favourable newspaper reviews are virtually impossible, the rebel either accepts or invites contumely or neglect' (Levitt 1998: 103). In questioning established directors such as Peter Hall, flying to Havana to direct the world premiere of *The Four Seasons* in 1968, turning down Prime Minister Harold Wilson's offer of a CBE (Commander of the Order of the British Empire), condemning critics for their lilliputian minds and suing the Royal Shakespeare Company in 1973 over their failure to produce his play *The Journalists*, Wesker showed he was a free spirit. Cumulatively, Wesker almost seemed to invite a backlash and he most certainly received one. Though his plays continued to be produced abroad, Wesker retreated both geographically and spiritually, ensconced within his cottage situated in the Welsh Black Mountains, yet still yearning for the early successes he had experienced on various London stages. When the 'wilderness' years finally receded, it was still through the revival of early work (such as productions of *The Kitchen* at the RCT in 1994 and the National Theatre in 2011, *Chips with Everything* at the National Theatre in 1997, *Chicken Soup with Barley* at the RCT in 2011 and *Roots* at the Donmar in 2013) rather than later work (Wesker 2011b). In a thoughtful obituary, fellow playwright David Edgar commented on this situation in that although 'his great early plays really were great [...] British theatre wasted his later work', a state of affairs that Wesker often bitterly lamented (Edgar 2016: n.pag.).

Wesker's ambivalent place within contemporary British drama can be further illustrated by the lack of updated scholarship since Reade Dornan's edited collection of essays in 1998 together with the aforementioned narrow range of revival productions. Likewise, only a fraction of Wesker's dramatic output tends to be studied (*Roots* was for many years a set A-level text), and he is still persistently remembered and discussed as the author of *The Trilogy*, three plays, staged between 1958 and 1960. This situation fails to accurately reflect both the range of genres Wesker's plays encompass and his willingness to experiment with a number of different styles – moving far beyond the frozen and incorrect image of being a naturalist playwright. Making extensive use of Wesker's deposited archive at the Harry Ransom Center (HRC) in Austin, Texas, this collection of essays aims to consider his long career as a playwright and to establish new insights to both his major as well as lesser known work.

To do so, the volume focuses on two central tropes that have guided Wesker's creative process since the early years: fragments and visions. Visions echo his initial battle cry to the Secretary of the British Trades Union, 'Vision! Vision! Mr Woodcock', in a bid to obtain support for the arts through the extraordinary initiative that became C42 in Britain (Wesker 1960a: n.pag.). Such visions are equally present in his plays where characters are moved to action by the utopian yearnings expressed by characters such as Ronnie in *Jerusalem* and Andrew Cobham in *Golden City* to John Carpenter in *Longitude* (2005).

Fragments also figure for Wesker as an equally positive force. For example, fear of fragmentation motivated Wesker not only to make sense of chaos by communicating to audiences and other artists throughout the C42 project, but also led him to experiment from the mid-1960s onwards with new theatre languages. Wesker claims that '[t]he arrangement of fragments is the artist's purpose in life' (Wesker 1970: 106), yet as Robert Gross points out in his study of *The Old Ones*, Wesker's explanation of this creative process 'remains shadowy' (Gross 1998: 234) in its relation to truth (Wesker 1970: 111). However, Wesker acknowledges how the search for clues shaped his first plays, 'digging back as far as possible to beginnings, in order to explain the present' (Wesker 1970: 113). This approach sheds light on his controversial use of flash-forward in *Golden City* and informs his last plays in various ways. For instance, he revisits impressions of personal neglect in

Groupie[2] where the curmudgeonly, once famous painter Mark Gorman is shaken out of his raucous inertia and self-pity by Mattie Beancourt, a 60-year-old version of the ebullient Beatie Bryant. They break down each other's barriers in passages that echo early tropes, from the sharing of food in an indoors picnic to the sharing of art and questioning of the place of the artist in a gallery.

In his last play, *Joy and Tyranny* (published in 2011), his arrangement of fragments has created a patchwork which bears testament, possibly, to the vision he held throughout his playwriting career. The text itself blends previous plays, including the prominent character and original excerpts from *Betty Lemon*, Connie's lines in *When God Wanted a Son* (1997) revised for the Comedienne's interventions as well as other characters and situations variously inspired by *The Journalists* or *Men Die Women Survive* (1992); it also borrows the episodic structure of *Chips with Everything*; it emphasizes Wesker's concern with musicality by subtitling the play, *à la* Strindberg, 'Arias and variations on the theme of violence'; it opens with a film that serves not only to establish the topic of violence – itself a theme running through his plays – but also to recall his partial training in film as the stage directions dictate the visual movement of the punch by a cinematographic reference: 'just as the bone thrown in jubilation into the air by the victorious ape in Kubrick's "2001" [*sic*] morphs into a space ship' (Wesker 2011a: 15). The play closes with an explosion, but the final words spoken are reminiscent of the lasting influence of Leah Wesker on her son and of an attitude that he carried throughout his career: 'I had a mother, a strong and tiny thing she was who gave me one piece of advice I never forgot. "Talk" she said. "Always say something. Something is remembered" ' (57). That this idea is expressed by Betty Lemon, a character that Wesker created as a metaphor '[f]or last days, last thoughts, last fights' (AW 1986), confirms the impression that in *Joy and Tyranny* he has weaved together pieces of his work which he wanted remembered (AW 1986: n.pag.).

Ultimately, what Wesker feared, and for which he condemned the Labour party in 1968, was 'fragmentation of vision' (Wesker 1970: 107), a fate which he publicly challenged in a letter titled 'Prole playwrights', a few months after the success of his first produced play, *Chicken Soup with Barley*:

> I didn't write *Chicken Soup* simply because I wanted to amuse you with 'working-class types' but because I saw my characters within the compass of a personal vision. I have a personal vision, you know, and I will not be tolerated as a passing phase.
>
> (Wesker 1959: n.pag.)

This book attempts to navigate between these two driving forces whereby fragments can become the best ways to understand Wesker's overall vision.

This is reflected in two parts, which address different periods of his career with alternate critical focuses. The first part, 'Early Visions', outlines portraits of Wesker's early career. As such it opens with two chapters, on C42 and on his relationship with playwright Harold Pinter, that frame the following case studies on three of his early plays: *Roots*, *Chips with Everything* and *Their Very Own and Golden City*. The second part, 'Unifying Fragments', examines alternative but connected facets of his life and later work, from his reputation as a 'difficult' playwright to the lasting importance of community in his plays. Building on previous studies by major Wesker scholars Glenda Leeming, Ronald Hayman, Robert Wilcher and Reade Dornan, the authors have proposed new insights and potential for future investigation.

Edward Bond's prologue to the critical chapters is both a personal account of his early recollections of Wesker and a vivid picture of the seminal impact that the RCT made on their own writing careers.

Another feature that contributes to the originality of the volume has been its recourse to extensive archival material. In 2018, the Harry Ransom Center (HRC) completed work on gathering the entirety of Arnold Wesker's archive. This consisted of 408 boxes acquired through four accessions.[3] Wesker himself in a mordant essay entitled 'What are we writers worth?' weighed his collected life's work at three and a half tonnes (Wesker 2010: 151). Wesker's archive, in much the same way as the collections of Samuel Beckett's papers at the University of Reading and Harold Pinter's collection at the British Library, has opened up exciting vistas offering researchers entirely new perspectives on the work of these writers. While the first two accessions of the Wesker collection were catalogued by 2004, the last two, dispatched in 2016 and 2018, still remain uncatalogued at the time of publication of this volume. However, Dr Eric Colleary, Curator of Theatre & Performing Arts at the HRC, granted unprecedented access to editor Anne Etienne. This has included access to previously restricted material. Many of the contributors have taken advantage of the materials deposited in the collection, and this volume represents the first stage in an 'archival turn' that offers both a major reassessment and the hope that it will promote further interest in the work of Arnold Wesker.

For his involvement in C42, Wesker was often called the English Planchon. While he must have been flattered, Wesker's early portrait of Roger Planchon betrays not only the extraordinary qualities he lends the Frenchman but also the impossibility to find a matching counterpart among his heroes, let alone himself:

> Consider one person with, say, the administrative capabilities of George Devine, the splendid vulgarity of Behan, the friendly belligerency of Lindsay Anderson, the gentle intelligence of Karel Reisz and the vision of Joan

Littlewood – all in one! Planchon seems to have just that, and he's a fine actor into the bargain!

(Wesker 1960b: n.pag.)

In his chapter, Lawrence Black charts the impossible task of leading C42 and argues that the contradictions that befell C42, in its push for a radical cultural agenda against personal, political, economic and radical counter-cultural forces, made its failure inevitable. In 1974, Jean-Louis Barrault's production of *Rabelais* at the Roundhouse (C42's London home) opened to the infamous protest of naked actors condemning the theft of the Roundhouse by bourgeois interests, claiming that 'The Roundhouse was meant to be used by workers […] It has been turned over to the commercial theatre' (AW 1974: n.pag.). Though Wesker, present with Barrault in the auditorium, was embarrassed by the event, one may infer that his abandonment of the C42 social and artistic project to coffee shop entrepreneur and former civil servant George Hoskins's commercial interests in 1970 hinged on the same realization: 'It is an over-simplification, but it is near enough to the truth to be said' (AW 1974: n.pag.). Yet, Black points to C42's legacy represented by the Roundhouse, as an emblematic and 'chic' venue that has endured to this day by reinventing itself beyond the initial C42 vision.

Graham Saunders's chapter traces the relationship, both personal and theatrical, between Harold Pinter and Wesker. Both were near contemporaries who grew up in the same Hackney neighbourhood in London's East End, and both came to prominence as representatives of the 'new drama' in Britain during the late 1950s. The chapter draws on correspondence from Harold Pinter's archive, which is held at the British Library. The correspondence is wide ranging and touches upon the dramatists' shared Jewish identity and their views on theatre. What emerges is an affectionate, if distant, relationship, but in this reappraisal, the use to which the pair are often used by critics as bookends to differentiate between the differing stylistic, thematic and political paths that British theatre took after 1955 is misplaced.

James Macdonald, who directed *Roots* at the Donmar Warehouse in 2013, recalls his trip to Norfolk, looking for the roots of the play with the assistance of Dusty (Beatie Bryant) Bicker's family. In his research on this school syllabus play that started as a commercial flop, Macdonald suggests that the legacy of Wesker is to have created a new form of drama: 'politics as it is lived by people'. At the same time, Macdonald also points out that the lasting beauty of the play resides in its lyricism. This ability of Wesker to have politics living on stage and to write theatrical poems is raised by French directors in a later chapter.

Echoes of C42 are evident in *Roots*, in the opposition between Beatie's and her family's cultural expectations; they are also to be found in *Chips with Everything*, as pointed out by John Bull in his case study of the context and development of

6

the play between 1960 and 1997. In *Chips with Everything*, Wesker's most commercially successful play in the United Kingdom, Bull argues that much hinges on the enigmatic character of Pip, Wesker's first upper-class figure who voices both his fascination and despair at the working classes' obsession for 'chips with everything'. Bull's chapter makes use of archival documents at the HRC to trace how Wesker shaped and changed this play about a group of RAF conscripts before the appearance of Pip very late into the writing process, possibly influenced by Brecht's *Galileo* in more ways than the play's structure.

Chris Megson's chapter resonates with evocations of C42 in that it looks at the theatrical illustration of Wesker's cultural endeavours with C42, *Their Very Own and Golden City* (1965), a play that Dexter deemed to be too close to Wesker's experiences and therefore refused to direct (Hayman 1973–74: 92). Disregarded by Dexter, it was similarly overlooked by the critics, repeating the fate of his previous play, its companion piece, *The Four Seasons* (1965). This period marked the beginning of Wesker's commercial and critical descent. However, Megson's meticulous study unpacks the play's merits against its controversial contexts and suggests its inclusion as a significant early example of being a state-of-the-nation play.

Wesker's career has undoubtedly suffered from his reputation for being disputatious and confrontational. While contemporaries such as John Osborne, John Arden and Edward Bond have also been portrayed as fellow members of the 'awkward squad', this reputation did not manifest itself until much later in their careers. By contrast, Wesker, with C42, made enemies from as early on as the 1960s in his battles with the trade unions and Harold Wilson's government. His close friend the novelist Margaret Drabble explains his tendency to fight as emerging from two impulses:

> unlike most people who feel hurt, he doesn't care who knows it: most of us are restrained by a kind of pride from answering back to our attackers, but not Wesker. He conducts long battles in newspapers: he is even prepared (and considers he ought) to take more serious offenders to court. [...] He doesn't merely brood, he takes action, which is what he was brought up to do.
>
> (Drabble 1975: 25)

Harry Derbyshire argues that the public attacks Wesker waged upon his critics was initially launched out of a sense of personal hurt before they became a point of principle. In the long run, the theatre Establishment prevailed because 'he [Wesker] refused to flatter the theatre elite' (Pascal 2016: n.pag.). For Derbyshire, the undiplomatic interventions serve to highlight the unspoken rules of British cultural discourse that Wesker had rashly transgressed to his great cost. As evoked by Saunders, Pinter and Wesker found themselves on opposing sides of the Iraq War debate, and Derbyshire's chapter examines Wesker's political views on a cluster of issues, including Israel, the Salman Rushdie *fatwā* and 9/11, which relate in complex ways to his cultural identity as a Jew.

Wesker had never been religiously observant – speaking as late as 1970, he had only just recently, it seemed, begun to gain a sense of identity as Jewish and with it a shared sense of suffering and persecution (Hayman 1970: 4–5). Yet, Jews and Judaism have always been an intermittent concern that runs through his work from *Chicken Soup with Barley* (1958) to *Blood Libel* (1996, written in 1991). In a memorial speech in 2016, Mike Leigh drew attention to Wesker's Jewishness, raising an overlooked alternative perspective to the angry young men of British theatre in the late 1950s:

> If you were a nice Jewish boy born in the 1940s and you were not called some-thing Old Testament like Michael, David or Jonathan, you would be Anthony, Leslie, or Jeffrey. Half a generation earlier the fashion had been the likes of Harold, Bernard or Arnold. [...] So imagine how exciting it was for the tiny handful of us who were concerned with [...] culture to discover that not just one but three young East End Jewish dramatists had burst onto the scene: a Harold, a Bernard and an Arnold!
>
> (Leigh 2016: n.pag.)

Sue Vice's chapter on the representation of Jewishness within Wesker's plays chooses to look at three examples from the latter part of his career in what she describes as 'case-studies of antisemitism in different national and historical con-texts'. All three – *Shylock*, *Blood Libel* and *Badenheim 1939* (2010) – are set at specific periods (medieval England, renaissance Italy and Nazi-occupied Austria, respectively), a strategy that Vice sees as a deliberate shift from plays such as *The Old Ones* (1970) in which Jewish characters feature, but the issue of Judaism or antisemitism is not at the forefront.

The professional controversies explored in Derbyshire's study most often stemmed from his work being disregarded by directors or critics in the United Kingdom. However, this reputation did not follow Wesker abroad, where his work met with more lasting success. While the international scope of his career deserves a volume in itself, Anne Etienne's chapter focuses on the case of France, a country where Wesker and his then girlfriend Dusty spent a year in 1956, at her request, in Paris. The chapter makes extensive use of archival material and interviews car-ried out with the directors of some of his plays to explore how the French audience knew and received his work. While it reveals occasional differences in opinions and of approach between Wesker and his French directors, it also reveals stark discrepancies in appreciations of the plays compared to the United Kingdom and a keen understanding of Wesker's creative process.

In an interview with a French journalist in 1968, Wesker expresses his writing process in visual terms: 'In organising facts, I modify them. For instance, I will darken the story to make more vivid the sudden explosions of light that set it aglow at specific points' (Schifres 1968: 98). This tendency to contrast can of course be found in his shift between monologues and snappy dialogues, the one enlightening or emphasizing the other, but also giving it the rhythm that will complement the play's colours. Wesker also had recourse to visual references when describing his plays' aesthetics. For instance, in comparing his historical plays, he suggested that with *Blood Libel* he 'wanted to build a drama out of large primary blocks rather than minute detail' to be found in the more naturalistic *Shylock* and *Caritas* (1981), concluding it to be 'the difference between naturalistic and abstract painting, between, say, Constable and Ben Nicholson' (AW 1991: n.pag.). His designer for *Annie Wobbler*, Pamela Howard, not only relates how their collaboration began but also brings to light and analyses the visual talent displayed in his little-known drawings. Much like he described his plays in visual terms, Howard points to the presence of the stage in the way he approached a space.

When Arnold Wesker came on a visit to University College Cork in 2004, he wanted to talk about his mother because of the pivotal influence she had had on him. Leah Wesker was the first woman in his life to find a theatrical representation as Sarah Kahn, and she was followed by Dusty as Beatie Bryant. Both Margaret Rose and Glenda Leeming have devoted groundbreaking studies to the woman plays, respectively, on the tradition of the monodrama and on his portrayal of women's experiences, analysing how his writing questions their sense of identity against dominant discourses (see Dornan 1998: 129–36; 194–08). Based on extensive archival and empirical research, Michael Fry's chapter tracks the figure of the dramatist in the one-woman plays, in various forms and habits. Indeed, Wesker acknowledged that *Betty Lemon* was a self-portrait, as discussed in Anne Etienne's chapter on French productions, and *Four Portraits – of Mothers* was further inspired by familiar stories rather than 'social objectives': 'One is my aunt. The unmarried one and failed one are based on people I know. The fourth mother is inspired by my wife' (AW 1983: n.pag.). Beyond these personal experiences, Wesker explained that he found 'women more interesting than men. They seem to me more courageous, more perceptive, more vivacious than men' (cited in Attallah 1997: 50). Though John Dexter had indeed suggested, 'it seems to me as though all that you've written belongs to a female and not a male', Fry's careful exploration of Wesker as a woman raises counterarguments (cited in Hayman 1973– 74: 95).

In her insightful article, Margaret Drabble noted that community was a dominant image in his plays: 'a family, a group of friends, even a group of National

Servicemen. They make community, often against the odds' (Drabble 1975: 28). In the final chapter, Robert Wilcher qualifies the recurrent theme of the community and the individual as 'Wesker's [contradictory] commitment to socialism and humanism' through a discussion that includes a wide range of work before ending in a detailed look at *Beorhtel's Hill* (1988), a community play involving the local residents of the new Essex town of Basildon. For Wilcher, in *Beorhtel's Hill*, the living community of townspeople as performers claim the play for themselves as an embodiment of its history – a culmination and distillation of the ideas that Wesker first developed in the *Trilogy*.

Ten years ago, Wesker e-mailed Anne Etienne his latest news: 'Chichester Festival Theatre have finally bought my new(ish) play GROUPIE for their next season; and the Royal Court are reviving CHICKEN SOUP WITH BARLEY for late 2010. Who knows, I may be discovered!' (Wesker 2009: n.pag.). This final exclamation encompasses Wesker's sense of tragic irony, which he defined as tongue-in-cheek humour, but also the acute awareness of his career at this point. He was in effect discovered all over again in those final years through successful productions on London's main stages of his early work. This collection of essays is an attempt at discovering Wesker in a theatre career lasting over fifty years by synthesizing unifying fragments to the portrait of a 'gentle man who fought for his ideals', a challenging writer whose plays were shot through with social and artistic visions (Nathan 2016: n.pag.).

Acknowledgements

Lady Dusty Wesker has contributed unstintingly to the volume in terms of her time in answering numerous questions. She has also granted access to her personal photographic albums that help to draw a fuller portrait of Wesker's domestic life and early career.

We would like to thank the staff at the Harry Ransom Center in Austin, Texas, the British Library, and the V&A Performance Collection. We are grateful to the School of English and to the College of Arts, Celtic Studies and Social Sciences, University College Cork, for their financial assistance, and to Professor Lee Jenkins for her support and encouragement.

NOTES
1. The dates throughout the book refer to the plays' first production, be it national or international.
2. Originally commissioned by Radio 4, it was first given a reading at the Chichester Festival Theatre in July before being broadcast in November 2001, with Barbara Windsor and

Timothy West directed by Ned Chaillet. Foreign productions followed, but every British attempt has foundered so far.

3. Throughout the book, references to the Wesker Papers at the HRC have reflected these four accessions. Therefore, AW refers to the first accession and AW2 to the second one, followed by the box and file code. The third and fourth accessions (AW3 and AW4) only have box numbers because they were uncatalogued at the time of writing.

REFERENCES

Attallah, Naim (1997), 'Never quite out of the wilderness: The playwright at sixty five', *Literary Review*, June, pp. 49–52.

Billington, Michael (2000), 'Never trust a therapist', *The Guardian*, 20 May, https://www.theguardian.com/culture/2000/may/20/1. Accessed 10 May 2019.

—— (2016), 'Arnold Wesker, the radical bard of working Britain', *The Guardian*, 13 April, https://www.theguardian.com/stage/2016/apr/13/arnold-wesker-radical-bard-of-working-britain-class-plays. Accessed 6 May 2019.

Dornan, Reade (ed.) (1998), *Arnold Wesker: A Casebook*, New York: Garland.

Drabble, Margaret (1975), 'Arnold Wesker – A Profile', *The New Review*, 1:11, pp. 25–30.

Edgar, David (2016), 'Arnold Wesker applied his life to his times – and showed us greatness', *The Guardian*, 13 April, https://www.theguardian.com/stage/2016/apr/13/arnold-wesker-playwright-david-edgar. Accessed 29 November 2018.

Gross, Robert (1998), 'Wisdom in Fragments: *The Old Ones*', in R. Dornan (ed.), *Arnold Wesker. A Casebook*, London: Garland, pp. 233–51.

Hayman, Ronald (1973–74), 'Interview with Arnold Wesker and John Dexter', *Transatlantic Review*, 48, Winter, pp. 89–99.

Leigh, Mike (2016), 'Our teenage hero – an appreciation', Wesker memorial, Royal Court Theatre, 9 October.

Levitt, Paul (1998), 'Well-nigh Wesker', in R. Dornan (ed.), *Arnold Wesker. A Casebook*, London: Garland, pp. 97–108.

Martin-Barbaz, Jean-Louis, and Etienne, Anne (2018), Telephone interview, 11 December.

Nathan, John (2016), 'Tributes to Sir Arnold Wesker', *The Jewish Chronicle*, 14 April, https://www.thejc.com/lifestyle/features/tributes-to-sir-arnold-wesker-a-gentle-man-who-fought-for-his-ideals-1.64103. Accessed 14 May 2019.

Pascal, Julia (2016), 'Sir Arnold Wesker obituary', *The Guardian*, 13 April, https://www.theguardian.com/stage/2016/apr/13/sir-arnold-wesker-obituary. Accessed 9 May 2019.

Schifres, Alain (1968), '*Racines* triomphera-t-il à Paris', *Réalités*, 275, December, pp. 98–100.

Thorne, Jack (2019), *The End of History*, London: Nick Hern Books.

Wesker, Arnold (1959), 'Letter: Prole playwrights', *New Statesman*, 28 February, p. 293.

—— (1960a), 'Vision! Vision! Mr Woodcock', *New Statesman*, 30 July, p. 300.

—— (1960b), 'Roger Planchon's theatre', *New Statesman*, 3 September, n.pag.

—— (1970), *Fears of Fragmentation*, London: Jonathan Cape.

—— (2001), *One Woman Plays*, London: Methuen.

—— (2009), E-mail to Anne Etienne, 11 December.

—— (2010), 'What are We Writers Worth', in *Wesker on Theatre*, London: Oberon, pp. 149–55.

—— (2011a), *Joy and Tyranny*, London: Oberon.

—— (2011b), 'It does feel as though the wilderness may be receding', Interview with Andrew Dickson, *The Guardian*, 10 June, https://www.theguardian.com/stage/video/2011/jun/10/arnold-wesker-chicken-soup-with-barley. Accessed 18 June 2019.

Wesker, Arnold Papers (AW) (1969), Letter from Claude Régy to Wesker, 14 May, Austin, Texas: Harry Ransom Center, Box 36.12.

—— (1974), 'Naked men ejected in theatre protest', *The Times*, 19 March, Austin, Texas: Harry Ransom Center, Box 31.5.

—— (1983), Draft interview with Patricia Niedzwiecki, July, Austin, Texas: Harry Ransom Center, Box 2.8.

—— (1986), Letter to Jean-Michel Ribes, 13 May, Austin, Texas: Harry Ransom Center, Box 102.9.

—— (1991), Notes on *William of Norwich*, 23 October, Austin, Texas: Harry Ransom Center, Box 19.8.

FIGURE 1: Arnold Wesker in the studio of Raul Martinez, Cuba, 1964. Photo by Luc Chessex.

Prologue: It Matters

Edward Bond

I first met Arnold at the Royal Court Writers' Group[1] together with John Arden,
Keith Johnson, Ann Jellicoe, Wole Soyinka and David Cregan. The group had originally been larger. John Osborne and other established writers were not active
in the group when I attended it. We held evening meetings once a week in a house
by Hammersmith Bridge on the Thames.[2] The organizer was then Bill Gaskill.
Later I learnt that George Devine, an original leader of the group, had said that
I was one of two writers he should get rid of because I would never do anything.[3]
Bill – and probably George Devine – decided we would not discuss the structure
and techniques of drama. Instead we should learn actors' problems and their practical techniques. Working as actors we would choose situations to improvise on.
It was useful, sometimes in surprising ways. In one improvisation, I and another
writer were shut in a space rocket and were to travel alone in it for the rest of our
lives. After lift-off, there was a tense silence. Suddenly, spontaneously, I started
to tap my fingers on my knee and hum dum-di-dum-di-dum. The room exploded
in laughter. No matter how complicated and extreme, whatever else happens
drama, if it is to be comprehensive and adequate, must come from simple things.
At another time, I improvised *King Lear*'s Gloucester. Gloucester was blind and
was supposed to think he had thrown himself to death off a cliff. Then he should
pass out. I threw myself off, but instead of passing out I got to my feet and staggered forwards, groping to find the cliff edge again and throw myself off it. That
second fall would have been immense. I couldn't do it, I am not an actor. But a
writer must imagine it. All reality would be in the second fall. All drama writing
comes from the second fall.

So improvising was useful. But I was deeply frustrated. I needed to learn in what
role drama cast the audience and how it did this. If I didn't know how, I couldn't
know why. If I didn't know why, then drama was only a story – it might be a con
trick, a book whose pages were turned by the wind. After the Second World War,
the Royal Court was a cultural lifebelt. Before the war, UK theatre had been in
the censor's straightjacket. It didn't struggle in it, it relaxed in it. Instead of tragedy, there could be sadness or melancholy; instead of unfillable desire, there were

15

adulterous weekends; its polite Georgian poetry was not meant to be understood by the chauffeur or the tram driver. The allies had defeated Germany, but from now on Europe would be haunted by the shadow of Hitler hanging round the death camps. Europe was a continent dripping with blood, the air thick with the ashes of buildings and people. Britain had looked into the abyss. But all major victories cause a revolution in the victor's society more profound than defeat in the enemy's. You may recover from defeat, but you are tempted by victory. The angry young men knew, if only incoherently, that the ultimate cause of the death camps was class society. Britain was a rigid class society. Viscerally the angry young men were angrier with their own society than with Hitler. They were ex-army working or middle class and some of the working class had been to university. They wanted a new drama uncluttered by tradition that could directly express their anger. Before the war continental avant-garde drama had changed, ultimately because of the great European political revolutions. Picasso wrote plays, Sir Alfred Munnings did not.[4] This new drama, especially in the work of Michel Saint-Denis, had radically influenced George Devine. He passionately wanted to bring it to the Royal Court. It was a mission. But who would write it? He commissioned plays from established British novelists.[5] It didn't work. The wish to recapture the past clashed with the need to create the new. The novelists-cum-playwrights created a respectable tedium. Osborne's *Look Back in Anger* (1956) exploded and blew all that away. *Look Back* contained a vicious attack on the middle class, who had been the patrons of pre-war theatre – but ironically that is the theatre it rejuvenated. Basically *Look Back* is a very middle-class play. And later it turned out that many of the new writers, in theatre and elsewhere, were reactionary.[6] At first this wasn't noticed. The shock of war couldn't be ignored, and to prove (if only to itself) that it was progressive the Royal Court strongly associated itself with CND and went on the Aldermarston pilgrimages.[7]

Harold Pinter was thought to bring to London the less effete 'vitality' of provincial theatre. His hatred of militarism was passionate and sincere – and he voted for Thatcher.[8] How could that happen, how could it possibly be? Thatcher was then the closest to being a fascist of any British prime minister. (Since then that position has been contested.) The remark is contentious. But we must learn to judge people and ideas not by what they at first present themselves to be but by what they must inevitably become. It matters and will matter more in the future. Thatcher and Reagan were responsible for Trump, Johnson, the 2008 financial collapse, Brexit, the new fascism in Europe and the horrors that are still on their way. Thatcher's smile in the notorious photograph of her in the gun turret of a tank shows all the cultural and psychological distortions, confusions and incomprehensions of our politics.[9] This ambiguity is in all Pinter's plays and in the corruption of our present establishment theatre. Ironically, the ambiguity is the core subject of drama

16

itself: the struggle for justice. And the human catastrophe is that drama – but only when it is logically and consequentially acted – is the one art that must authenticate itself morally and even politically. It comes directly from the primary neonatal brain. Bad drama is a time bomb under society. But we don't even have that. We have an entertainment industry. A eunuch's fig leaf.

To be fair to Pinter, he did write a play called *Betrayal* (1978) – but it was not about the betrayal of a society, or the dead sacrificed in war, or a generation of young playwrights, it was about one of his own marital infidelities. *Betrayal* was a West End success. Not every writer is fortunate enough to make money out of their infidelity.

Wesker could never have voted for Thatcher. It is impossible.

I owe a lot to the Royal Court Writers' Group. I also owe a lot to my frustration with it. Beyond Sloane Square dramatists were struggling to create a modern drama uncorrupted by ambiguities. Bill Gaskill's autobiographical account of his time as its Artistic Director unconsciously records the Royal Court's own ambiguities.[10] His theatrical life-blood was driven by the classics and their great interpreters – Edith Evans, Sybil Thorndike, John Gielgud. The nuances of their diction and expressiveness revealed the unstated. How you said it compensated for how little you said. Really it was all an echo of the pre-war theatre that the Court was supposed to replace. At the same time, the Court had to accommodate this subtlety with the new, often brash and obscene, theatre from America. To give an example, a play in which grotesque characters with huge papier-mâché heads scrawled obscenities on the set's walls.[11] Edith Evans did not scrawl lavatory lewdities on walls.

First it was necessary to get rid of the Lord Chamberlain's censorship. It was a matter not only of 'bad' language but also of the actions the 'badness' of the language demanded. The censorship was a means of using theatre to lie, not a means of preserving cultural standards. When the Lord Chamberlain tried to ban my early work, I refused the customary compromise of trading one word for another or one incident for another. When his censorship was abolished, it became possible to be more honest. But I was still frustrated. I did not know what drama's role was – not just the story of the play but how, by bringing the profound to the surface, drama was prior to daily reality.

I had a simple plan: a structure of drama. My first play (*The Pope's Wedding* in 1962) was homage to the life in early medieval British drama and literature. Then I wrote a pentad cycle of plays that related to Shakespeare's cycle. In it he had laid out the site of drama. I started not with a history but a contemporary play – *Saved* (1965). The next four plays were: *Early Morning* in 1968 (modern English history and eternity), *Narrow Road to the Deep North* in 1968 (colonialism and salvation), *Lear* in 1971 (because in it Shakespeare sought to combine the two problems – the social and the personal – that fracture each other) and to end *The Sea* (1973). *The Sea* is in the place of *The Tempest* (*c*.1610). But I ended it not in reconciliation and resolution but in a coming war, in mid-sentence, not in the silence of peace but of the battlefield, as if the soldier had been shot in mid-sentence. The cycle mapped out the problem and responsibility of contemporary drama. Bill Gaskill found no point in any of it. I knew his craft intimately and had written *Narrow Road* specifically for him. He said it meant nothing to him and declined to direct it. The director chosen in his place was good.[12] But the main actor had made his part bombastic, empty bravura. The day before the play was to open, I spoke to Gaskill. That afternoon he stood alone in the stalls. The actor was alone on stage. For three hours Gaskill took him through the play. Every line, incident and word in it. Nothing wasted. He was calm. Ruthless. Lucid. Awesomely precise. In perfect control. He totally changed the actor's performance and its effect in the play. It was startling. I've never seen anything so extraordinary. Yet when I first gave Gaskill the play, he had said he didn't understand it. Gaskill was the best stage director of my lifetime. But the opportunity to start a new drama was missed. The war's violence was too great, peace too demanding, the new world too threatening. Perhaps there was still even a remainder of pre-war capriciousness. Gaskill left the Court to join Max Stafford-Clark and the Joint Stock Company. That was the sort of theatre that was no longer needed – Stalinist dilettantism. One of Bill's closest colleagues said, 'Bill has finally taken the Court off the map'. The Royal Court was lost. It still is. I briefly tried to work with the Royal Shakespeare Company and the Royal National Theatre (incidentally Sir Peter Hall also voted for Thatcher, and his great ambition was to find and direct a new successful West End-Broadway musical). I was dismayed by the directors' mechanical shallowness and the reaction forced on them by their ambition to work on Broadway and in Hollywood. I went abroad and worked mostly in France.

I write about Wesker but till this sentence I've used his name only once. But all the time I've been writing intensely about him and with a collegiate closeness.

To do its real work, theatre must be an Institution of all theatre workers. No one theatre worker is any good without the other good workers. The Royal Court could not build an 'Institution of Drama', a stage on which Wesker could have radically influenced culture and made it human. 'Institution' not in the sense of a rigid structure, 'Institution' in the sense of a group of people interested in improving the work of each other. Drama is the logic of reality – it has, you may say, its own purpose, or that at the least it shares the purposes of humanness, and if you abuse it, it first trivializes and corrupts you and then destroys you. I think that there has never been a generation of young UK dramatists as gifted as the present one. If they are wasted, then many other things will be wasted.

Wesker was from an Eastern European family. He knew about war and persecution and that peace may be as destructive as war. War has never led to peace and all peace has led to war. Knowing that made him a dramatist. In him there was a whole generation's hunger for humanness, and I think that hunger can't be lost or fully satisfied. He had a decency and a sensitivity that seemed to stun the air around him like the stillness after an explosion. He is dead but his plays breathe. I have an image of him. One evening after leaving the Royal Court Writers' Group, we crossed Hammersmith Bridge. He had an inflated blue balloon. Sometimes the occasion produces the right prop. He climbed an ornate Victorian lamppost at the foot of the bridge. He was not slim, even a bit overweight, but he shimmied up the lamppost to tie the balloon to the top. We walked away and he left the balloon to be found there by people going to work in the morning.

NOTES

1. The Writer's Group was originally set up by the Royal Court's first Artistic Director George Devine in January 1958, after which it was taken over by William Gaskill. The Group broke up in 1960. See Philip Roberts, *The Royal Court and the Modern Stage*, Cambridge: CUP, 1999, p. 63.
2. Little and McLaughlin locate the meetings being held 'in an old paint shop in Flood Street, Chelsea'. See Ruth Little and Emily McLaughlin, *The Royal Court Theatre: Inside Out*, London: Oberon, 2007, p. 43.
3. This has been well documented. William Gaskill has spoken about Devine's dislike of Wesker's work in Gesdnam A. Doty and Billy J. Harbin (eds) *Inside the Royal Court Theatre, 1956–1981: Artists Talk*, London: University of Louisiana Press, 1990, p. 47 and Philip Roberts, *The Royal Court and the Modern Stage*, Cambridge: CUP, 1999, p. 72. Wesker has also spoken about Devine not understanding his work. See Harriet Devine, *Looking Back: Playwrights at the Royal Court 1956–2006*, London: Faber, p. 284.
4. Sir Alfred Munnings (1878–59) was a celebrated British artist who specialized in the painting of horses, often within the context of warfare.
5. Most notably these included Angus Wilson's *The Mulberry Bush* (1956) and Nigel Dennis's own stage adaptation of his novel *Cards of Identity* (1956) and a later play, *The Making of Moo* (1957).
6. Apart from Osborne, John Wain, Kingsley Amis and John Braine, whose novels *Hurry on Down* (1953), *Lucky Jim* (1955) and *Room at the Top* (1957) associated them as Angry Young Men in the 1950s, but later saw them becoming increasingly reactionary in their views.
7. Members of the English Stage Company who involved themselves in the CND Aldermaston protest walks included Peter Gill, George Devine, Ann Jellicoe, Keith Johnston, John Osborne, Anthony Page, Wole Soyinka and Arnold Wesker.

8. Harold Pinter and Peter Hall (as Bond later points out) both voted for Mrs Thatcher's 1979 government, partly out of their mutual disgust at the union actions that resulted in a series of disruptive strikes at the National Theatre. Pinter has subsequently spoken about bitterly regretting his decision action within weeks of casting his vote. See Michael Billington, *The Life and Work of Harold Pinter*, London: Faber, 1996, p. 306.

9. A photograph taken on 17 September 1986 when Mrs Thatcher visited a NATO training camp in Fallingbostel, near Hamburg Germany.

10. Bond is referring to William Gaskill's *A Sense of Direction: Life at the Royal Court*, London: Faber, 1988.

11. It is likely that Bond is referring to a visiting production in 1969 to the Royal Court by the American Bread and Puppet Theatre with their production *The Cry of the People for Meat*.

12. Jane Howell.

PART 1

EARLY VISIONS

FIGURE 2: Arnold Wesker in front of the Roundhouse, July 1967. Photo by William Glenesk.

1

Radical Chic? Centre 42, the Roundhouse and How Culture Countered Wesker in the 1960s

Lawrence Black

Centre 42 (C42) was Arnold Wesker's 1960s' odyssey – preoccupying his emotional and creative energies, and in the end ultimately draining them. The fame Wesker found in *The Trilogy* (1958–60) gave a platform to launch a bold cultural-political initiative. *The Trilogy* depicted working-class life and segued Jewishness, political belonging and socialism. Arguing that art and culture were central to the Labour movement's progress in a 1960 Trades Union Congress (TUC) motion (no.42), Wesker's initiative ran local festivals in 1961 and 1962. In 1964, it inherited the Roundhouse in North London, which became its spatial and symbolic home. By 1970, C42 came to the end of the line – struggling to synthesize and enhance working-class cultural life, failing to secure funding from the unions and Arts Council of Great Britain (ACGB) and superseded by other popular and counter-cultural activities at the Roundhouse.

Exploring C42's diverse activities and volatile narrative in itself resembles in some ways a social history of the 1960s. In the opening piece of *Radical Chic & Mau-Mauing the Flak Catchers* (1970), Tom Wolfe's account of a Black Panther gathering with the liberal elite of Manhattan society at composer Leonard Bernstein's apartment in 1970 is suggestive of the same contradictions inherent in C42 (Wolfe 1970). There was a similar air of 'radical chic' to C42: a socialist playwright wanting to take art to the workers but marooned in a London post-industrial building which was envisaged as C42's base, together with a glamorous cast of (sometimes) supporters and (supposed) political and artistic allies. The argument here is that whilst C42 nurtured varied cultural activity, it was thwarted by countervailing tastes, practices and policy agendas. The wider culture – artistic, but also political, financial, personal and popular – also countered Wesker's vision.

Wesker's 1960s: Cultural and Political Context

Wesker's sixties celebrity was notable. He was close to Arts Minister Jennie Lee and Prime Minister Harold Wilson as well as a member of the government's Youth Service Development Council from 1960 to 1966. *Tatler* profiled him in 1965 and by 1967 *Roots* was an A-level text. During the tumultuous summer of 1967, Wesker was offered and declined a CBE. *Roots*' off-Broadway run in 1961 had critics comparing Wesker to Clifford Odets (Anon. 1961b). His play *Chips with Everything* was a Broadway hit in 1963 – 'as rollicking as Sgt. Bilko' and casting Wesker as part of 'the British invasion' (Anon. 1963c: n.pag.). The buzz was such that Wesker sold the film rights for £10,000 in 1964 to kick-start the Roundhouse appeal by sponsoring a pillar and some bricks (AW 1963b).

Wesker was the personification, a *cliché* even, of the 1960s radicalism. Active in the Campaign for Nuclear Disarmament (CND) and a founder of the Committee of 100 in 1960 along with Doris Lessing, Lindsay Anderson, Shelagh Delaney and John Osborne, Wesker marched to Aldermaston, was arrested on a sit-down protest and served a month in Brixton Prison in 1961 (AW 1960a; Wesker 1995: 610, 619). While critical of the Soviet Union, Wesker visited Cuba in 1964 and 1968, and although he condemned Castro's persecution of homosexuality, the British-Cuba Association headquarters was situated at the Roundhouse (Wesker 1969: 15, 21).[1]

C42 and the Roundhouse were part of the 1960s' DIY ethos of social innovation and underground entrepreneurialism (Curtis & Sanderson 2004: 1) and the stages for the dramas and debates about popular, elite and counter-cultural content: London and the regions, the role of the state and the post-industrial use of buildings. Longer-term, it can be argued that they became the model for arts centres and for forging 'culture' as a political terrain.

In another register, C42 cast itself as a cultural wing of the New Left – an intellectual-activist political formation that from 1956 proposed an alternative vision of socialism to both social democracy and Soviet communism. Culture was the New Left's keyword, and C42 assumed that culture, in both content and practice, should be political. Yet, most accounts of the New Left point to a waning of this ideal in its 'second' generation, where it turned from 1962 to theory rather than such practice as the Soho Partisan café, Left Clubs, new wave cinema or Wesker plays at the Royal Court (Rustin 1989: 117–28).

This relationship can be found in the *May Day Manifesto* movement (1967–68), a revival of the 'first' generation New Left – Wesker was a signatory of the original 1967 *New Left May Day Manifesto* (Ponnuswami 1998: 138). Yet, despite being edited by Raymond Williams, it said little about 'culture'. This extended to its critique of 'Labourism', in which it argued that it was not just a hostile culture that marginalized the left in national life, but that the British Labour Party and trade unions by comparison with European social democracy were too narrowly focused on parliament and wages, lacking a broader presence in civil society or ideological strategy for cultivating this. Yet, Jennie Lee as Minister for the Arts (1964–70), 1962's Festival of Labour (Black 2016) and modernizing Labour MPs like Tony Crosland and Roy Jenkins indicate that it was not lack of interest, resources or will but rather popular cultural preference and the wider political culture that constrained Labour's cultural progress (Black 2007: 149–62).

The Labour Party, like Wesker, were firm believers in a cultural hierarchy that it trusted Britons might be enticed to ascend. As with much of the permissive legislation enacted in the 1960s, arts policy was at odds with popular opinion; distinctively, it endeavoured to not only modernize traditional arts but also promote access to it, particularly in the regions. Jazz, much in evidence at the Festival of Labour and made eligible for Arts Council funding in 1967, was about as modern as its tastes ran to. Lee's 1965 Arts White Paper extolled how 'in the world of jazz the process has already happened; highbrow and lowbrow have met' (Cmnd. 2601 1965: para. 71). This agenda was challenged by self-made commercial pop culture, not to mention the counter-culture that emerged in late 1960s Britain.

By contrast, C42 was less permissive and more prescriptive, defending folksy-proletarian culture as well as elite forms such as classical music. Contemporary critics such as John McGrath and later critics like Mulgan and Worpole felt that for C42 'the problem was of taking existing art to the workers, not trying to create new forms of art' (Mulgan & Worpole 1986: 28–29).

Roots and knots

Wesker's animus and the impetus behind C42 was that theatregoing was a minority pursuit compared to mass audiences for cinema and television. 'Is anybody listening?' he wondered in *The Modern Playwright or O, Mother, Is It Worth It?*, the 1960 pamphlet he sent to every Trade Union leader (Wesker 1970: 13). In this, Wesker railed against the industrial relations satire film *I'm Alright Jack* (1959) and condemned the Labour movement for offering little alternative to cultural habits – 'a neglect [...] almost immoral' – and instead focusing its efforts almost entirely on material improvement for its members (Wesker 1970: 17).[2] For Wesker this was an impoverishing outlook, since 'if we are not to be materially exploited neither should we be culturally exploited'. Wesker saw exemplars of cultural well-being in 'the Gorkis, Chekhovs, Millers, the Balzacs and Steinbecks, the Beethovens and the de Sicas, the Van Goghs and the Louis Armstrongs' (Wesker 1970: 18). Socialism, for Wesker and the writers of his generation (Rebellato 1999: 11), meant 'not merely an economic organization of society but a way of living', and Labour and the unions were perpetuating the fragmenting of work and leisure (Wesker 1970: 17).

The birth of C42 is well documented (Black 2010). At the 1960 TUC, a motion drafted by Wesker and Bill Holdsworth, active in the Hemel Hempstead Left Club, called for the involvement of trade unions in cultural activities (Wesker 1960c: 67). The motion was moved by Ralph Bond, who told of attending an International Confederation of Trade Unions Film Festival, featuring Scandinavian, West German, Austrian and American films – but not a single British contribution, he was 'sad to say' (TUC 1960: 435). When a speaker backing the motion was interrupted by the Congress President – 'I hope delegates will be brief as I want to take the economic section after this' – this served to demonstrate the motion's critique of dominant materialist outlooks and coalesced support for it (TUC 1960: 438).

C42 posters proclaimed that 'All Art should be Free – it is an experience not a commodity' and reasoned that 'the principle of free art, like free education and medicine, would be accepted within a couple of decades' (AW n.d.a: n.pag.). Novelist Doris Lessing told the first C42 council of management how '[u]nder the glossy mask of false prosperity which is the face of Britain now, people are being starved [...] 95% of the people are educated away from art' (AW 1961c). Wesker proved relentless in urging Harold Wilson to consider the arts as a way of improving Labour's image during the 1964 election campaign (AW 1964c). Wilson responded that his famous 1963 'white heat' speech had really been about technology generating the potential for leisure (AW 1964d: n.pag.). Jennie Lee, the Minister for Arts and Culture, initially endorsed Wesker's 'brave idea' that if politicians and economists had 'failed to rescue us from the torpor of a subtly totalitarian culture, the only thing left is to give the poet his chance' (Lee 1962: 95–96).

Yet, Wesker and C42 were often seen as patronizing to working-class cultural tastes. Wesker once told the Finsbury Theatre Society in 1963 'that the British public was philistine' (Anon. 1963a: n.pag.); in 1970, John McGrath, founder of the radical 7:84 theatre company, and briefly a member of C42's council, condemned Wesker's crusade, claiming that 'the idea [...] that culture is a product to be sold by culturally-conscious (therefore superior) artists and intellectuals to a culturally starved (therefore inferior) workers, is based on the bourgeois concept of culture' (McGrath 1970: n.pag.).

Such attitudes were implicit in C42's cultural repertoire and preferences. Wesker's pet hates included the furore around the Beatles and intellectuals who 'pretend to like Elvis' (Wesker 1971: 5). In *Youth Service Magazine*, he explained: 'that the music of Bach is superior to the music of Elvis Presley [...] an indisputable fact that Presley himself would admit' (Wesker 1964: n.pag.). In

Chips with Everything (1962), we see the Wing Commander's chagrin when the men chose folk music in preference to Elvis – an echo of Beatie in *Roots* trying to educate her mother to appreciate Bizet.

Commentators like Richard Hoggart were similarly wary of American mass culture. Yet, C42 also exhibited what, in *The Uses of Literacy* (1957), Hoggart warned was a 'middle-class Marxist' tendency found in the early New Left type: 'a nostalgia for those "best of all" kinds of art, rural folk-art or genuinely popular urban art, and a special enthusiasm for such scraps of them as he thinks he can detect today [...] part-pitying and part-patronizing working-class people' (Hoggart 1958: 5). In this sense, Wesker's C42 could be seen as practicing radical chic, *nostalgie de la boue* as Wolfe also terms it, romanticizing exotic primitive culture. C42's politically progressive, culturally traditional amalgam exalted indigenous national cultures in highly selective ways. It aimed to recover 'authentic', traditional working-class experience just as this was reckoned to have evaporated or mutated. Significantly, the multiculturalism of 1960s Britain only faintly registered on C42's radar. C42 was an exercise in cultural defence against new forms of popular culture as much as against elitism – anti-establishment, but at the same time defending traditional 'authentic' forms and struggling to rival mainstream commercial culture. Its only non-classical musical tastes, folk and jazz, were of the 'trad' (acceptable American) type, countering electric pop – although at the start of the 1960s, there was a revival in both, with popular and radical resonance (McKay 2005; Horn 2009; Mitchell 2014).

The activities for which the Roundhouse would become controversial and (in)famous later in the 1960s were very different from the early offerings at C42's festivals between September and November 1962 in Nottingham, Birmingham, Leicester, Bristol, Hayes and Southall and (in 1961) Wellingborough. Standard C42 fare included: pub and workplace poetry readings from Dannie Abse, Laurie Lee and Christopher Logue (AW 1962c); folk music from Ewan MacColl, Peggy Seeger and A. L. Lloyd and art and sculpture displays (including Barbara Hepworth and L. S. Lowry) in shops and community centres. The National Youth Theatre performed *Hamlet* ('Shakespeare's Jimmy Porter' as festival pamphlets dubbed it), and a theatre folk ballad *The Maker and the Tool* (1962) was constructed by Charles Parker from workplace recordings (Watt 2003: 43–46). Wesker's short play *The Nottingham Captain* (1962) was written for the festivals with ACGB funding and dealt with the defeat of the 1817 Pentrich Luddite rising. It was scripted to a part-jazz (by David Lee, later musical director on BBC TV's *That Was the Week That Was*) and part-classical score (ACGB 1962). Jazz came from the Fortytwo Big Band, led by Tommy Watt. The sixteen-piece's repertoire included the 'TUC twist' and 'Wesker Jumps In' and was well enough regarded to record with Columbia Records in 1964 (Green 1962: 1).

27

Yet, this folksy, nostalgic cleaving to some authentic workers' culture did not impress all. Playwright Shelagh Delaney, admired by the New Left and initially a supporter of C42, increasingly wondered why it 'seem[s] to think that 100 years ago, everybody was speaking poetry in pubs' (Anon. 1962: n.pag.). Working-class artists, such as Ron Dellar in *New Left Review*, felt 'resentment' when portrayed as 'romantic misfits whose works could only be [...] appreciated by an [...] upper middle class minority' as much as when they had to debase their art by contributing to 'glossy magazines' (Dellar 1961: 60).

C42's answer to such concerns was to organize itself as a vanguard, 'a cultural hub in London which by its approach and work will destroy the mystique and snobbery associated with the arts':

> If we do not succeed an army of highly powered commercial enterprises are going to sweep into the leisure hours of future generations and create a cultural mediocrity [...] a nation emotionally and intellectually immature, capable of enjoying nothing, creating nothing and effecting nothing. This is not an idle prophecy; it is a fact in the making.
>
> (AW 1962a: n.pag.)

In addition to creating a space to nurture 'the best professional artists' (AW 1962a) and a new popular audience for the arts (not vice versa), C42 rethought spectators as more active participants (AW 1962a: n.pag.). Wesker believed that 'given the right opportunities, art will return as the natural function of any community; without it a community is soulless and in the end easily exploitable'; 'a vote in a democracy may be the individual's weapon against political abuse, but [...] art can strengthen a man's personality against spiritual abuse' (AW 1962b: n.pag.). There was a clear theory to the nomenclature of a *Centre* 42 prior to the Roundhouse.

Roundhouse: The rise and fall

Built in 1847 by Robert Stephenson as a turning house for locomotives, developments in rail design eventually rendered the Roundhouse obsolete. From 1869 until fashion tycoon Louis Mintz acquired the leasehold and gifted it to C42 in 1964, it was a liquor warehouse (Foster 1971: 43). In 1954, it was categorized as a Grade II listed building. Plans for the Roundhouse, once it was acquired in 1964, were outlined by Wesker in the *Allio Brief*. This provided French theatre designer René Allio and architect Paul Chemetov with guidelines for redesigning this former railway shed as a multipurpose, state of the arts centre. Allio had worked on Roger Planchon's Théâtre de la Cité in Lyon and Malraux's Centres Dramatiques

Nationaux. Chemetov led the *Atelier d'urbanisme et d'architecture* in Paris and had worked on the new French Communist party HQ (Joly 1973: 58–63).

The *Allio Brief* 'evoke[d] the atmosphere' and aesthetics of C42's vision (Wesker 1970: 52). Architectural excellence was imperative; C42 artists ought to be 'war-like, audacious, gay, courteous, brilliant – and no doubt drunk' and the Round-house 'a place of pleasure and marvelous revelation' and 'efficient, effective, func-tional', including meeting rooms for local Co-ops, trade unions, church and youth groups (Wesker 1970: 55). The building should relate the artist and the audience more intimately than in traditional theatres and 'result in developing a new and informed audience' (Wesker 1970: 58). Unlike Allio, Wesker liked 'the idea of sceptical youngsters lounging around in a building where there is music, theatre and debate in full swing' and felt there ought to be 'a jellied eel stall, the FortyTwo fish and chip shop, the bookstall... And the drinking bar [...] must be available [...] as a pub throughout the day' (Wesker 1970: 59). More militantly, the Round-house was to be the place where if artists were to

> forge a new language that will make society recognize its responsibilities to the arts – it should be here. If they are to acquire that confidence that will eliminate the artist's nervous twitch of apology for his so-called 'inessential' profession – it should be here. And if all this adds up to a cultural revolution and if this revo-lution has a seat – it should be here.
>
> (Wesker 1970: 60)

Yet, it can be argued that '[t]he notoriety and achievements of the Roundhouse came *despite* C42 more than *because* of it' (Etienne 2016: 141, original emphasis). Indeed, the 'sorts of popular culture the Roundhouse housed for financial expedi-ency' superseded C42's vision (Etienne 2016: 141). The Roundhouse would not have happened so easily in a non-1960s context, yet the same context also under-mined C42. Whereas it foundered, other politically engaged theatre companies developed away from London, for instance 7:84, Red Ladder and The People Show (Itzin 1980: 4–5). However, C42 was a precursory model for numerous local arts centres and 'carrot-cake' cinemas – such as, variously, the Dagenham Roundhouse or Bristol's Arnolfini, which found its present site in a former tea warehouse in the city centre docks in 1975 – often located in regenerated industrial buildings.

Harold Wilson had gifted the Roundhouse George Hoskins (a coffee shop entrepreneur and former civil servant) and Robert Maxwell, MP, already reputed for his unscrupulous business practice (Anon. 1966), allegedly to lend gravitas to fund-raising initiatives (AW 1965a). A DIY ethos remained from C42's regional festivals, which not even the business nous of Hoskins and Maxwell could dispel. In January 1967, the Greater London Council declared that 'the present condition of the premises falls short of the required standard' (AW 1967a: n.pag.). Efforts to put things on a more commercial footing institutionally uncoupled C42 from the Roundhouse Trust. This saw the Roundhouse used variously for TV, adverts, ice shows, Campaign for Real Ale festivals and a British Film Institute-*Sunday Times* 'cinema city' exhibition, visited by Harold Lloyd and Gene Kelly.

Without secure funding or cultural roots, C42 and its property were also overrun by popular and counter-cultural activities, far from the blend of high-end culture or authentic-folk-proletarian culture Wesker envisaged. Dubbed 'the cathedral of the permissive society', the Roundhouse was a trip through the 1960s (Anon. 1971: n.pag.). It hosted two key London counter-culture events: the 1967 Dialectics of Liberation conference and the launch of *International Times* (*IT*) in 1966. Neither was designed by C42, but its rates made the Roundhouse cheap to hire. Jim Haynes, an *IT* editor and founder of London's ArtsLab and Edinburgh's Traverse Theatre, argued that Wesker's financial ambitions for converting the Roundhouse overrode C42's cultural output. At the same time as the Dialectics conference took place Wesker was at a fund-raising tea party at Downing Street with political leaders and entertainment impresarios like Sir Billy Butlin and Lew Grade. This coincidence of the Dialectics happening and the No.10 tea party encapsulated the cultural chasm between the vision of C42 and the day-to-day life of the Roundhouse (Green 1988: 119; Cooper 1971).

The 1960s Roundhouse was evidence of class, status and culture in flux as new money and lifestyles, and new artistic forms, flourished. By 1971, performances included a rock version of *Othello* and Peter Brook's trapeze interpretation of *The Tempest* (1968), bands such as The Doors and The Who and Andy Warhol's first play, *Pork* (1971).

The Roundhouse, more soberly, was also a political venue favoured by 1960s radicals. In 1967, it hosted the anti-Vietnam War 'Angry Arts' week, sponsored by Jonathan Miller and Vanessa Redgrave, featuring Ewen MacColl, Peggy Seeger and Harold Pinter, and recorded as a TV documentary (Anon. 1967b: n.pag.). It was also used by anti-Apartheid groups, *Black Dwarf*, and the Revolutionary Socialist Student Federation conference in November 1968, addressed by Daniel Cohn-Bendit. The schizophrenic nature of the venue was such that it also hosted 'high' cultural events like the British School at Rome Painting Group and record-ings of Beethoven by the New Philharmonia Orchestra. There was a frisson to the Roundhouse – its radical chic was encapsulated in the fact that it was a scene to be seen at and not where the common herd frequented (AW 1971: 27–31).

By 1969, the Roundhouse had become louche, a rowdy place. That year, the GLC Public Services Entertainment sub-committee refused an extension of an all-night music licence (Anon. 1969a). When the Roundhouse lost its Camden Council subsidy in 1970, this was the final rupture between C42 and the Roundhouse (AW

1971: 18). Relating his decision to resign to the architect Paul Chemetov, Wesker wrote that the 'building has a certain cachet in London […] every slick enterprise wants to hire it', but he now had 'nightmares about it' (AW 1970: n.pag.).

Friends (and foes and funds)

Away from such dramatic gestures, much of the story of C42, the Roundhouse and Wesker was concerned with a running battle to win the argument for a particular vision of culture and to win material support to practically enact it. Neither proved easy. The six 1962 Festivals had left C42 £40,000 in debt, which made Mintz's offer of the Roundhouse particularly appealing in lending C42 not only an artistic space, but also a permanent base. Yet, it also left C42 with the task of fund-raising to convert the Roundhouse into a cultural hub. Lord Harewood (the Queen's cousin and director of the Edinburgh Festival) launched the appeal at the Roundhouse in July 1964 in the presence of Mintz, Wilson and James Callaghan, the Chancellor of the Exchequer (AW 1964e). Harold Pinter, John Osborne and the TUC's George Woodcock and Vic Feather turned down invitations (AW 1964f). The target was £590,000 (approximately £11.3 million in 2018) to be funded from national and local government, the public, trade unions, charities and business.

Despite arguing in 1963 that trade unionism needed to address spiritual as well as material poverty, Vic Feather (1963: 124), the TUC's Assistant General Secretary, proved a thorn in C42's side. According to the British Film Institute's Stanley Reed, when C42 was mentioned to him in 1962, Feather bemoaned 'eccentrics knocking on the doors of the TUC' (AW 1962d: n.pag.).[3] Wesker had urged the new TUC General Secretary George Woodcock in 1960 to show 'vision' (Wesker 1960b: n.pag.), but by 1963, Woodcock bemoaned C42 for being 'long-haired and starry-eyed' (Anon. 1963b: n.pag.). Two years later, Wesker retaliated by branding the TUC 'old men […] paralyzed by the narrowness of your preoccupations' (Wesker cited in Coppieters 1975: 47). The hostilities meant that the TUC ceased to support C42.

C42 called on local authorities to contribute, as permitted by the 1948 Local Government Act. However, with the London County Council (LCC) expanding into the GLC between 1963 and 1965, many local authorities deferred such decisions. In 1966, Bromley Councillor Raymond Pope denounced C42 as a 'proletarian piffle' and any donation as 'throwing […] public money down the kitchen sink' (Anon. 1966: n.pag.). The GLC and LCC were minded to hear how the ACGB felt about C42 before committing (AW 1963a). Likewise, the ACGB's Chairman Lord Goodman was keen to see match-funding for any ACGB support (AW 1966a).

The Gulbenkian Foundation donated £10,000 early in 1962 and £3,000 in 1964 (ACGB 1964). Business patronage was also forthcoming from the ITV Companies Association Committee of Review of Grants to the Arts and Sciences. After 1964, business interest diminished as central ACGB funding and support increased (ACGB 1968). The Arts Council's Secretary General, Sir William Emrys Williams, had suggested that 'Weskerism' was a 'false doctrine', premised on mass interest in the arts and told Wesker that business would want to see that C42 was 'a sound and sane organization' (AW 1964b: n.pag.). C42 submitted four unsuccessful bids to the ACGB by 1967. Ultimately, Goodman confessed his personal dislike of the C42 project to the ACGB and LCC (ACGB 1965).

Wesker's celebrity and charisma gave the movement early impetus, enabling him to assemble union leaders Ted Hill, Frank Cousins and Bill Carron plus Doris Lessing, Tom Maschler and Jennie Lee on C42's first Council of Management (AW 1961b). C42 was based on personalities as much as ideas long before its aspirations, directed to a primarily trade union audience, faded. Much energy was expended on schemes like the 1965 Stars Committee fronted by John Lennon, Vanessa Redgrave, Spike Milligan and Fenella Fielding (AW 1965b; Anon. 1965). If Wesker's abrasive personality attracted controversy, his core concept of a cultural hub was no less contentious since it implicitly questioned current government policy and the dominant structures of artistic production. This explained why C42 was received so coolly by many otherwise politically or creatively sympathetic. Doris Lessing spoke as early as 1961 about 'a great deal of malice being spread [...] about C42' (AW 1961a: n.pag.). Lessing reported that George Devine, the Royal Court's Artistic Director who had facilitated Wesker's breakthrough works, 'seems to see this as an attack on himself' (AW 1961a: n.pag.).

Wesker's talent for ingratiating himself with the famous and the influential meant that the 'Friends of C42' was bedecked with Lords, Ladys and Sirs as well as the Countess of Albemarle and luminaries John Berger, Sidney Bernstein, Gerald Gardiner, Peter Hall, Cleo Laine, J. B. Priestley, Alan Sillitoe, C.P. Snow, Kenneth Tynan and Raymond Williams (AW 1971: 40–41). Most audacious was an approach to Prince Philip. Wesker explained he would 'sooner have built 42 on the pennies and pounds of many hundreds and thousands', but this was not forthcoming (AW 1965c: n.pag.). He visited Buckingham Palace in May 1965, where Prince Philip blamed government funding of sports and arts for reducing the interest of private or business patrons. Wesker's request was rejected (AW 1965d). In another instance Wesker simply pleaded for a millionaire to back him (AW 1966b).

C42 always generated as well as hosted cultural debate – and amidst the evidence of putative or fleeting friends and the uncertainties induced by its aura of radical chic, it is worth noting there were plenty who not only ignored but were downright hostile to either Wesker's vision or the workings of the Roundhouse. Noel Coward, a critic of the 'dustbin school of drama' (Anon. 1961a: n.pag.), disparaged Wesker's efforts in 'all those dreary English towns organizing dreary festivals for those dreary people' (Anon. 1964: n.pag.). Other cultural warriors saw C42 as more sinister. In 1968, Mary Whitehouse drew attention to 'the head-quarters of the left wing organization "Centre 42"', adding that 'the Roundhouse is used for activities of the "anti-university"' and had hosted a conference on the '"dialectics of liberation" [...] whose neo-Marxist ideas have kindled much of the present unrest in Europe' (NVALA 1968: n.pag.).

But even C42's relationships with its friends were fraught. Wesker's hostility to pop music, including the Beatles, has been noted, but Lennon's association was keenly sought. Peter Sellars was listed amongst the Friends of C42, but *I'm Alright Jack* was regularly cited as unworthy of the Labour movement because it suggested trade unionists were self-interested, cynical and lazy. Impresario Jack Hylton was also a 'Friend', but Wesker dubbed him a 'cretinizing' cultural influence (Green 1962: 7) and told Goodman he would 'prefer to have Hylton's assurances in the bank' (AW 1962e: n.pag.). On the eve of the No.10 tea party, Wesker enjoined the Gulbenkian's Jim Thornton: 'let us hope that the industrial thugs who gather at Downing Street will be touched with your enlightenment' (AW 1967d: n.pag.).

The New Left was as unforthcoming with ideological sustenance as the TUC or ACGB. Relations had been close – Wesker wrote in the first *New Left Review* (Wesker 1960a) and touted his project as 'another focal point of activity' to match CND (Wesker 1960c: 47). Yet, actress and later Labour MEP Janey Buchan wrote to Wesker in 1960 explaining she had 'prodded Stuart Hall and *NLR* until I'm sick' to participate in the burgeoning fringe at the Edinburgh Festival (AW 1960b: n.pag.). She despaired of the New Left's London-centrism and felt that '*NLR* need their heads looking at because they could have the most tremendous stage ready-made for them' (AW 1960b: n.pag.).

Relations with Lee also faltered (Hollis 1997: 246–96). Although Lee noted that Wesker 'agreed with me that an urgent priority is to try to set up counter-attractions to the influences of commercial television, betting, drugs' (AW 1967c: n.pag.), Wesker's outburst at June 1967's Labour Arts and Amenities group meeting sealed the fallout (JL 1967: n.pag.). The group chair told Lee: 'C42 is suffering from 'Jenniecide' [...] Arnold is under the delusion that you are conspiring with Ted [Willis] to kill the C42 project' (HW 1967a: n.pag.).

Goodman then undermined C42 with the Prime Minister. He had 'never felt much enthusiasm for the project', since it was

> in direct contradiction to a policy [...] cultivated by Jennie and myself [...] that
> we do not impose our views or any central views on the local regions and [...]

that pre-packaged London culture dispatched all over the place is the exact reverse of what we are trying to establish.

(HW 1967b: n.pag.)

The July 1967 tea party at 10 Downing Street came a month after Wesker's accusations against Lee. Donations totalled almost £80,000 (AW 1971: 41–42). This amounted to a survival rather than a development package, confining C42 to a virtual entity, existing in name and imagination alone.

Wesker's suspicions that C42 had ended up as 'tenants of the Roundhouse, rather than having a prior claim on it, [...] hood-winked by tycoons, railroaded by commercial imperatives and deserted by [...] Lee and the TUC' (Black 2010: 167) were not unfounded (AW 1966c). Ted Willis, TV playwright and Labour Lord, was a longstanding foe of C42. He had suggested that it merge with Unity Theatre in 1963, and in a 1966 interview with Susan Barnes (partner of Labour MP Tony Crosland) in *The Sun*, Willis berated Wesker for suggesting that 'to write for television would be dipping his pen in mud' (n.pag.). Willis felt Wesker suffered from a 'messiah complex', seeing 'himself in shining white robes coming down [...] the Old Kent Road and converting everybody there to Bach and Beethoven' (1966: n.pag.). Such 'hysterical sincerity' was 'patronizing' (Willis 1966: n.pag.).

Other critics argued C42 was too profligate and that cultural output should always precede the needs of funding and a permanent base. Again, Willis was among their number, writing in *Tribune*: 'Wesker seems to think that he alone has the tablets of stone [...] on art and the rest of us are either philistines or cheats'. He insisted C42 needed to 'show us in deeds not words' (Willis 1967: n.pag.). For Mike Kustow, the ICA (Institute of Contemporary Arts, where he was Director from 1967 to 1971) was artistically superior and ArtsLab more 'successful as a meeting place' (Anon. 1969b: n.pag.). In fact, the uncoupling of the Roundhouse and C42 was apparent to most commentators from 1967 onwards. *London Look* (Anon. 1967a) were wowed by the spectacle and presence of the building but put-off by its ambitious funding demands and felt C42 was essentially a landlord to other cultural providers. *Jackie*, the teenage magazine for girls (itself evidence of how the Roundhouse was a fixture in popular youth culture), observed that with its late-night bars and psychedelic lighting, the Roundhouse was 'a really jumping scene' but during daytime reverted to 'the rather solid sign of a social and cultural arts centre' (Anon. 1967c: n.pag.).

The popular reception C42 elicited proved equally constraining. C42's local festivals met the uneven reception that the project as a whole encountered. J. B. Priestley was supportive of Wesker's 'noble simplicity' and efforts to counter 'admass' but imagined Halifax workers faced with C42's cultural fare remarking, 'ah couldn't make head nor tail of it' (Priestley 1965: n.pag.). For his part, Wesker saw in Priestley 'a popular touch which seems to have eluded me' (Wesker 1995: 144).

Conclusions

Interviewed by Catherine Itzin and Glenda Leeming for *Theatre Quarterly* in 1977, Wesker conceded (indeed almost felt 'fulfilled' by) the suggestion that 'your earlier career seems to be slightly overshadowing your later career' (Wesker 1985: 100). C42 and the Roundhouse were the buffers against this earlier success. Wesker at least thought that C42 had 'created a spirit and focused attention on the arts in a way that has inspired' (AW 1968: n.pag.). Itzin reckoned that as fringe theatres and arts centres flourished in the 1970s, C42 had 'come true, independent of its originators' and foreshadowed the heyday of radical theatre (agit-prop, avant-garde, feminist, black, gay) in the 1970s (Itzin 1980: 103–15). Wesker tended to look back in anger. In 1967, he reflected: 'I have been too charming or innocent in my dealings with "the powers that be"' (AW 1967b: n.pag.).

Like many contemporaries, historical comment on C42 has tended to judge it harshly. For Coppieters, the idea of a Centre controlled by artists was radical enough to generate political unease, threaten commercial dictates and question artistic hierarchies – its potential was 'betrayed' by elite opposition and union antipathy (Coppieters 1975: 51). By contrast, Marwick notes that efforts to transform the Roundhouse into a political theatre 'inevitably flopped' (Marwick 1998: 343). The terms of such perceived 'failure' disclose much about the pattern, and limits, of the 1960s' cultural revolution. Nonetheless, this chapter's argument moves beyond such a simple dichotomy to see Wesker as thwarted by wider cultural tastes and emerging practices, the broader political culture and by the project's own contradictions: in short, culture(s) countered it. In addition, whilst C42 fell short in its own terms, it served to inspire as a model for others after 1970.

What C42 lacked in cultural provision (once in the Roundhouse it is hard to envision precisely *what* C42's output was to be), it made up for with a vision. Its legacy was here rather than in its own cultural turns in the 1960s – in modelling rather than realizing the cultural turn. Wesker would return to Buckingham Palace to collect a knighthood in 2006. By then the Roundhouse had undergone many changes: it had remained culturally iconic but dishevelled in the 1970s (Preston 2005), failed in efforts to become a black arts centre with GLC support in the 1980s, became subject to preservation by English Heritage in the 1990s and reopened in 2006 as a renovated, bespoke arts centre, with private financial backing, as well as English Heritage and Arts Council support. Echoes of C42 and Wesker resounded: Pink Floyd offered financial support, there was a sponsored brick scheme and a 'studio 42', whose first play was the suggestively titled *The Foolish Young Man* by Jeremy Weller. Politics was apparent in that it hosted US radical filmmaker Michael Moore's first UK stand-up performance, albeit one that ended in claims of Moore being short-changed by the venue and organizers

(Brooks and Clarke 2003). This all tied in with the 1990s' and 2000s' New Labour rhetoric of the creative industries. If this was a cultural revolution, it was not as Wesker planned or envisaged, and while he nourished and hosted it, he ended up being consumed by it. Radical, mostly; chic, definitely!

NOTES

1. For critics like Bernard Levin, all this meant that 'on political matters' Wesker 'has a brain made of apfelstrudel' (Levin 1970: n.pag.), a culinary reference borrowed from Wesker's *The Four Seasons* (1965).
2. In the original address to the 1960 Oxford Drama Festival on which the pamphlet was based, Wesker's rhetoric extends to calling the film 'a sick cultural manifestation' (see AW 1960c: n.pag.).
3. This animosity did not prevent Wesker from using Feather as one of the inspirations for the character of Victor in *Love Letters on Blue Paper* (1977).

REFERENCES

Anon. (1961), *New York Times*, 26 February.
—— (1961b), *The Nation*, 25 March.
—— (1962), *Sunday Citizen*, 23 September.
—— (1963a), *The Guardian*, 9 February.
—— (1963b), *The Observer*, 14 July.
—— (1963c), *New York Daily Post*, 28 October.
—— (1964), *Daily Mail*, 5 June.
—— (1965), *Daily Mail*, 21 July.
—— (1966), *Kentish Independent*, 6 May.
—— (1967a), *London Look*, 28 January.
—— (1967b), *Morning Star*, 3 July.
—— (1967c), *Jackie*, 22 July.
—— (1969a), *Holborn Guardian*, 21 March.
—— (1969b), 'Mike Kustow, ICA', *The Guardian*, 5 December.
—— (1971), *She*, October.
Arts Council of Great Britain (ACGB) archives (1962), ACGB to Wesker, 29 November, London: Victoria and Albert Museum, Box 34, File 89.
—— (1964), Gulbenkian press release, 14 February, London: Victoria and Albert Museum, Box 34, File 208.
—— (1965), Abercrombie to Goodman, 12 October, London: Victoria and Albert Museum, Box 34, File 89.
—— (1968), ACGB grants, 1964–68, London: Victoria and Albert Museum, Box 38, File 42.

Black, Lawrence (2007), 'Arts and crafts: Social democracy's cultural resources and repertoire in 1960s' Britain', in I. Favretto and J. Callaghan (eds), *Transitions in Social Democracy*, Manchester: MUP, pp.149–62.

—— (2010), *Redefining British Politics: Culture, Consumerism and Participation, 1954–70*, Basingstoke: Palgrave.

—— (2016), 'Festival of Labour', http://www.labourpains.group.shef.ac.uk/the-festival-of-labour-1962/. Accessed 19 October 2018.

Brooks, Xan, and Clarke, Sean (2003), 'Pressurised Moore "cracks" at Roundhouse', *The Guardian*, 7 January, https://www.theguardian.com/film/2003/jan/07/news.seanclarke. Accessed 16 April 2020.

Cmnd. 2601 (1965), *A Policy for the Arts: The First Steps*, London: HMSO.

Cooper, David (ed.) (1971), *The Dialectics of Liberation*, Harmondsworth: Penguin.

Coppieters, Frank (1975), 'Arnold Wesker's Centre Fortytwo: A cultural revolution betrayed', *Theatre Quarterly*, 5:18, pp. 37–54.

Curtis, Helene, and Sanderson, Mimi (eds) (2004), *The Unsung Sixties: Memoirs of Social Innovation*, London: Whiting & Birch.

Dellar, Ron (1961), 'Centre 42', *New Left Review*, 11, pp. 60–61.

Etienne, Anne (2016), '"Visions don't work"? The role of Wesker's theatre and Centre 42 in 1960s' British culture', *Studies in Theatre and Performance*, 36:2, pp. 130–44.

Feather, Vic (1963), *The Essence of Trade Unionism*, Oxford: Bodley Head.

Foster, Michael (1971), 'The Roundhouse', *Architectural Association Quarterly*, 3:1, pp. 43–55.

Green, Benny (1962), 'Big band noise for C42', *Scene*, 4, p. 1.

Green, Jonathan (1988), *Days in the Life: Voices from the English Underground 1961–71*, London: Pimlico.

Hoggart, Richard (1958), *The Uses of Literacy*, Harmondsworth: Penguin.

Hollis, Patricia (1997), *Jennie Lee*, Oxford: Oxford University Press.

Horn, Alasdair (2009), *Juke Box Britain*, Manchester: Manchester University Press.

Itzin, Catherine (1980), *Stages in the Revolution: Political Theatre in Britain since 1968*, London: Methuen.

Joly, Pierre (1973), 'Oscar Niemeyer joue avec la faucille et le marteau', *L'Oeil*, 219, pp. 58–63.

Jones, Mervyn (1966), 'Labour and the arts', *New Statesman*, 18 February, pp. 220–21.

Lee, Jennie (1962), Letter in *Encounter*, 1 August, pp. 95–96.

Lee, Jennie Papers (JL) (1967), Labour Arts and Amenities committee, 19 June, Open University, Milton Keynes, File 4/1/2/8.

Levin, Bernard (1970), *Daily Mail*, 6 March.

Marwick, Arthur (1998), *The Sixties*, Oxford: Oxford University Press.

McGrath, John (1970), 'Reviews: Friends and enemies', *Black Dwarf*, 14:35, 12 June, p. 15.

McKay, George (2005), *Circular Breathing: The Cultural Politics of Jazz in Britain*, Duham, NC: Duke University Press.

Mitchell, Julia (2014), 'Subterranean Bourgeois Blues: the 2nd English Folk Revival, 1945–70', Ph.D. thesis, London: University College London.

Mulgan, Geoff, and Worpole, Ken (1986), *Saturday Night or Sunday Morning? From Arts to Industry*, London: Comedia.

NVALA Annual Convention (1968), May, National Viewers' and Listeners' Association (NVALA) archives, Colchester: Essex University Library, 2000 accession, Box 7.

Ponnuswami, Meenakshi (1998), 'Histories of the New Left: Arnold Wesker and the angrier young men', in D. Reade (ed.), *Arnold Wesker: A Casebook*, London: Routledge, pp. 137–62.

Preston, John (2005), *Kings of the Roundhouse*, London: Viking.

Priestley, J. B. (1965), 'Gay with the arts?', *New Statesman*, 23 April, p. 639.

Rebellato, Dan (1999), *1956 and All That: The Making of Modern British Drama*, London: Routledge.

Rustin, Mike (1989), 'The New Left as a social movement', in Oxford University Socialist Discussion Group (eds), *Out of Apathy*, London: Verso, pp. 121–27.

TUC (Trades Union Congress) (1960), *Annual Conference Report*, London: TUC.

Watt, David (2003), '*The Maker and the Tool*, documentary performance and the search for a popular culture', *New Theatre Quarterly*, 19:1, pp. 41–66.

Wesker, Arnold (1960a), 'The Kitchen', *New Left Review*, 1, pp. 32–37.

—— (1960b), 'Vision! Vision! Mr. Woodcock', *New Statesman*, 30 July, p. 300.

—— (1960c), 'Trade unions and the arts', *New Left Review*, 5, p. 67.

—— (1964), 'Art: therapy or experience', *Youth Service Magazine*, January, p. 47.

—— (1969), 'Aie Cuba! Aie Cuba!', in *The New Man in Cuba*, London: British-Cuba Association, pp. 1–5.

—— (1970), *Fears of Fragmentation*, London: Jonathan Cape.

—— (1971), 'It's an illusion', *Ark*, Spring, p. 5.

—— (1985), *Distinctions*, London: Jonathan Cape.

—— (1995), *As Much as I Dare: An Autobiography*, London: Arrow.

Wesker, Arnold Papers (AW) (n.d.a), C42 Posters, Austin, Texas: Harry Ransom Center, Box 133.1.

—— (n.d.b), T. Watts, 'Jazz', Austin, Texas: Harry Ransom Center, Box 134.2.

—— (1960a), Founding meeting, Committee of 100, Austin, Texas: Harry Ransom Center, Box 119.1.

—— (1960b), Buchan to Wesker, c. August, Austin, Texas: Harry Ransom Center, Box 136.9.

—— (1960c), Scrapbook on his work, Austin, Texas: Harry Ransom Center, Box 107.7.

—— (1961a), Lessing to Wesker, c. June, Austin, Texas: Harry Ransom Center, Box 136.8.

—— (1961b), C42 Council of Management minutes, 20 July, Austin, Texas: Harry Ransom Center, Box 136.8.

—— (1961c), 'A cultural revolution: 1st stage', C42 management minutes, 12 October, Austin, Texas: Harry Ransom Center, Box 147.5.

————— (1962a), *Centre Forty-Two: First Stage in a Cultural Revolution*, Austin, Texas: Harry Ransom Center, Box 141.9.

————— (1962b), 'Draft appeal for funds and the 1962 series of People's Festivals', Austin, Texas: Harry Ransom Center, Box 137.4.

————— (1962c), 6-city festival pamphlets, Austin, Texas: Harry Ransom Center, Box 150.1.

————— (1962d), Reed to Wesker, 27 April, Austin, Texas: Harry Ransom Center, Box 137.3.

————— (1962e), Wesker to Goodman, 25 November 1962, Austin, Texas: Harry Ransom Center, Box 144.11.

————— (1963a), William Hart to C42, 8 August, Austin, Texas: Harry Ransom Center, Box 143.7.

————— (1963b), Open Road films to Wesker, 19 November, Austin, Texas: Harry Ransom Center, Box 134.3.

————— (1964a), Leslie Ash Lyons to Henshaw, 9 May, Austin, Texas: Harry Ransom Center, Box 134.7.

————— (1964b), Report of meeting (Williams-Wesker), 2 June, Austin, Texas: Harry Ransom Center, Box 154.9.

————— (1964c), Wesker to Wilson, 29 June, Austin, Texas: Harry Ransom Center, Box 154.8.

————— (1964d), Wilson to Wesker, 1 July, Austin, Texas: Harry Ransom Center, Box 154.8–9.

————— (1964), Harewood's Roundhouse launch address, n.d., Austin, Texas: Harry Ransom Center, Box 154.8.

————— (1964f), Roundhouse launch invites and correspondence, Austin, Texas: Harry Ransom Center, Box 144.10.

————— (1965a), Wesker to Hoskins, 11 April, Austin, Texas: Harry Ransom Center, Box 132.6.

————— (1965b), Wesker to Lennon, 18 and 26 May, Austin, Texas: Harry Ransom Center, Box 144.6–7.

————— (1965c), Wesker to Duke of Edinburgh, 19 January, Austin, Texas: Harry Ransom Center, Box 142.7

————— (1965d), (The Duke's reply) Sir John Hunt to Wesker, 19 July, Austin, Texas: Harry Ransom Center, Box 142.7.

————— (1966a), Hoskins to Maxwell, 5 January, Austin, Texas: Harry Ransom Center, Box 136.4.

————— (1966b), 'Millionaire appeal', Austin, Texas: Harry Ransom Center, Box 133.1.

————— (1966c), Wesker's memo to C42 council, 24 February, Austin, Texas: Harry Ransom Center, Box 137.4.

————— (1967a), GLC Report, 27 January, Austin, Texas: Harry Ransom Center, Box 133.6.

————— (1967b), Wesker to David Mercer, March, Austin, Texas: Harry Ransom Center, Box 150.7.

————— (1967c), Lee to Hoskins, 31 May, Austin, Texas: Harry Ransom Center, Box 146.10.

————— (1967d), Wesker to Jim Thornton (Gulbenkian) 19 July, Austin, Texas: Harry Ransom Center, Box 144.8

—— (1968), Memo, Council of management, May, Austin, Texas: Harry Ransom Center, Box 149.1.

—— (1969), Berman to Hoskins, 18 April, Austin, Texas: Harry Ransom Center, Box 157.6.

—— (1970), C42 Council of management, 31 October, Austin, Texas: Harry Ransom Center, Box 148.6.

—— (1971), Roundhouse Trust, *First Report 1965–71*, Austin, Texas: Harry Ransom Center, Box 156.5.

—— (1960), Holdsworth-Wesker correspondence, Austin, Texas: Harry Ransom Center, Box 5.6.

Willis, Ted (1966), *The Sun*, 15 February.

—— (1967), *Tribune*, 2 June.

Wilson, Harold Papers (HW) (1967a), Ben Whitaker MP to Marcia Williams, 12 June, Oxford: Bodleian Library, Box c.872.

—— (1967b), Goodman to Wilson, 30 June, Oxford: Bodleian Library, Box c.872.

Wolfe, Tom (1970), *Radical Chic & Mau-Mauing the Flak Catchers*, New York: Farrar, Straus and Giroux.

FIGURE 3: Arnold Wesker, *c*.1959.

2

Introducing Mr Harold Wesker

Graham Saunders

Theatrical contemporaries

On 27 June 1998, Harold Pinter received an uncharacteristically short letter from his playwriting contemporary Arnold Wesker. The letter contained a clipping from *The Jewish News*, publicizing a collection by the photographer Erroll Jackson, focusing on Jewish artists. Included was a photograph of a youthful looking Arnold Wesker in a literary pose besides a typewriter, but wrongly captioned as Harold Pinter: 'When are they going to get it right?' (HP 1998a: n.pag.) writes Wesker, to which in his reply Pinter compliments Wesker on his handsome looks (HP 1998b).[1] After Pinter's death in 2008, Wesker also recalled once being sent a letter addressed to 'Harold Wesker' and on another occasion being asked at a British Council function in Rome whether he was still married to Lady Antonia Fraser (Wesker 2009).

However, dominant histories of post-war British theatre have mainly concentrated on Wesker and Pinter's differences, using the pair as convenient markers of a perceived stylistic and thematic divergence. Wesker becomes one of the politically committed angry young men of the 1950s writing socio-realist drama, whereas Pinter (despite sharing some early associations with the group, coming mainly from his realistic depiction of everyday speech) becomes more closely associated with the European drama that emerged after the war, popularly known as the Theatre of the Absurd.

Wesker has always been hostile to such demarcations, especially regarding the question of realism. For example, in a 1997 article for *The Sunday Times*, following a disappointing visit to Peter Hall's new production of *Waiting for Godot*, Wesker noted that after Hall's first London production in 1955, Beckett's play had subsequently been 'used to polarise definitions of art' (Wesker 1997: n.pag.). Stephen Lacey in his study of British realist theatre notes that from relatively early on in his career, Wesker 'wrestl[ed] with some of the essential problems of the form' (Lacey 1995: 105). For example, in a 1965 letter to the journal

Gambit, Wesker points out that himself and Pinter share common ground with regard to 'the limitations of human beings' (Wesker 1965: n.pag.). Yet, Lacey also supports the more widely held view that using realism as the basis for a critique of society puts Pinter's drama in the 1950s and 1960s in direct opposition to Wesker (Lacey 1995: 143).

Wesker acknowledges some of these differences in December 1980 when he writes to Pinter asking him to consider directing his new play *Caritas* at the National Theatre: 'Our writings have gone very different ways and for many we stand at opposite ends of the spectrum', but he adds, 'curiously [our work has been] fuelled by a common background' (Wesker 1980: n.pag.). Both in fact were near contemporaries (Pinter b. 1930; Wesker b. 1932); each grew up in East End Jewish families, with fathers who both worked in the garment industry. Both also made their playwriting debuts in 1957 (Wesker with *The Kitchen* and Pinter with *The Room*), although it was Wesker who first came to prominence when *Chicken Soup with Barley* was staged at the Royal Court in London the following year. By contrast, Pinter's *The Birthday Party*, which premiered that same year, suffered a poor critical reception. Wesker's 1980 letter to Pinter goes on to recall other 'strange parallels and coincidences' from their background and careers:

> Our Hackney schools – Grocer's[2] and Upton House; the Laura Place girls-in-brown (a circle of whom we both shared)[3] telling me about you in *Macbeth*[4] which they insisted I see and did and was so impressed with. Both of us applying to RADA, winning a place and having to apply for an LCC grant. You were awarded one, I wasn't. Somehow – I don't know how – we knew each other as we passed on the way to those auditions. Then a memory of you in the back of the stalls at the Royal Court having watched a rehearsal of one of the TRILOGY and telling me 'you know yours is just the kind of play I'd love to act in' [...] And do you remember the awful ordeal of posing for Cecil Beaton? I'd just been through it and you were next in line. I passed you coming out and warned you how embarrassing it was going to be.
>
> (HP 1980: n.pag.)

Reflecting on Arnold Wesker's work in 1970, Ronald Hayman gives what reads like an end-of-year school report on its particular strengths and weaknesses: the former includes its warmth, humanity, sincerity, passion, bravery, honesty, energy, enthusiasm and concern. Weaknesses include didacticism and a tendency 'to let the social problems distract him from his characters' personal predicaments'; other perceived flaws include verbosity, excessive emotion (where passion and instinct outweigh intellect), combined with naivete. Ronald Hayman observes that sometimes these qualities led to 'brilliant formal inventions, [yet] he is neither self-critical nor very conscious of technical problems' (Hayman 1970: 13). Read in this light, Pinter's work seems antithetical in every respect: interactions between his characters range from guardedness, insincerity, mockery, lack of concern for others and sometimes outright hostility. Against the emotional incontinence associated with Wesker, Pinter's writing has a formal disciplined quality, notably in its precision of language – rarely is this spontaneous as it is in Wesker's plays, but more often calculated on his characters' intent of gaining advantage over others. Comparing the two in 1970, Pinter's drama still gave no indication of wanting to address social issues.

Yet on occasions, each have strayed into the other's territory. Wesker makes mention of this in the aforementioned 1980 letter when he writes:

> the chemistry of our different (though fuelled by a common background) [...] may have crystallized in CARITAS. I'm not sure I can put my finger on it but there is a rightness about our coming together over this play which strikes my imagination very forcibly.
>
> (HP 1980: n.pag.)

In truth, it is difficult to see how *Caritas*, based on the life of Christine Carpenter, who in 1329 took vows as an anchoress and lived the remainder of her life in a walled-up cell built into the church of Shere, shares any perceptible stylistic or thematic similarities with Pinter. It is perhaps then unsurprising that despite admiring *Caritas*, Pinter declined Wesker's offer to direct his play.[5]

However, if Wesker had made the same approach in 1965 with *The Four Seasons*, Pinter might have reacted differently, as it more readily shares territory that was starting to appear in Pinter's work at this time and even seems to anticipate some of the future directions he would go on to take. Wesker's play, a poetic exploration of a love affair over the course of one year, was a radical departure in style from the socio-realism of *Roots* (1959) or *Chips with Everything* (1962). One of its unusual features, compared to what had gone before, was its ambiguity; we never know, for example, the identity of the owner of the remote cottage at which Adam and Beatrice stay or why it remains empty for a year; likewise, we never learn how the couple met; Beatrice is also completely silent in the first segment of the play, and there is an absence of any social or political commentary. *The Four Seasons* could in fact be seen as an antecedent to the three short plays (*Landscape*, *Silence* and *Night*) that Pinter wrote between 1968 and 1969, which also incorporate poetic form to chart and explore the failure of relationships. However, it is difficult to imagine Pinter including the Lawrencian moment in *The Four Seasons* where Beatrice covers a sleeping Adam in bluebells (Wesker 1990b: 80). Yet, this examination of a love affair over a prolonged span would be something

Pinter would return to again in *Betrayal* (1978), although its use of time frame in the narrative would be both longer and more experimental, starting in 1977 at the end of the affair between Jerry and Emma and subsequently moving back in scenes that retrace its start in 1968.

In a similar vein, occasionally critical comparisons have recognized shared likenesses. For instance, a 1961 essay by Clifford Leech sees the pair as complementary in terms of the approach Wordsworth and Coleridge took in their poetry collection *Lyrical Ballads* (1798). For Leech, Wesker is Wordsworth, 'who wishes us to see the things around us more sharply than we normally do, to sympathize with other men', while Pinter is Coleridge, 'the man who wants to penetrate beneath the skin of observable fact, to explore a dream-world which has a valid relationship with the world of doing and conscious thought' (Leech 1968: 14).

A more direct synthesis can be found in Wesker's *The Kitchen* (1959) and Pinter's *The Dumb Waiter*, produced the following year. Despite its cast of 25 to Pinter's two, the characters in both are dehumanized as they attempt to supply the demands of their offstage customers. In Wesker, this leads to Peter sabotaging the gas supply to halt a never ceasing flow of demands from the kitchen, while in Pinter, it is the mechanism of the dumb waiter itself that entraps the two hitmen, before finally delivering its message for Gus to execute Ben. In this light, it is perhaps unsurprising that William Baker's *Harold Pinter Chronology* records him attending Stephen Daldry's Royal Court revival of *The Kitchen* in March 1994 (Baker 2013: 210). However, Pinter might have been surprised to discover he was the subject of pre-production talks in which Wesker and Daldry had seriously considered asking Pinter to play Marango, the restaurant's proprietor. In one letter to Stephen Daldry, Wesker writes, 'Harold [Pinter] is not a wild idea – I just don't think he'd consider it a good career move! But he'd be perfect. Powerful and bewildered!' (Wesker 1994: n.pag.).

Daldry's decision as the Royal Court's incoming Artistic Director to direct a landmark play from its 1950s golden period, whilst simultaneously bringing on a host of new dramatists, including Sarah Kane, Mark Ravenhill and Joe Penhall, can be read as a statement of intent – demonstrating both an awareness of the theatre's past, (and by association Wesker's place within it), together with a desire to create a new golden age. Pinter's place within that golden age is less secure and more complicated. Although some accounts of the period argue for Pinter's inclusion (Dukore 1988: 4; Kitchin 1960: 119–22), others consider any similarities cosmetic, save for Pinter happening to emerge at the same time as people like Wesker, John Osborne and Ann Jellicoe, together with a shared interest in ridding the English stage of the upper-middle-class speech and settings that up until 1956 had been so dominant (Esslin 1982: 267; Knowles 2001: 74).

Bridges, pauses and silences

Another principal difference between Wesker and Pinter concerns the views both hold regarding the form and function of dramatic language. Something of this can be found in Wesker's response in October 1999 after Pinter had sent his new play *Celebration* to read. In a later note to his children (posted on the script), Wesker considers it to be amongst Pinter's finest plays (AW4 1999). In his letter to Pinter, Wesker writes:

> I took the play to bed with me last night. I found it very sad. Those people with nothing to say and nothing to celebrate. The waiter is a wonderful creation. With the longest speeches he too has nothing to say, just sad boasts. I hope your actor realises that's the star part. Very good luck and thank you for the preview.
>
> (HP 1999: n.pag.)

By contrast, characters in Wesker's plays have a great deal to say – much of it celebratory – such as Beattie Bryant in *Roots* extolling the virtues of love-making in the afternoon (Wesker 2001: 91) or describing Bizet's *L'Arlésienne* suite as 'full of living' (Wesker 2001: 135). Although the plays also have their share of disillusioned characters, such as the eponymous Shylock who suffers under the anti-Semitic laws of Renaissance Venice, earlier he effusively expresses his faith (in a speech lasting two pages in the text) on the endurability of the printed word, likening it to an underground spring 'full of blinding questions and succulent doubts. [...] Unsuspected. Written! Printed! Indestructible!' (Wesker 1990a: 229).

To find such humanist sentiments in the work of Harold Pinter would be inconceivable, nor would he endorse Beattie Bryant's belief in *Roots* (albeit parroting the words of her boyfriend Ronnie Kahn) that words and language are 'bridges, so you can get safely from one place to another' (Wesker 2001: 91). In Pinter, language is never emancipatory: bridges in his plays are precarious, shifting and sometimes dangerous structures that fail to convey his characters safely from one place to another. Whereas Wesker's characters constantly reappraise their words to communicate exactly what they feel – such as Beattie Bryant's celebrated final speech at the end of *Roots*, where she begins to use her own words and ideas for the first time – Pinter's characters often hide their true intentions behind a carapace of language. Pinter has always refuted this interpretation, saying his characters communicate only too well (Knowles 1995: 12); yet, this only seems to occur at moments of direct confrontation or crisis, such as the knife fight between James and Bill in *The Collection* (1961) (Pinter 1977: 151–53) or Teddy stealing his brother Lenny's cheese roll in *The Homecoming* (1965) (Pinter 1991a: 71–72).

In a 1997 letter to the editor of *The Sunday Times* after being asked to write a reappraisal of Beckett's *Waiting for Godot*, Wesker refers to a public talk given by Pinter at the Hay-on-Wye Literary Festival where he draws a likeness to himself and Samuel Beckett in regard to both using fewer and fewer words in their plays as they grew older (AW 1997). One of the praiseworthy qualities associated with Beckett's and Pinter's work has been the ways they demonstrate the unreliability of language as a communicative tool; yet this is also something that Wesker, for all his belief in the transformative power of language, was aware of from early on. For example, in *I'm Talking about Jerusalem* (1960), Ada Kahn bitterly mocks her brother Ronnie's optimistic metaphor of language as bridges: 'Useless bloody things words are. Ronnie and his bridges! [...] Wait till he's older and he learns about silences – they span worlds' (Wesker 2001: 206). Pinter makes much the same point in an often-cited 1962 speech 'Writing for the Theatre', where he observed: 'I think that we communicate only too well, in our silence, in what is unsaid' (Pinter 1991b: xiii). While Wesker's stages are often filled with noisy debate and argument, such as the Kahns' house *in Chicken Soup with Barley*, by the end of the play we might feel inclined to interpret all this activity as part of the second type of silence that Pinter identifies in language. Whereas in the first nothing is said, but meaning is clear, in the second nothing is communicated despite 'a torrent of language [...] being employed' (Pinter 1991b: xiii).

Yet, Wesker can also be adept at employing the first type of silence when needed. For example, in *Roots* we encounter long breaks when nothing is said, such as the silences between husband and wife Jimmy and Jenny Beales, interspersed with brief exchanges on how each spent their day (Wesker 2001: 86–87). While taciturn characters like Bert Hudd in *The Room* (1957) or Aston in *The Caretaker* (1960) are a hallmark of Pinter's early work, they can also occasionally be found in Wesker, such as the monosyllabic Mr Bryant in *Roots*, who as his wife aptly observes, 'don't ever talk more'n he hev to' (Wesker 2001: 126). In another scene in the play, as Beattie and Jenny wash the dishes together, Wesker includes the stage direction, '*This is a silence that needs organizing [...] The silences are important – as important as the way they speak*' (Wesker 2001: 93). Yet, it is telling that Wesker feels the need to communicate the meaning behind the silence through a stage direction, whereas in Pinter's plays no clues, besides punctuation, are given. This is something that the critic John Russell Brown notes in his comparison of the two dramatists, observing that Wesker uses silences as 'indications of personal and social limitations' rather than providing 'clues to hidden power or tension' (Brown 1972: 164).

Dramatists of conviction

Regarding their views on theatre in general, there is more that unites than divides Harold Pinter and Arnold Wesker. One of their shared beliefs concerns authorial proprietorship, especially when it is challenged by directors who claim the right to alter or cut stage directions and dialogue. One exchange of letters between the pair is especially informative on this matter, concerning as it does a dispute between Pinter and fellow playwright David Mamet when Pinter directed the first London production of his controversial play *Oleanna* in 1993. According to Lia Williams, who played Carol in the production, Mamet rewrote the ending (which sees the student's university tutor physically assaulting her), after his wife, Rebecca Pidgeon, who originally played the role, started getting abuse from audiences. In the original ending, Carol continues to condemn her attacker immediately after the assault, whereas in the rewritten ending, she simply says, 'Well that's right' after being beaten up, followed by a blackout (Batty 2005: 204). Pinter was convinced that the original ending was the right one, and finally, despite misgivings from Mamet, this was the version used in the London production.

Following a telephone conversation over the matter, Wesker writes to Pinter:

> Thank you for sharing this information about the Mamet play with me. I was intrigued. And on reflection – confused. You are absolutely right to believe that the writer's job is not to do what the audience wants him to do, and there is no doubt in my mind that his original ending is the superior one [...] The confusion arises in me because although I agree with you about the ending, to have gone against Mamet's wishes raises grave implications. I think about the quote I often use of your – stirring and justified – outburst over 'Old Times' in Rome: '*Let me remind you that a play is not a public property. It belongs to its author under the international law of copyright.*' I would like to think that had I been Mamet I would have been persuaded of your view of my original intention, but had I not been and had I felt strongly enough I might have taken out a court injunction to stop the play opening. What would *you* have done? [...] I suppose part of the answer must be that if Mamet cared sufficiently about the ending he'd have made absolutely certain you were in possession of the text he'd sanctioned. A production of *The Kitchen* had to be cancelled half way through rehearsals in Athens because they'd started without asking me and I had made changes to the text after my production of it in the States. I didn't want the old version performed. It sounds as though Mamet was being careless. Surprising. Or else he secretly suspected his original ending was the right one and he was ashamed to have

been bullied into surrendering it. What a difficult moral quandary. I'm glad I didn't have to face it.

(Wesker 1993: n.pag., original emphasis)

Pinter replies, emphasizing that Wesker has misunderstood their telephone conversation. Mamet had originally given permission for the original ending to be used, only changing his mind after receiving a letter from Pinter stating that without the original ending being reinstated he could not direct the play; Mamet relented, albeit reluctantly (HP 1993).

Part of the reason why Wesker (mistakenly in retrospect) takes Pinter to task is because the subject has always been a particularly sensitive one for him. For instance, he has written that a dramatist should, if they wish to, have first rights over directing inaugural productions of their plays (Leeming 1983: 15), and characteristically he has written at length on the matter (Wesker 1985: 74–83). In partnership with John Dexter, Wesker found his ideal director – someone who instinctively seemed able to serve his own vision. However, the partnership ended acrimoniously after Dexter directed a Broadway production of *The Merchant* (subsequently retitled *Shylock*) in 1977. Likewise, Pinter also established a fruitful partnership with Peter Hall, first at the RSC and later at the National Theatre during the 1960s and 1970s; however, unlike Wesker, he has been more fortunate, both in subsequent directors such as David Leveaux, Sean Mathias and Katie Mitchell and in the positive critical reception afforded to him as a director of his own work and the work of others. This has not been so forthcoming when Wesker has directed his own plays, at least not in the United Kingdom, and it is interesting to note that on two occasions in their correspondence Wesker has asked Pinter to direct his plays, *Caritas* and *Denial* (2000) (HP 1980; 1993).

One of the most widely noted differences between the two dramatists has been their approach to politics. In a 1961 *New Theatre Magazine* interview with Harold Pinter, Wesker's name was directly mentioned as a contemporary associated with socialist theatre, followed by a question about whether politics interested Pinter. His answer in many respects defined the reception of his work until the mid-1980s:

> I find most political thinking and terminology suspect, deficient [...] I object to the stage being used as a substitute for a soap box, where the author desires to make a political statement at all costs and forces his characters into a fixed and artificial statement at all costs and forces his characters into fixed and artificial postures in order to achieve this [...] I don't care for didactic or moralistic theatre. In England I find this theatre, on the whole, sentimental and unconvincing.

(Thompson 1961: 9)

It is hard not to see these criticisms as levelled directly at Wesker himself, which in turn have been repeated by others. For example, Pinter's aversion to sentimentality has been repeated by Arnold Hinchliffe, who considers Wesker's depiction of working class characters to be ridden with naïve romantic clichés (Hinchliffe 1967: 24). Elsewhere, Christopher Bigsby makes a distinction that the working classes in Pinter's early work become 'simply one more ironic tool [...] between language and referent' (Bigsby 1981: 395), while Michael Billington in his biography of Pinter makes a variation on the same point, arguing that whereas Wesker's *Trilogy* emerges from his position as a 'disillusioned socialist', Pinter by contrast 'wrote from the vantage point of sceptical enquiry' (Billington 1996: 88).

This is evident in the 1961 interview when Pinter is asked for his views on Wesker's recent initiative with the British Trades Union movement in setting up Centre 42 (C42) to promote arts and cultural activities for its members:

> To me, this seems to be happening on the other side of the moon. I mean, I can't fix the matter as having any grave or significant import for me. I suppose it's a laudable attitude from certain points of view, but these points of view simply do not interest me.
>
> (Thompson 1961: 9)

That same year Pinter refines these views in a well-known speech delivered at the National Student Drama Festival: 'If I were to state a moral precept it might be: beware the writer who puts his concern for you to embrace, who leaves no doubt of his worthiness, his usefulness, his altruism' (Pinter 1991b: xi). Although careful to point out that he does not wish to 'propagate a phoney war between hypothetical schools of playwrights' (Pinter 1991b: xi), the speech has subsequently been interpreted by some as a public disassociation from Wesker and the other Royal Court dramatists (Batty 2005: 30).

In turn, Wesker has criticized Pinter's lionization by critics who praise his work for its qualities of ambiguity over social comment. Wesker was prompted after novelist and playwright John Mortimer's review of Martin Esslin's study of Pinter, *The Peopled Wound* (subsequently retitled *Pinter the Playwright*). Against the qualities Mortimer found so praiseworthy, Wesker counterargues that in drama other needs exist

> not for the mystery to be solved [...] but to be illuminated in part [...] To stay and indulge in 'the mystery' is to reduce art to an intellectual parlour game, an emotional quiz, to make a jigsaw out of tragedy and a mere oddity out of all human behaviour.
>
> (Wesker 1985: 20)

However, it would also be wrong to say that Pinter has been entirely lacking in political consciousness. Interviewed in 1966, he recounted how, after watching a television programme in which a group of American politicians commented on the progress of the Vietnam War: 'I wanted very much to burst through the screen with a flamethrower and burn their eyes out and their balls off and then enquire from them how they would assess this action from a political point of view' (Pinter cited in Smith 2005: 61). Despite clearly feeling impassioned about the subject, in the same interview Pinter still remained sceptical about theatre's ability to report on the conflict with any more clarity than other media (Smith 2005: 63). In fact, he seemed just as outraged when giving an account of attending Peter Brook's production of the Vietnam protest play *US* (1966): 'I don't like being subjected to propaganda, and I detest soapboxes [...] The chasm between the reality of the war in Vietnam and the image of what *US* presented on the stage was quite preposterous' (Smith 2005: 62–63).

Pinter's abandonment of an early play *The Hothouse* (1958), claiming it was too ideologically driven in its satire on bureaucratic state-sanctioned violence, only to return to it more favourably in 1980[6], is illustrative of the change in attitude Pinter underwent during this period. Yet, he has always remained consistently suspicious of didacticism, mainly because the process of creation for Pinter is also a largely unconscious one. This perhaps explains why recognizably political plays such as *Party Time* (1991) have been interspersed with a return to the memory plays of the early to mid-1970s with *Moonlight* (1993) and *Ashes to Ashes* (1996), the latter being an amalgamation of the two forms.

Subsequently, Pinter rejects the earnest humanism, the romanticism and the striving for utopias that define much of Wesker's oeuvre. An assessment of Pinter's other writings and public speeches on subjects ranging from American foreign policy to the torture of political dissidents around the world means that while one cannot doubt his sincerity on these issues, it does not always come through in his drama. Even *Mountain Language* (1988), a play clearly motivated by outrage against politically repressive regimes, offers few possibilities for optimism or evidence of the struggles for change that Wesker often strives for.

In terms of their political activism, it would not be unfair to describe both men as iconoclasts. With the notable exception of Wesker's collaboration with the British Trades Union Congress and Harold Wilson's 1964–70 Labour administration in trying to establish C42 or Pinter's association with PEN – an organization that campaigns for writers facing persecution around the world – neither have affiliated themselves directly to a political cause or movement. While both could be broadly described as coming from the Left, both have at times gone against consensus thinking. Perhaps as an outcome of the lack of support shown to C42, after 1970, Wesker became critical of the trade union closed shop, which he saw as an abuse of power. This view was also shared by Pinter during the industrial dispute that interrupted the opening of the National Theatre's new home on London's South Bank in 1976 and in no small part led him (in a decision he very much came to regret) to voting for Mrs Thatcher's government in 1979 due to its commitment to curb union power. Pinter's decision was much criticized at the time, as was Wesker in 1971 when he gave permission for his plays to be performed in South Africa during the apartheid regime (Wesker 1985: 181–85). This independence of mind has also been combined in both with a willingness to accept the consequences of their actions. In 1961, Wesker was arrested for an act of civil disobedience at a demonstration organized by the Committee of 100 and spent a month in Drake Hall open prison. Pinter also risked imprisonment when he refused to do National Service on the grounds of being a conscientious objector.

The pair came together in January 1988 when they both wrote a letter to the *Guardian* newspaper criticizing it for its lack of reporting on the eight-year sentences with hard labour given to members of the Turkish Peace Association (Pinter and Wesker 1988). The need to draw attention to the plight of prisoners of conscience, and particularly those of writers, was a cause that both have supported. However, in 2003, they came into conflict, at least through the media, when each presented opposing views over the war in Iraq. Originally a piece for the BBC World Service, their responses were later transcribed by the *Wall Street Journal* in the United States and *The Sunday Times* in the United Kingdom. Pinter, a highly vocal critic of both American and British involvement in the conflict, included a specially written poem entitled 'The Bombs'. Wesker, in his original letter to the *Guardian*, while denouncing Saddam Hussein as a tyrant, imagines the dictator's delight at the anti-war movement:

> I've got the leading artists and intellectuals of Europe and America to march and sign petitions helping me to perpetuate the tyrannical oppression of my people [...] and best of all I've got Osama Bin Laden calling for suicide attacks against my enemies and Harold Pinter writing verses against my enemies.
>
> (Wesker 2003: n.pag.)

While Pinter's reaction to Wesker's letter is not known, Wesker's scepticism of the anti-war movement chimed with that of Simon Stephens, one of the millennial generation of British playwrights. Stephens has written that his play *Motortown* (2006) set out to challenge the liberal consensus amongst the sort of theatregoers who attended the Royal Court (Stephens 2009: xvii). This was couched using the same argument Wesker employed, whereby the anti-war movement 'managed, at times, to argue its way into defending the sovereignty of a mass murderer' (Stephens 2009: xvii). While Pinter might have felt compelled to write a poem about the devastation created by the bombing of the people of Iraq, it is also worth remembering that he was notably absent in the late 1950s when Wesker, together with fellow playwrights John Osborne, John Arden and Shelagh Delaney, marched in solidarity at a number of CND demonstrations against the far greater threat posed by the proliferation of nuclear weapons.

Jewish dramatists

Despite such disagreements, Arnold Wesker and Harold Pinter both share a common cultural background as East End London Jews. Wesker drew attention to this shared heritage when he wrote to congratulate Pinter on hearing the news that he had been awarded the 2005 Nobel Prize for Literature: 'Congratulations! Glad they chose one of the Hackney Jew boys!' (HP 2005: n.pag.). While for both, Judaism as a religious practice was never to play any part in their lives, both have acknowledged a sense of Jewish consciousness, although in a 1970 interview, Wesker confessed to only recently gaining a sense of belonging to a community with a shared sense of suffering and persecution (Hayman 1970: 4–5).

Yet, like so much about the two dramatists, both display very different attitudes regarding their sense of Jewish self-identity. Signs of this can be found in their correspondence. For example, in 1992, after a request from Wesker, Pinter contributes £250 towards tuition costs at the Guildhall School of Music and Drama for a Russian student who has been forced to leave her home country due to antisemitism (HP 1992). However, in an earlier letter, written in February 1984, Pinter declines Wesker's request for him to join The Israeli Cultural Institute, an organization Wesker had been trying to set up with the help of what he calls other 'high powered people (mainly Jewish) in the arts', based on the model established by bodies such as the British Council and Goethe Institute. The letter is interesting as it not only outlines Wesker's position on Israel at the time but also assumes that 'like me and a large section of Anglo-Jewry (as well as Israel society), you're probably critical of much Israeli policy'. However, he also adds, 'If you agree it's a country of inhabitants vibrant with artistic, intellectual and moral energy as no other in the area then you'll be concerned about its beleaguered and isolated situation' (HP 1984b: n.pag.). Although in his reply Pinter gives no response to his own position on Israel, elsewhere he has spoken out against the arrest and detention of both Palestinians and its own citizens critical of the regime (Smith 2005: 104–5). Wesker also published several articles that discuss both the place of Judaism in his own work as well as his attitude to Israel and its place in the world (Wesker 1985: 252–87). In his reply to Wesker's letter, Pinter regrets that he is unable to participate, saying that while Israel is a concern to him, other political commitments also call on his time; he ends by saying that although he identifies as being Jewish, he remains many other things as well (HP 1984a). These sentiments seem in accord with a 1991 interview where, recalling his East End background, Pinter also comments: 'I didn't go around proclaiming myself a Jew, although I always was a Jew and remain so' (Pinter cited in Batty 2005: 97).

While he has spoken about his formative years spent in the East End of London, Pinter has never been compelled to draw directly on these experiences in the same way that Wesker has done in plays such as *Chicken Soup with Barley* or *The Old Ones* (1972), which draw on Jewish family life. Ronald Hayman points out that the production of *Chicken Soup With Barley* coincides with Pinter's early work, where characters such as Rose in *The Room* and Meg in *The Birthday Party* also appropriate the same language of 'the dominating, nagging, working class Jewish mother figure' that we see in Wesker's characterization of Ada Kahn (Hayman 1970: 23). Hayman's view in turn may have been influenced by a rare outing that saw Wesker as a critic when in February 1960 he reviewed Pinter's *The Birthday Party* for *The Jewish Chronicle*, after the play text had been published by the theatre journal *Encore*. Wesker's piece is interesting, not only because it is one of the earliest examples of a substantial piece of critical writing on *The Birthday Party* but also because he was amongst the first not to reject the play out of hand as an infuriating puzzle, as so many other reviews had done. Rather, Wesker perceptively reads the play as being about how society punishes individual non-conformity. However, with *Chicken Soup with Barley* clearly in mind, Wesker also goes on to say, 'Pinter is a Jewish writer and this is a play out of his own experiences in the Jewish community' (Wesker 1960: n.pag.). Writing to Pinter in 1980, Wesker reminds him of both the review and his reaction to it: 'I'd reviewed THE BIRTHDAY PARTY for the J.C. [*Jewish Chronicle*] – and favourably, but you told me later I'd got it all wrong!'[7] (HP 1980: n.pag.). Wesker returns to the review in 2009 for a memorial piece on Pinter for the journal *Jewish Renaissance* saying, 'I defended the play but worried over its coy avoidance of the Jewish milieu against which the play made most sense' (Wesker 2009: n.pag.). Others in turn have said the same about *The Homecoming* (1965), including actor Warren Mitchell, who played the role of patriarch Max in Peter Hall's 1991 revival, who saw the play centring around a London Jewish family (Billington 1996: 325). Pinter has always strongly refuted any such associations, although he has spoken about it being prompted by the situation of a Jew marrying a non-Jew and bringing her back to meet his family (Billington 1996: 163).

Judaism has been something Wesker has returned to periodically during his career – for example, *Shylock* (1976), *Blood Libel* (1996) and *Badenheim 1939* (1987) have all examined historical examples of anti-Semitic societies. By contrast, Pinter's approach has always been less direct, although he has spoken about how

Ashes to Ashes (1996) came about after reading Gita Sereny's *Albert Speer: His Battle with Truth* (1995), and in the past he had adapted Fred Uhlman's novel *Reunion* (1989) for film and directed Robert Shaw's play *The Man in the Glass Booth* (1967), both of which concern the persecution of Jews during the Nazi period.

As Wesker points out in his memorial article on Harold Pinter, their relationship was based more on a fond acquaintanceship than close friendship (Wesker 2009). William Baker's highly detailed *Pinter Chronology* records just three meetings between the pair between 1975 and 1986, yet, judging by their slim correspondence held in the British Library's Harold Pinter archive, there exists a mutual respect and affection. The style of the letters also provides good indicators of the differences that can be found elsewhere through the voice and tone used in their dramatic work. Wesker's letters are friendly, effusive and often lengthy, while Pinter's are more terse and non-committal. Writing in his influential study *Anger & After*, John Russell Taylor comments that over and above any dramatist of his generation it is impossible to extricate Wesker the playwright from Wesker the man (Taylor 1969: 147). By contrast, it is far harder to detect autobiographical stands in Pinter's plays, although recent public access to his extensive archive has shown that autobiographical incidents frequently haunt much of the work.

Wesker, in his memorial to Pinter, felt that this guardedness extended towards a reluctance to let life and humanity into his work, something he saw as an inherent weakness:

> Each successive play seemed a parody of the previous one. Every character was a Pinter-character, never allowed to be itself. He had stumbled upon a trick of dialogue that became a restrictive mannerism, which mannerism – strong and recognizable – led to 'Pinteresque' entering the language. But I found none of his characters loveable. Sweet or tender, or even intellectually interesting... 'I could never write a happy play', he is quoted as saying. Why? It is a strange confession. What was there about joy that was such an anathema to him? Audiences come away from a Pinter play not having been made to think or feel, but to guess. We don't end up arguing about, or being moved by, his view of the human condition, instead we argue about what was happening on stage.
>
> (Wesker 2009: n.pag.)

It is here that Wesker perhaps comes closest to pinning down the differences in form and content between his own work and Pinter's. While Wesker's stages resonate with memorable characters busily engaged in the business of living, Pinter's curiously anonymous creations often circle one another suspiciously in enclosed rooms in which the outside world rarely intrudes.

Given the worldwide regard in which Pinter's work is held, Wesker realized that the view expressed in his memorial to Pinter would always be likely to remain a minority one; certainly within the pantheon of dramatists Pinter's star continues to shine considerably more brightly than Wesker's. However, both careers have been marked by highs and lows – after *The Homecoming* in 1965, despite keeping occupied adapting screenplays, as well as acting and directing, Pinter felt unable to write anything for the theatre save two short plays, *Landscape* (1968) and *Silence* (1969). It was not until *Old Times* in 1971 that Pinter managed to produce a full-length play. While Wesker did not encounter writer's block, much of his energies during the 1960s were expended on running C42, until he resigned in 1970. In between, two plays *The Four Seasons* (1965) and *Their Very Own and Golden City* (1965) were poorly received at their British premieres. Despite occasionally receiving poor critical notices, notably for *Betrayal* (1978) and *Moonlight* (1993) (which have subsequently grown in critical standing), Pinter's career since *Old Times* has been one of almost unbroken success. While Wesker's work has remained popular abroad, ironically it was only towards the end of his life that three acclaimed revivals – *The Kitchen* at the National Theatre and *Chicken Soup with Barley* at the Royal Court, both in 2011, and *Roots* at the Donmar Warehouse in 2013 raised his critical standing. Yet, whereas revivals of work from every stage of Pinter's career has been the norm, for Wesker, revivals of his work in the United Kingdom at least continue to be drawn from the early part of his playwriting career.

However, it is worth ending with one of the last exchanges of correspondence between the two men that took place ten months before Pinter's death in December 2008. In the January of that year, Wesker had published a collection of poems entitled *All Things Tire of Themselves*, in which five were dedicated to Harold Pinter. While the reasons for this dedication are unclear, Wesker sent the collection to Pinter, from which he received the following reply, rather aptly, on Valentine's Day:

Dear Arnold

What a pleasant surprise to receive your book of poems. I was very touched that five were addressed to me. But I like the poems very much. They are so simple, so direct – and poignant.

Congratulations!
Yours Harold

(AW4 2008: n.pag.)

NOTES

1. The Harold Pinter estate does not allow direct quotations from his letters held in the British Library archive. I have abided by this and instead have summarized content only.

2. Here Wesker is using the original name, The Grocer's Company School, before it was renamed in 1906 as Hackney Downs School.

3. Wesker is referring to a Clapton Secondary School for Girls in Hackney. Jacky Hymans in *Hooped Skirts and Ponytails – A Fifties Memoir* writes the following: 'Laura Place girls had a raw deal: their uniforms consisted of a brown tunic, yellow blouse, brown blazer – and brown knickers, a horrific idea for any girl' (Hyams 2016: 90).

4. Wesker is referring to a school production of *Macbeth* at Hackney Downs Grammar school in 1947, where Pinter played the eponymous role.

5. Wesker's letter had initially been prompted by Peter Hall's suggestion that Pinter, as an associate director at the National Theatre, might want to direct *Caritas*. However, Mark Taylor Batty records that despite also being offered the choice of Thomas Otway's Restoration tragedy *Venice Preserv'd* (1682) and Brian Friel's new play *Translations* (1980), Pinter opted to direct an earlier abandoned play of his own, *The Hothouse* (Batty 2005: 63).

6. Pinter returned to the play later in 1995, playing the part of *Roote* in a production at the Chichester Festival and subsequently at the Comedy Theatre in London.

7. In the review Wesker simply assumes that Stanley is having an affair with Meg, his landlady.

REFERENCES

Baker, William (2013), *A Harold Pinter Chronology*, Basingstoke: Macmillan.

Batty, Mark (2005), *About Pinter: The Playwright and his Work*, London: Faber.

Bigsby, Christopher (1981), 'The politics of anxiety: Contemporary socialist theatre in England', *Modern Drama*, 24:4, pp. 393–03.

Billington, Michael (1996), *The Life and Work of Harold Pinter*, London: Faber.

Brown, John Russell (1972), *Theatre Language: A Study of Arden, Osborne, Pinter and Wesker*, London: Allen Lane.

Drake, Sylvie (1985), 'Acting is just like old times for Pinter', *Los Angeles Times*, 29 October, https://www.latimes.com/archives/la-xpm-1985-10-29-ca-13277-story.html. Accessed 10 April 2020.

Dukore, Bernard (1988), *Harold Pinter*, 2nd ed., Basingstoke: Macmillan.

Esslin, Martin (1982), *Pinter: The Playwright*, 4th rev. ed., London: Methuen.

Hayman, Ronald (1970), *Arnold Wesker*, London: Heinemann.

Hinchcliffe, Arnold (1967), *Harold Pinter*, Basingstoke: Macmillan.

Hyams, Jacky (2016), *Hooped Skirts and Ponytails: A Fifties Memoir*, London: John Blake Publishing.

Kitchin, Laurence (1960), *Mid-Century Drama*, London: Faber.

Knowles, Ronald (2001), 'Pinter and Twentieth-Century Drama', in P. Raby (ed.), *The Cambridge Companion to Harold Pinter*, Cambridge: CUP, pp. 73–86.

—— (1995), *Understanding Harold Pinter*, Carolina: University of Carolina Press.

Lacey, Stephen (1995), *British Realist Theatre: The New Wave in Its Context 1956–1965*, London: Routledge.

Leech, Clifford (1968), 'Two Romantics: Arnold Wesker and Harold Pinter', in J. R. Brown and B. Harris (eds), *Contemporary Theatre: Stratford-Upon Avon Studies 4*, rev. ed., London: Edward Arnold.

Leeming, Glenda (1983), *Wesker: The Playwright*, London: Methuen.

Pinter, Harold (1977), *Plays: Two*, London: Methuen.

—— (1991a), *Plays: Three*, London: Methuen.

—— (1991b), *Plays: One*, London: Methuen.

Pinter, Harold Archive (HP), London: British Library

—— (1980), Letter from Arnold Wesker, 10 December, ADD MSS 88880/6/4.

—— (1984a), Letter to Arnold Wesker, 13 February, ADD MS 88880/654.

—— (1984b), Letter from Arnold Wesker, 10 February, ADD MSS 88880/654.

—— (1992), Letter from Arnold Wesker, 3 January, ADD MS 88880/6/12.

—— (1993), Letter to Arnold Wesker, n.d., ADD MS 88880/6/12.

—— (1998a), Letter from Arnold Wesker, 27 June, ADD MS 8880/6/47.

—— (1998b), Letter to Arnold Wesker, 1 July, ADD MS 8880/6/47.

—— (1999), Letter from Arnold Wesker, 9 October, ADD MS 8880/6/19.

—— (2005), Letter from Arnold Wesker, 14 October, ADD MS 88880/11/5.

Pinter, Harold, and Wesker, Arnold (1988), Letter to *The Guardian*, 2 January.

Smith, Ian (2005), *Pinter in the Theatre*, London: Nick Hern.

Stephens, Simon (2009), *Plays: 2*, London: Methuen.

Taylor, John Russell (1969), *Anger and After: A Guide to the New British Drama*, London: Methuen.

Thompson, Harry (1961), 'Harold Pinter replies', *New Theatre Magazine*, 2:2, pp. 8–10.

Wesker, Arnold (1960), 'Plea for a play', *The Jewish Chronicle*, 12 February.

—— (1965), Letter from Arnold Wesker, *Gambit*, Summer, p.14.

—— (1985), *Distinctions*, London: Jonathan Cape.

—— (1990a), *Volume 4: Shylock and Other Plays*, London: Penguin.

—— (1990b), *Volume 2: The Kitchen and Other Plays*, London: Penguin.

—— (1997), 'On the shelf', *The Sunday Times*, 31 August.

—— (2001), *Plays 1*, London: Methuen.

—— (2003), Letter to *The Guardian*, 14 February.

—— (2009), 'Harold Pinter: Thoughts and memories', *Jewish Renaissance*, 8:3, p. 47.

Wesker, Arnold Papers (AW) (1994), Letter to Stephen Daldry, 11 January, Austin, Texas: Harry Ransom Center, Box 48.6.

—— (1997), Letter to Georgie Greg, 29 July, Austin, Texas: Harry Ransom Center, Box 48.6.

Wesker, Arnold Papers (AW4) (1999), Note on Copy of Script by Harold Pinter of *Celebration*, n.d., Austin, Texas: Harry Ransom Center, Box 3.

—— (2008), Letter to Arnold Wesker, 14 February, Austin, Texas: Harry Ransom Center, Box 3.

FIGURE 4: Arnold and Dusty Wesker, Paris, mid-1970s.

3

Roots: A Political Poem

James Macdonald

Arnold was a poet. *Roots* is a love poem – to a person, to a place, to a family, to a landscape. And to the possibility of transformation, of self-improvement, of change. It is the story of Beatie Bryant returning home to her family of farm workers in Norfolk, full of the joys of London and culture and most of all her Socialist boyfriend Ronnie. It is a description of a world that Arnold, disguised as Ronnie here, came to know through Dusty and her family. In many ways it is his most purely observational play. So much of what he saw and heard would be completely new on a British stage. That kitchen sink, those particular rural voices and most of all that action. Here and elsewhere, Arnold really invented the work play, a completely original and truthful moment in world theatre, much imitated: politics as it is lived by people.

He wrote a lot of this play in the front room of the family's tied farm cottage, whilst Ma Bryant – Bicker was Dusty's real family name – cooked and chatted to neighbours in the next room, giving her wonderful running commentary on illnesses and scandal and any passing lorries and buses. The rhythm of this life is beautifully and artfully caught. Everything takes as long as it takes, from peeling vegetables to making sponge cakes to filling a tin bath. The women practically never stop working, the men are spent husks in chairs. Talking is something that happens to fill the doing. And whilst it is easy to think of Arnold as being a wordy writer, he also had an uncanny ear for silence, for the unspoken.

This particular world of work is long gone – though the Bicker family still live in the area. On a research trip, Dusty's nephew Keith incredibly graciously talked to our company of actors about the family, filled us in on who had been outraged by Arnold's depiction of them in the play and described how the playwright had given Ma Bicker a signed copy of his play about her world – which she placed on a windowsill and never read. The farm estate that once employed 35 people is now managed by two men mounted on huge machines. Then Keith showed us round the village, the gravel pits and finally the cottage itself, where a minibus full of theatre folk descended on an unsuspecting retired couple from Yorkshire who had just that week moved in. No blue plaque – they had no idea a great work of genius had been written in their tiny living room. (Bizarrely, the wonderful Royal Court playwright Lucy Kirkwood lives in the same village – and she had no idea either…).

But back in the day, the Royal Court never quite trusted Arnold's plays enough. They made him open in Coventry – twice. In fact, Tony Richardson took Arnold out to lunch round the corner from Sloane Square in La Poule au Pot and told him what he and Devine thought needed to be done with *Roots*: *You can't spend three acts talking about a character who never turns up* – (two years after *Waiting for Godot*, this…) *Condense what you've got and write a new last act in which Ronnie comes through the door.* Arnold sensibly told them to fuck off. And so… back to Coventry.

Arnold's one note to me was: it's a lyrical play. It is indeed written with an extraordinary sensibility to sound and rhythm, and its central act contains a brilliant running debate about the value of popular and classical music – with excerpts sung and played on Beatie's Dansette. Beatie is an innocent, but her eyes are wide open and she is constantly making discoveries – shyly realizing that she is an artist – or… *isn't your nose a funny thing, and your ears* – and most crucially of course, at the heart of the play, in her grief and rage at Ronnie's betrayal and her family's indifference – accidentally discovering articulacy, her own voice. A political ideal embodied in a moment of extraordinary theatrical power.

Arnold also shared with me his one disappointment in the way the play had been received – audiences did not seem to like Ronnie! But actually as a dramatist what he had done was instinctively brilliant. Up to a point Ronnie, ventriloquized by Beatie, is charming and a clown – as indeed he is in person elsewhere in *The Trilogy* – but the play's argument is stronger if we come to mistrust him here, as Beatie's family do. Beatie must discover her own sense of truth.

In 1960, the person who understood Arnold's project best was someone I did not even know was a theatre critic – Ted Hughes:

> At bottom Wesker is a naive lyrical poet, full of joy, in love with individuals and all the minute details of their lives, and with the moment-to-moment chance to live. He is also an analytical realist: he sees how people neglect their chances, let their feelings die, lose contact with life and with each other, sinking into routine and indifference. In the collision of the poet and the analyst lies his suffering. He can't just give people up, he loves them too much, but he can't bear to see the way they let themselves down either. His 'socialism', his message, takes the form of a desperate public exhortation – wake up and live… He possesses a musical gift: his passages of dialogue sometimes take on the inevitability of a delicate kind of poetry, and this is directly related to the most remarkable thing about

these plays and certainly the thing to be grateful for: the food of love which sustains them... Wesker's 'socialism' is something close to a poetic intuition, a concern with the life at the root of all parties and opinions.

(Ted Hughes, *The Nation*, 19 November 1960: n.pag.)

I wanted to finish with Arnold's voice; it is the little note at the front of the playscript. For me it catches his unique generosity of spirit:

Actors and Producers – please

My people are not caricatures. They are real (though fiction) [...] The picture I have drawn is a harsh one, yet my tone is not one of disgust - nor should it be in the presentation of the plays. I am at one with these people: it is only that I am annoyed, with them and myself.

(*The Trilogy*, n.pag.)

FIGURE 5: Following the Wesker 68 festival in Tokyo, Wesker frequently wore his Japanese jackets into the early seventies. Photo by Torbjörn Gustafson.

4

The Enigma That Is Pip:
A Character under Construction
in Wesker's *Chips with Everything*

John Bull

Art and experience – the boundaries become blurred.

(Wesker 1994: 256)

My memory, as a would-be rebellious teenager, of seeing the original production of Arnold Wesker's *Chips with Everything* (1962), after its transfer from the Royal Court to the Vaudeville in 1963, is that my instinctive reaction to it was to find in it the spirit of opposition to an oppressive system of authority. When I attended the 1997 revival at the National Theatre, I still found something of that original spirit, but was perhaps struck less by the call to resistance, and more by the creation of order. The play consists of a series of oppositions and pairings, but these are never realizable as a part of a dialectic structure. There is nothing other than a theatrical conclusion, and that in itself will prove worthy of examination.

In this chapter, I first contextualize the moments of its inception. I then trace the history of the play, from its source in the experiences of the playwright as a Royal Air Force (RAF) National Service conscript through the attempt to create a novel out of those experiences, through the first draft of a play drawing from the failed attempt at a novel, *The Conscripts* in 1960, to the first performances of *Chips* in 1962. I do so with an awareness that the passing of time has also changed the way in which the play is and can be read. And above all else, I do so realizing that the central problems that the play presents – and its essential fascination – lie in the figure of Pip. After considering the different ways in which Wesker sought to present a character, with whom he both did and did not identify, I look at Pip as, in part, a response to Brecht's *Galileo*, as a would-be rebel faced with his own Inquisition.

The Conscripts

When Arnold Wesker's *Chips with Everything* opened at the Royal Court Theatre in London on 27 April 1962, not only was it the fifth of his plays to be produced professionally, but it was the fifth of his to be produced at that theatre. Bolstered by the Royal Court bringing back his trilogy (*Chicken Soup with Barley, Roots* and *I'm Talking about Jerusalem*) in a single season in 1960, Wesker – in a proposal that mirrored the Centre 42 (C42) plan to stage festival events in a series of cities across the United Kingdom – offered eight other civic theatres the opportunity to open simultaneously with the London production. In the event, only Glasgow accepted the invitation, though Geoffrey Ost at the Sheffield Playhouse also begged leave to join the party.

The play would be concerned with the process, from arrival at the camp to the final passing-out parade, of a group of young men embarking on their National Service in the RAF. It follows the progress of one hut of men as they pass through the tough and dehumanizing initial process of training. Although Wesker does not make the point too obviously, there is a regional diversity in the young working-class recruits. The exception is Pip, an ex-public schoolboy who has chosen to be enlisted with the men, rather than offering himself up for officer training, as would be expected from someone of his background.

A would-be rebel against the system, Pip resists the officers' attempts to get the men to perform a rock 'n' roll number at the Christmas Eve party in the NAAFI (Navy, Army and Air Force Institutes, the social and recreational centre for the other ranks) and persuades them to give first the solo recitation of an old Scottish lay and then a defiant choral version of an ancient rebel folk song; he leads the men in an organized night-raid on the coke store and refuses to embark on bayonet practice, risking a court martial and prison, before eventually acceding and accepting his fate as a potential officer. Paralleling his narrative is that of conscript 279 Washington, known as Smiler because he cannot help smiling: 'I'm not smiling, Corporal, it's natural, I was born with it' (24).[1] Picked on and punished, he eventually attempts to desert, before returning, beaten, to the camp, with the prospect of having to stay on to complete his training, while his colleagues having supported him in defiance of the officers, successfully and triumphantly take part, perfectly drilled, in the passing-out parade.

The slickness and efficiency of this final scene is characteristic of the entire production, both in 1962 and in the 1997 National Theatre revival. For Callum Mill, the director of the 1962 Glasgow Citizens Theatre production,

[t]he purely mechanical running of the play requires ingenuity and imagination. The action of the play is limited to an RAF training camp – but the scene moves swiftly and continuously from the hut – the focus of the life of the place – to the parade ground, to the NAAFI, to the Lecture Hut, to the C.O.'s Office, to the Guard Room, to the coke yard, to the road beyond, back and forth, *from* bed *to* bed, from morning to night to the constant tempo of marching feet, the orders of the strident N.C.O.s and the songs of the displaced.

(Mill 1962: 23)

Jocelyn Herbert's brilliantly open set design at the Royal Court was predicated on her central premise that *Chips* was 'very much an inside/outside play' (Courtney 1993: 51) and was greatly aided by the subtle lighting changes and by one of the director's first big decisions: 'John Dexter got the idea of the soldiers drilling to overcome the difficulty of opening the hut, and in the end the drilling went right the way though the play and he got someone from the army to come and instruct the actors' (Courtney 1993: 51). In fact, a great part of the first of the five-week rehearsal period was spent on drilling the men (Dexter 1962: 32). In 1997, the director, Howard Davies, reinforced this effect by having the stage covered in gravel. What this constant and seamless activity does – the men being ordered to their beds at night and shouted at to get out of them the following morning in a single piece of dialogue from Corporal Hill, who is responsible for training them, for instance – is to emphasize the conveyor-belt way in which they are being moulded and shaped from raw intake to well-drilled men, from individuals to a single organized unit: moving, as the Corporal says at the final parade, 'as one man, as one ship, as one solid gliding ship' (71).

Now, it is important to stress the direct context of the action, for obviously – as many critics noted from the outset – the process of initiation, and its ramifications in terms of class relations (officers and men), was rightly open to a wider interpretation: the camp as a microcosm of the state. One of the most vociferous analyses of this sort came from the anonymous reviewer in the *Financial Times*:

Mr Wesker has chosen an RAF recruit station as his scene. But his play, of course, is not 'about' the RAF. It is not just a crude attack upon the way officers treat the men. It is not even 'about' the class system though this is nearer the point. What the play does is to bring into sharp focus the moral and spiritual damage which our class relationships do to people as people.

(Anon. 1962: n.pag.)

However, not only is the play grounded in the very fact of National Service, but, unless that reality is created on stage, the larger resonances would ring hollow.

The practice went back to the Second World War and the National Service (Armed Forces) Act of 1939. National Service, as it came to be known, continued after the war, requiring most non-university bound men to enrol for two years. The call-up ended at the very end of 1960, and the last National Servicemen were demobbed in May 1963, just one year after *Chips* opened.

Chips would prove to be the most commercially successful play of Wesker's entire career in the United Kingdom. But it had been a hard-fought success. Although the English Stage Company (ESC) at the Royal Court had staged his first play, *The Kitchen*, in its original form as a Sunday night production without décor in 1959, it was initially extremely reluctant to put on any of the three plays in *The Trilogy* and did so only after they had premiered at the Belgrade Theatre Coventry (Bull 2012: 174). This reluctance initially extended to *Chips* (Wesker 1994: 258), but in the event it did premiere at the Court. Its success, following the staging of the complete *Trilogy* and the full-scale production of the revised and enlarged *Kitchen* in 1961, ensured that he had become established as second only to John Osborne as the corner-stone of the ESC's critical and financial credibility. Indeed, at the end of 1962, the director, John Dexter, talked of the work, even before its transfer to the West End, as having 'given to Arnold and myself and the boys, security for almost the first time' (Dexter 1962: 32). By July 1963, after the play had successfully transferred, there was already a total surplus of £1,695 'after paying off both production costs and the cost of the transfer to the Vaudeville Theatre', where it was averaging £700 a week profit (ESC 1963a: n.pag.). Its importance to the ESC cannot be underestimated. Indeed, the minutes show that 'of the twelve productions presented during the year only one, *Chips With Everything*, had been a financial success' (ESC 1963b: n.pag.). As well as having the highest take-up of seats in the financial year ending 31 March 1963 (94 per cent), it made nearly £10,000 profit (Findlater 1981: Appendix II). This is worth putting in context: although the Arts Council of Great Britain's contribution to the company in 1962–63 was £20,000, this was double that of the previous year and just about matched by *Chips'* contribution.

However, by June 1963, things at the Court were running less smoothly, and 'the situation had deteriorated greatly' (ESC 1963b: n.pag.). Negotiations for a US transfer had been underway for a while, held up by the demands of American Equity, and they 'were waiting to hear how many of the company would be allowed to play in the States' (ESC 1963a: n.pag.). In the event, when it opened at the Plymouth Theatre on Broadway on 1 October 1963, it did so with the original director and stage designer, John Dexter and Jocelyn Herbert, but with only three of the Court cast still in place, George Innes as Cannibal (Archie), Ronald Lacey as Washington (Smiler) and Corin Redgrave as the Pilot Officer. To the relief of the Court, the production was 'guaranteed against loss by the American management prior to presentation in the States' (ESC 1963b: n.pag.). Yet, although it played for a total of 149 performances at a succession of theatres, *Chips* did not enjoy the same degree of success across the Atlantic that it had in London. Nor, perhaps, was that too surprising. Even when the play was revived at the National Theatre in London in 1997, an American critic writing for the *Wall Street Journal* was aware of the inherent problems in making the transfer, having to explain to his US readership what square-bashing was and that chips were otherwise known as French fries, the title of the play meaning that 'the smallest of the many linguistic and cultural barriers [...] must be breached to a non-British audience' (Levy 1997: 11). For above all, this was a British – some might say English – play aimed solidly at a British audience, and this is even truer for the original 1962 production than it was for the 1997 revival.

It is not simply that the terms needed explaining to an American audience, it is that the play only really makes sense at a narrative level when it is contextualized in terms of contemporary Britain. Timing is everything. When *Chips* opened, the end of the Second World War was just seventeen years earlier, but it was beginning to recede as an immediate memory for an increasing percentage of the population. The years in between 1945 and 1962 had initially featured many cinematic 're-enactments' of the war: in particular, two films based on the exploits of the RAF, *The Dambusters* (1955) and *Reach for the Sky* (1956). What now seems most significant about these films, and others, was that they were extremely British in their reading of the struggle and that it was a struggle that was being not only organized but also almost exclusively fought by an officer class. In reality, however, the military opposition to Germany was largely populated by the lower ranks, who not only were mostly not career servicemen but had been conscripted into the various forces after 1939 and the National Service (Armed Forces) Act. There was an acute difference between being conscripted to fight against a declaredly fascist enemy in the war and being part of a series of attempts to string out the last remnants of Britain as a colonial power – the Suez fiasco of 1956 being perhaps the rather obvious end of that particular line. Martin Priestman points out that by 1960 (when Wesker started work on his play), government was still very much in the hands of the Conservative Party:

> the armed forces, earlier a vital focus of much left-wing idealism, now seemed increasingly to represent a belated attempt to reinforce right-wing values not only overseas but at home. Through 'national service', a generation of young men could be systematically reintroduced to the class division between officers and troops, with the NCO's hard-earned power to bully those below in the name of those above as the upper limit of working-class aspiration.
>
> (Priestman 1998: 222)

Whatever more general truth this contains, there can be no doubt that for very many of its participants – perhaps a majority – National Service in peace-time seemed more of a chore, an unwelcome break from family life and work, than an honour or a duty. Popular culture reflected this move.

In 1956, the Boulting Brothers' film comedy *Privates on Parade* gave evidence of a cultural shift as far as popular entertainment was concerned. Set in a post-war world that allowed for a plot that included recovering Nazi loot, it was concerned with the antics of a group of army National Servicemen who are precisely not of the officer class, a point that is emphasized by having the male lead, played by Ian Carmichael, as an undergraduate conscript who fluffs his officer selection board. In box-office terms, it was the second most popular UK film of the year, the first being *Reach for the Sky*. In 1957, two years after the first commercial television station had started to broadcast, a new comedy series, *The Army Game*, started on ITV. It ran highly successfully until 1961, but, unlike *Privates on Parade* – to which it was clearly much indebted, it was set in an army camp that had no link to the events of 1939–45 and centred on the comic antics of a group of somewhat reluctant, as well as incompetent, conscripts, permanently to thwart and to frustrate the efforts of those of superior rank to control them. It in turn provided the model for what would be the very first of the *Carry On* films, *Carry on Sergeant* of 1958, whilst the following year Anthony Newley began his climb to stardom in *Idol on Parade*, another National Service conscripts romp, in this instance referencing Elvis Presley's induction into the US army. Interestingly, Fiona Sturgess has argued a more serious case than usual for the *Carry On* films as examples of quasi-social documentation:

> Carry On films were by no means radical social documents, but they nonetheless reflected the collapse of the age of deference and the strides made towards social equality. [...] These shallow, knockabout comedies had at their heart a mistrust of authority, and never missed an opportunity to skewer the pomposity of supposed superiors.
>
> (Sturgess 2019: n.pag.)

A scene that was excised from the original Royal Court production of *Chips* (and from all published versions of the play), though staged in Sheffield, could easily have popped up in a more farcical form in *The Army Game* or *Carry on Sergeant*:

> The conscript-hating Wing Commander puts the men on fatigues, their task being to work through a load of bricks, chipping concrete off of them and transferring them from one wheelbarrow into another. The squad instantly organise

themselves and perform the job with robot efficiency, while the enraged officer shrieks abuse at them for their inability to work together.

(Wardle 1962: n.pag.)

This scene mirrors the famous coke-stealing scene, where Pip organizes the men in his hut to put their training and discipline to a more personal use to keep their stove alight and allow tea to be made. And, of course, the audience finds humour in these acts of subversion.

However, the narrowness of the gap between a *Carry On* gag and Wesker's play could be seen in the National Theatre's 1997 revival when, in scene 3, Corporal Hill's command not to actually march – 'I want you only to take a step forward, just pretend got that? Some dimwitted piece of merchandise is sure to carry on. Now then, watch it, SQUAD – by the front – quick MARCH!' (24) – is followed by precisely what he had anticipated including, much to the audience's pleasure, one man actually marching off-stage and out of sight. Indeed, Michael Billington lamented that the cast of a 1970 touring revival of the play 'were handicapped by an audience in Cambridge that had come apparently expecting a Brian Rix farce' (Billington 1970: n.pag.).

This movement away from an upper and officer class to a broadly working-class perspective clearly has its roots in much larger social and political models in the post-war context, and other cultural manifestations can be found in the novel or in movies and in post–*Look Back in Anger* theatre. Indeed, the four plays of Wesker that preceded *Chips* can be seen as both exemplars of this move and as key components in its development. It is this combination of factors that makes it perhaps less surprising to discover that there was not just one play about National Service duty in the RAF but two opening in London in April 1962. As well as Wesker's play, a fortnight earlier Henry Livings had had his *Nil Carborundum* staged at the Aldwych by a Royal Shakespeare Company that had, after Peter Hall's appointment as Artistic Director in 1958, embarked on a policy of putting on contemporary work for the first time: a move that can be seen, incidentally, as a challenge to the Royal Court Theatre – where all of Wesker's early work had played – as a champion of new theatre. Despite their common setting, the two plays are very different, and this provides a convenient point at which to start to analyse what Wesker, and also what his audiences, thought that his play was attempting. Though Livings clearly had a serious intent in *Nil Carborundum*, to show, in Harold Hobson's words, 'the (for him) enormous and portentous futility of military activity', this was really no more than, in their own way, what both *The Army Game* and *Carry On Sergeant* were about (Hobson 1963: 10). The action centres on the unravelling of a mock invasion exercise, and the overriding emphasis is on comedy, largely of the farcical variety. Although Livings is evidently recalling his own time as a National serviceman, there is no sense that he is documenting it. Both Livings and Wesker had been conscripted into the RAF, but the latter is far closer to his material – and this is where the problems start.

Never trust the author?

In September 1997, a friend, Roy Shaw, sent Wesker a press cutting of his own review of the revival of *Chips with Everything* at London's National Theatre. In the margin, Shaw had written: '<u>This</u> critic you shd [*sic*] read. He speaks well of the play, but invokes D. H. Lawrence to claim that he understands it better than you later did!' (AW3 1997: n.pag.). He is referring to the end of the review, where Shaw had written that the 'glamour, the resounding music' of the concluding passing-out parade, with the once ill-organized men now perfectly drilled, was a stark contradiction of the savage attack on the establishment mounted throughout the rest of the play.

> Much later, Wesker recalled his National Service as a 'mesmerising experience' which he ended up by enjoying. That is not the impression the play gave me. 'Never trust the artist. Trust the tale', Lawrence warned and went on to say, 'The function of the critic is to save the tale from the artist who created it.'
>
> (AW3 1997: n.pag.)

Now the critic's recall of Lawrence's famous declaration from his 1923 *Classics of American Literature* is interesting for many reasons. Shaw concludes by advising that his readers go and 'form your own opinion', with the implication that there is no single answer. However, it also points to a distinction that is crucial in considering all of Wesker's early work; or, rather, it points to a distinction that is in practice impossible to make, between the experience of the artist and the narrative of his life and the experience of his characters and the narratives of their lives. The very first sentence of Glenda Leeming's *Wesker the Playwright* opens thus: 'Of all modern dramatists Arnold Wesker must be one of the most – if not *the* most – personally involved in his own work' (Leeming 1983: 1, original emphasis). Indeed, we know that the playwright was drawing directly from his own experiences as an RAF national serviceman between 1950 and 1952 – the same years, coincidentally, that Henry Livings used for his *Nil Carborundum* – but the relationship between the lived experience and the play is a complicated one, notwithstanding the apparently quasi-documentary structure of it.

Though both plays can be seen to derive from the authors' own initial experiences of RAF National Service (albeit at different training camps), there is an immediacy about *Chips* that is entirely lacking in *Nil Carborundum*. For, though Livings is clearly drawing, at least in part, on his memories of being at the training camp, Wesker in contrast is drawing from material created by him at the time:

> I was determined to get something out of the experience. A novel! I would write a novel about square-bashing. Every day of the eight weeks I wrote home to someone [...] and I asked them to keep all the letters which I'd gather later as material for this landmark in English literature destined to make my fame and fortune. Eight weeks' worth of letters were collected [...] while I wrote my exposé of military malevolence.
>
> (Wesker 1994: 252)

In the event he had no interest shown by potential publishers, and he abandoned the project until *The Trilogy* had been staged by the Royal Court.

> I was scouting around for my next play and remembered what lay in the bottom drawer, and on re-reading it, it struck me: each chapter was the scene of a play. *Chips with Everything* was born – square-bashing as a metaphor for conformity, suppression of the individual spirit, the civilised defusion of protest.
>
> (Wesker 1994: 253)

Well actually, it was not *Chips* that was born but the outline of a play to be called *The Conscripts*, the very title of which is indicative of Wesker's initial interest in documenting the individual and collective experiences of the men from within, rather than from without, as the eventual title suggests. This is emphasized by the earliest listing of the conscripts, whose names are accompanied by brief signifiers: as 'Wilfe – Crude; and Andrew – Scottish and tender' (AW2 1960a: n.pag.). What is apparent from this early list is that Wesker conceived of the men as possessing specific and different characteristics. He was interested in the conscripts as individuals. At this point, the only one who has yet to be thus briefly described is Pip, who was clearly still a character very much under construction for Wesker, a character without any revealed characteristics. This cast list is accompanied in the Wesker archive by a 'Sequence' document headed *The Conscripts*. Although the chronology follows pretty well that of the play as eventually staged – with one small change from the 'new years eve' to the 'Christmas eve party' made by Wesker – there are just 13 scenes (as opposed to the 23 in *Chips*), commencing with 'Entry and fear' and ending with the passing-out parade (AW2 1960a: n.pag.).

When Wesker's biographical *As Much as I Dare* was published in 1994, it contained a chapter entitled '2496288 AC/2 Wesker', dealing with his time in the

RAF and in particular the first eight weeks of basic training.[2] This curious chapter opens with Wesker describing the wait for enlistment:

> Call-up papers were awaited. It was an event. [...] In the signing-on office sat a tired sergeant asking the same question of every nervous pimpled youth. Not all of us were nervous – just as I suppose not all of us were pimply – but a new regime was awaiting us; many shat themselves, others made sure their tongues were well in place.
>
> (Wesker 1994: 249)

It then breaks into a full page of theatrical dialogue, complete with stage directions, between 'Me' and 'Sergeant', a dialogue in which, during the Sergeant's attempts to document full details of the new arrival, Wesker's family origins are revealed as not only not British but neither pronounceable nor spellable: he is sent away to fill in the form independently. It is perhaps not too surprising that Wesker, by this time an established playwright, should use this comic format to make his point, but the issue becomes more problematic once he starts to describe the details of his basic training. These prose recalls are continually interrupted by direct quotations from the dialogue of the published version of *Chips*: it is as if the two were interchangeable, as if Wesker's experiences dating from the early 1950s could be directly translated into a play dating from the early 1960s. However, the Wesker who is writing the play from 1960 on is not the same young recruit who was undergoing National Service ten years earlier – something that would not matter so much if the playwright did not make it so difficult to separate the two. Here are two key moments in the chapter. Like Pip in the play, Wesker had initially refused to take part in bayonet practice: 'After the stupid bullying, after the pain of marching and marching and about-turning and smashing hard feet on tarmac [...] I found I couldn't take any more' (Wesker 1994: 254). This is followed in the chapter immediately by the Corporal's response, taken directly from the play:

> Even officers must go through this. Everyone, but everyone must know how to stick a man with a bayonet. The occasion may not arise to use the fucking thing but no man passes through this outfit till he's had practice.
>
> (Wesker 1994: 254–55)

I say 'taken directly', but it is not. In 1962, the Corporal's bayonet was a 'scorching thing' – as Wesker had corrected it to in the first hand-written draft of *The Conscripts* in 1960 – though it became a 'fucking thing' in 1997, when new sensibilities abounded (AW2 1960b: n.pag.). However, it is more complicated than this. After Wesker has run through the Corporal's full command – ending 'ON GUARD!

Run, scream, lunge', he reconsiders: 'Without the letters in front of me I cannot say this was word for word what Corporal Hall (stage name Corporal Hill) said to us. It is certainly more so than less' (Wesker 1994: 245). He then explains that 'my new friends, the other conscripts [...] had mixed feelings about my actions', before giving us the entire confrontation between Pip and one of the play's conscripts, Andrew, who accuses him of making heroic gestures to impress his fellow hut-mates. The playwright may not be alone by this time in realizing that

> [s]omething strange is going on here. I selected, compressed, shaped, extracted an essence hoping to create a truth about the experience of those square-bashing days. Not the whole truth, not the only truth – we've already accepted he impossibility of achieving that – but something, a flavour, a poetic moment with resonance; and now I'm using these extracted, highly stylised scenes as autobiographical stand-ins. I'm not even sure if such a scene took place between me and my Scottish hut-mate whose real name was Bill – or whether it was a conversation with myself. Art and experience – the boundaries become blurred.
>
> (Wesker 1994: 256)

In general terms, Wesker is not saying anything in the least contentious about the relationship between art and experience. However, it is the way that the playwright jumps between prose recall and theatrical quotation that makes it interesting, because in both these examples, although Wesker is the subject of the prose narrative, it is Pip who is the subject of the theatrical one: and it is Pip, as is agreed on all sides, who is the most complicated character in the entire play. Indeed, it is the very presence of this character that moves the central thrust of the play away from a sympathetic account of the *Conscripts*, as titled in the hand-written draft (AW2 1960b), to a critical one: the new title, *Chips with Everything*, coming from Pip's first intervention into the action.

In the second scene, set in the NAAFI, the new conscripts are already aware that they have, in the shape of Pip, something of a superior cuckoo in the nest. His response to being needled is to go on the attack:

PIP: Look old son, you're going to have me for eight painful weeks in the same hut, so spend the next five minutes taking the mickey out of my accent, get it off your chest and then put your working-class halo away because no one's going to care – OK?

CHAS: Where you from then?

PIP: My father is a banker, we idolise each other. I was born in a country house and I'm scorching rich.

(19–20)

Except that in the 1997 revival, on stage – though not in the prompt copy in the National Theatre archives – Pip claims to be 'fucking rich', the only time he uses the Corporal's favourite adjective in the play, perhaps a directorial response to Hill's final words in the preceding first scene: 'Anybody object to swearing?' (18). As this short scene develops, it is Chas who is the most antagonistic, assuming after Pip's declaration that he will be doing officer training and offering to knock him down. But it is the ill-fated Smiler – 'You don't mind being a snob, do you?' (20) – who unwittingly prompts Pip into his long recall of being forced to walk through the East End of London, and drinking a cup of tea 'from a thick, white, cracked cup' (20), and experiencing the uncared-for squalor that was the café. 'And then I saw the menu, stained with tea and beautifully written by a foreign hand, and on top it said [...] "Chips with everything". Chips with every damn thing. You breed babies and you eat chips with everything' (21).

Now, this long speech not only breaks into the largely naturalistic dialogue of the play prior to this, but it evidences the playwright's direct intervention into the play, in a role that he did not and could not have played in the training camp in 1950. Wesker had already used the phrase 'chips with everything' in a disparaging speech delivered by the grill chef Gaston in *The Kitchen* (Wesker 1976: 23), but he had even then borrowed it from elsewhere. In 1957, Tom Maschler had edited what turned out to be a highly influential collection of essays by prominent contemporary writers and thinkers, *Declaration*. Wesker had been particularly struck by the essay 'Get Out and Push' written by Lindsay Anderson, the director who would shortly give John Dexter a copy of *Chicken Soup with Barley* for potential production. In the opening paragraph, Anderson had written: 'Let's face it; coming back to Britain is always something of an ordeal. It ought not to be, but it is. And you don't have to be a snob to feel it. It isn't just the food, the sauce bottles on the café tables, and the chips with everything' (cited in Wesker 1994: 460). It is worth noting that it is not just the play's title that has been appropriated from this. The quotation also seeks to answer the question of Smiler's – 'You don't mind being a snob, do you?' – with Anderson's assertion, 'You don't have to be a snob to feel it'. And this at a time in Wesker's life when he was seriously grappling with issues of class and culture as the C42 project stuttered uneasily into life.

This implicit tension between the supposedly low aspirations of the working-class in cultural terms that would certainly include food for Wesker and the much-sneered at niceties of ruling class life is of key importance in the play. It is, after all, precisely the expectation that the conscripts will offer rock 'n' roll at the NAAFI party that is the basis for Pip's intervention and the basis for the relationship between Chas and Pip. Initially the most hostile to Pip and his privileged life, by scene 6 Chas listens in awe as he hears Pip recount a potted history of the American and French Revolutions, intermixed with a story about how his family became rich. The corporal intervenes, 'I bet you just made that up as you went along.' Pip's response, 'That's right, Corporal, the French Revolution was a myth', does not necessarily mean that the family part of the narrative is true, but Chas is eager to hear more anyway:

> CHAS: Tell us more, Pip, tell us more stories.
>
> PIP: They're not stories, Charlie boy, they're history.
>
> CHAS: Well, tell us more then.
>
> PIP: What's the use?
>
> CHAS: I'm asking you, that's what's the use. *I'm* asking you.
>   (PIP *picks up his webbing to blanco. The others withdraw and pick up what they were doing.* CHARLIE *is left annoyed and frustrated.*)
>   (34)

Pip and Chas have two further sequences of dialogue in the play. In the first (Act I, scene 8), the latter is more intent on establishing some kind of relationship with his hut-mate, talking of them as 'us', but is increasingly ready to argue with him, a development that was emphasized in the 1997 production by having Chas in possession of a live mic, so that his becomes the louder voice:

> CHAS: Let me bloody finish what I was going to say, will you! You don't listen! You don't bloody listen! [...]
>
> PIP: I'm sorry, I take it back, don't shout, I'm listening.
>
> CHAS: I didn't say *I* thought it'd be easier if I was more educated – I said *you'd* think it'd be easier, I thought *you'd* think it. And I was just going to say I disagreed – then you jumped.
>   (45)

By Act II, scene 9, Chas is concerned about how Pip might have been 'persuaded' into undertaking the bayonet practice and keen to be taught economics. However, the role of teacher rejected – 'Ask someone else' – Chas finally articulates his class-based analysis at Pip:

> Someone else. Someone else. It's always someone else, you half-bake you, you lousy word-user you. Your bleedin' stuffed grandfathers kept us stupid all this time, and now you come along with your pretty words and tell us to fend for ourselves. You clever useless leftover you. Oh, you're cocky, aren't you – Ask someone else. The truth is – you're scared, aren't you? You call us mate, but you're a scared old schoolboy. The pilot officer was right, you're slumming. You're a bleedin' slummer.
>   (66)

And, although Pip has the last word in this scene – 'You're a fool, Charles, the kind of fool my parents fed on, you're a fool, a fool' (66) – the equilibrium has changed, and Chas has found a political voice.

This is not a dialectical debate: their positions are ultimately irreconcilable, even if Chas is later to act where Pip no longer can. In a strongly critical review of the 1962 Glasgow production, Peter Hamilton recognizes the importance of the relationship, but in arguing that Wesker was attempting some kind of dialectical resolution, he completely misses the point:

> [T]he passages in which Wesker presents the struggle to communicate between Pip and Chas are distinguished by a total adequacy of expression to the clarity of his insight and are without question the work of a major writer. Wesker the propagandist finds it intolerable, however, that there should be no resolution of the situation and offers us his prescription – a political pill for a spiritual disease. The attempted union of the two Wesker personae is a conjunction of incompatibles and the advance which the author makes in this play is such that he must surely soon abandon the didact, for not to do so demands that he compromise his integrity.
>
> (Hamilton 1962: 25)

The two are on opposite sides of the class divide, and Wesker has said of their relationship that 'Chas and Pip are me in conflict' (Rees 1997: n.pag.). Wesker is not writing as a propagandist or a didact, and to understand why and how this is not the case is to open up the question of Pip's role in the play: for it is apparent that Pip, whilst not representing Wesker, is in a rather complicated manner effectively a mouthpiece for the playwright. An extreme expression of this view was given by a correspondent in the *Times Literary Supplement* in 1962: 'Pip is plainly a later version of Mr Wesker's Ronnie, but a Ronnie who has come up in the world a bit' ('A Correspondent' 1962: n.pag.). It is an interesting connection, for it is worth recalling that, like Pip, Ronnie frequently comes across as sounding arrogant. It is a quality that has been noted about Wesker's public pronouncements, including by himself:

> Perhaps I shouldn't be talking about this, but it seems as if the personality of the man has got in the way of the work. For reasons which I really don't think I understand, I do seem to arouse hostilities and irritations.
>
> (cited in Leeming 1983: 3)

The other qualities that mark Pip out from his fellow conscripts, and are remarked upon by them, are his 'posh' accent and his facility with language. Again, we might see connections with the playwright.

In his account of his initial refusal to undertake bayonet practice, Wesker recounts his meeting the Squadron Leader:

> The AC/2 sitting the other side of his desk was a very different kind of fish from those who swam constantly before his gaze – though National Service must have netted all sorts. Coming from no upper class I spoke like one – confident, articulate, well read.
>
> (Wesker 1994: 257)

Elsewhere, that he spoke 'without a trace of London or other accent [...] he attributes to the influence of his elder sister Della who went to a good local school' (Leeming 1983: 6).

Situating Pip as a theatrical arriviste, ten years after the events in the RAF camp, makes sense of the ambiguous and sometimes contradictory role that he is called upon to play. Before the coke-stealing escapade, Pip assures the men that there are '[n]o, no risks. Efficient, precise, but humane. They happen to be the only qualities for absolute power. That's what we want – absolute success but without a price' (49). But in the first draft of *The Conscripts* (1960), Pip had a more radical take on the project: 'These qualities have never been combined. [...] *They're* the qualities for absolute power – we want absolute success but without a price. It's possible – I'm going to prove it' (AW2 1960b: n.pag., original emphasis). What we have at this point is a far more determinedly rebellious Pip, one who might just go the whole way in his struggle with authority. As if in recognition of this, in the 1997 revival, the notion of a political rebellion that was 'efficient, precise but humane' was excised completely and emphasis laid entirely on the empirical success of the raid without any of its wider implications: 'No, no risks. Absolute success but without a price. Coke in ten minutes, with no one caught, and no one but us the wiser. Trust me?' So, we move in three different phases between apparently determined rebel, a qualified rebel and a clever man who simply knows how to get the coke.

After the event, Pip's mates rightly praise him for his leadership, but he then turns on them in what must be said to sound very much like a piece of straight Wesker polemic almost outside of the context of the play:

HILL: Well, don't you always need leaders?
PIP: Always, always!
HILL: Yes, always, always!
PIP: Always, always, always! Your great-great-grandfather said there'll always be horses, your great-grandfather said there'll always be slaves, your grandfather said there'll always be poverty and your father said there'll always

81

be wars. Each time you say 'always' the world takes two steps backwards and stops bothering. And so it should.

(51)

Impressive though this is, it should be noted that none of it actually deals with the question that the Corporal asks. Furthermore, in the third dialogue between Pip and Chas (quoted above), the latter will turn the argument about forebearers on its head – 'Your bleedin' stuffed grandfathers kept us stupid all this time': it is not the ignorance of the working-class, but the oppressive control of the ruling-class that is the real issue for Chas. Education, both its lack and its potential, are as crucial to the play as they were to Wesker in his own political agenda, including the development of C42.

In contrast, Smiler's 'education' through the play will do no more than allow him to become the exemplar of the naked brutality that lies beneath the training (education) process. Picked upon almost from the outset, the necessary sacrificial lamb, by Act II, scene 3 he finds himself in the guardroom on jankers (military punishment), his stay extended as he is abused and bullied by the double-act of Corporals. 'That'll do for the first lesson. Tomorrow we'll have some more. We'll break you Smiler, because that's our job' (56). In a truly harrowing scene, the echoes of Pip's words from the previous scene, 'You're a fool, Charles', mixing with the taunts to Smiler – ' You're no good lad', etc., rising to a crescendo (66) – Smiler temporarily deserts. In 1962, he occupied a mid-front-stage position, as a spotlight picked him out frantically running on the spot, as if in momentum. His long and distressed speech is one of hopeless defiance and defeat and ends with him re-entering the hut utterly destroyed. Events then take a very interesting turn:

> (CHARLES *and* PIP *are as we left them.* SMILER *is now with them.*)
> SMILER: The bastards won't believe it's natural. Look at me!
> (*A very broken* SMILER *stands there.* SMILER *turns to* PIP *for help.* PIP *approaches him and takes him gently in his arms. They sway a moment.*)
> SMILER: Wash my feet for me.
>
> (68)

Not for the first time, Christian mythology is invoked by Wesker, here embodying Smiler as the tormented Christ figure. He collapses and Pip starts to take off his shoes, but is abruptly halted by Chas, 'Leave him. I'll do it'. And from this point, Chas takes control, refusing any help with Smiler, and leading the refusal to allow him to be taken back to the guardroom. Pip's role as natural leader has been usurped by the friend that he was unable to educate.

Of course, Pip has been through his own process of being 'broken', and the terms on which he is broken, as well as many aspects of the play's staging, give substance to Wesker's response to the question 'You preach in your work?' in an interview in 1960:

> Not preach, but it may sort of come up. I take a situation in which an individual tries to do a job on his own, and I show how he fails. [...] That's how Brecht works. I've just got on to him. Thank God I have written four plays before reading about Brecht.
>
> (Weatherby 1960: n.pag.)

The second sentence could describe Pip's progress in the play well, so it would be useful to think about why Wesker should have coupled it with the sudden interest in Brecht. Shortly after *Chips* premiered, an interesting article appeared anonymously, as was still the practice, in *The Times*. Headed 'Heroes of Conscience in the Theatre', it sought to link Wesker's Pip with relatable 'heroes' in other recent plays – John Osborne's Luther, Terence Rattigan's Ross, Robert Bolt's Thomas More and Jean Anouilh's Becket. To this list could and should have been added Bertolt Brecht's *Galileo*, for his play received its first London production at the Mermaid Theatre from 16 June to 1 October 1960. It was one of the first plays by Brecht to be staged in English in the United Kingdom, following the visit of the Berliner Ensemble in 1956. It is impossible to believe that Wesker had not attended a performance, for it was an event of equal theatrical importance to the staging of his own complete trilogy, as was made clear by the poet and cultural enthusiast Sylvia Plath in a letter home dated 24 June 1960: 'Arnold Wesker's trilogy is in the middle of playing here, so we'll try to see it. Do you know his things? Also Brecht's Galileo, which I don't know at all. Soon, soon' (Plath 2018: 156).

In Act I, scene 4 of *Chips*, Wesker consciously recalls Brecht's play, as the Wing Commander and the Pilot Officer attempt to persuade Pip that he should put himself forward for officer training. When he refuses, Corporal Hill is called into the hut and told – clearly as a way of putting pressure on Pip – that his men are 'slobs' and must be punished with extra drilling. The Corporal immediately orders the men to double mark time, and the stage direction informs us: '*They do so for one minute. Exeunt at the double. The Inquisition resumes*' (59). Galileo had been shown the tools of the real Inquisition, so that Wesker's use of it here is both deliberate and pointed. Soon after, Pip responds to the jibe that he is slumming and that he feels guilty for his privileged upbringing with the riposte, 'A rather outdated cause to be a martyr for, don't you think, sir?' (58–59). It is not the last time that Pip will be associated with the concept of martyrdom. In Act II, scene 6, after the refusal to do bayonet practice, he is confronted by Andrew, who tells him that neither he or his hut-mates are impressed by his stand. Pip insists that he is not 'interested in the public spectacle' and that it is his decision, and his alone. In the dialogue that follows, Andrew tells him not to make 'heroic gestures' and that he 'can't bear your martyrdom – that's what it is; I don't think I can bear your look of suffering', and Pip denies both that he is suffering and that he is a martyr (61–62).

In the event, of course, Pip does agree to obey the Corporal's order to charge, and he does become a trainee officer; in that sense he, like Galileo, is broken. However, whereas Brecht makes it very clear what Galileo had hoped to achieve, in Pip's case it is not always evident to him, to an audience and perhaps to Wesker himself what the motivation might be. However, the way in which Pip unravels towards the end is revealing. Chas has taken responsibility for Smiler's well-being and rebukes the others' pessimism, continuing the theme of innocence tainted: 'For Christ's sake, give over – you talk like he was dead or something. Come on, help cover him' (69). 'With a sort of ritual' he is lovingly got into bed, and he and not Pip assumes the role of martyr at this point. The command of the Pilot Officer that Smiler be removed to the guardroom is loudly countermanded by Chas – 'YOU'LL LEAVE HIM BE!' (70) – and Pip suggests 'that you don't touch one of them' before changing from his airman's uniform to that of an officer, in an action that recalls scene 12 of *Galileo*, where a comparable assumption of power and status takes place in the Vatican: 'Pope Urban VIII, formerly Cardinal Barberini, has received the Cardinal Inquisitor. During the audience he is being robed' (Brecht 1963: 100).

Having assumed his new form of leadership, Pip uses it to ease the situation by involving the men:

> We won't let him, will we Charles – because you're right. Smiler has been badly treated, and you are right to protect him. It's a good virtue that, loyalty. You are to be commended, Charles all of you; it was a brave thing to do, protect a friend.
>
> (70)

This special mention of Chas confirms him as the new 'leader' of the men. However, this was not the original intention. In the first draft from 1960, not only does Chas not receive a mention, but Pip concludes the play as very much the successful rebel, directly threatening the officers with physical force if they attempt to take Smiler, and with no assumption of the role of officer. It is an extraordinarily different climax to the action.

> I said you won't touch one of us. There are nine of us to three of you and as long as we are all together as a hut you won't touch one of us. We can crush you Wing Commander, are you beginning to realise that. [...] Your victory is

tomorrow, when we have passed out and you can post us to different places. Be satisfied with that, and tomorrow you can divide us and turn your smiles on us. But it would be very unsubtle and crude to act now wouldn't it. Your victory is tomorrow – with one difference, that we have learned your tactics and are prepared.

(AW2 1960b: n.pag.)

So, in 1960, Wesker contemplated Pip as neither martyr nor victim, but as a successful, if temporary, leader of men. The first draft then finished as the 1962 production finished, with the passing-out parade, but with one significant difference. Not only has Pip not donned officer gear, but after the union jack is raised, it falls to the Pilot Officer, and not Pip, to read the dismal list of postings: and, whilst the other seven (Smiler having to do another three weeks' training) are firmly located, in December 1960, when he completed the first draft, Pip has a question mark after his designated future on the Officer Training Course. Just perhaps, he will not take the course. Just perhaps, he will continue his rebellion. In other words, at this point Wesker is still flirting with the idea of a Galileo who refuses to be cowed by the Inquisition.

The difficulties that critics and audiences have had with locating the specifics of Pip's motivation derive then firstly from the changing relationship that his creator, and to a considerable extent theatrical alter ego, has with the character. Originally, there was no Pip, and then he arrived around 1960 a fully formed rebel. But by 1962, the power of the Inquisition would prevail, as a demonstration of Wesker's determination to show how the ruling class succeeded in keeping things essentially unchanged. By 1997, all traces of the original national training process that started the playwright off on his long journey have been effectively erased. The Pip that we are left with is ambiguous, an ideologically slippery creature – possibly by accident as much as design, a product of changing historical and political circumstances, and of changing intent on his creator's part – and audiences in the future will continue to be required, in true Brechtian fashion, to continue thinking, to continue puzzling long after they have left the theatre. Who, what, how and why is Pip?

NOTES

1. To avoid repeated citations, subsequent quotations from the play-text are taken from the Penguin edition (Wesker 1963). Page references for quotations are provided in parentheses.
2. There was an RAF colleague of Wesker's called Pip: he was refused training as a pilot because he was 'boss-eyed', and whereas Wesker may possibly have taken his character's name from him, he did not take anything else (Wesker 1994: 251).

REFERENCES

'A Correspondent' (1962), 'Art and reality', *Times Literary Supplement*, 18 May.

Anon. (1962), '*Chips with Everything* review', *Financial Times*, 30 May.

Billington, Michael (1970), 'Chips with Everything: Arts, Cambridge', *The Times*, 28 October.

Brecht, Bertolt (1963), *The Life of Galileo*, London: Methuen.

Bull, John (2012), 'Arnold Wesker: The *Trilogy*', in D. Pattie (ed.), *Modern British Playwriting: the 1950s*, London: Methuen, pp. 171–97.

Courtney, Cathy (ed.) (1993), *Jocelyn Herbert: A Theatre Workbook*, London: Art Books International.

Dexter, John (1962), 'Chips and Devotion', *Plays and Players*, December, p. 32.

English Stage Company (ESC) minutes (1963a), THM/273/1/2/8, 23 July, London: Victoria and Albert Museum.

——— (1963b), THM/273/1/2/9, 17 June, London: Victoria and Albert Museum.

Findlater, Richard (ed.) (1981), *At the Royal Court: 25 Years of the English Stage Company*, London: Amber Lane Press.

Hamilton, Peter (1962), 'Glasgow production', *Plays and Players*, July, p. 25.

Hobson, Harold (1963), 'Introduction' in *New English Dramatists: 6*, Harmondsworth: Penguin, pp. 7–20.

Leeming, Glenda (1983), *Wesker the Playwright*, London: Methuen.

Levy, Paul (1997), 'Back to basic: Wesker play revived', *Wall Street Journal (Europe)*, 12 September.

Mill, Callum (1962), 'Wesker in twelve days', *Plays and Players*, July, pp. 23–24.

Plath, Sylvia (2018), *The Letters of Sylvia Plath: Letters Vol 2: 1956–63,* London: Faber.

Priestman, Martin (1998), '*Chips with Everything*: A snob's progress' in R. W. Dornan (ed.), *Arnold Wesker: A Casebook*, New York: Garland, pp. 221–24.

Rees, Jasper (1997), 'Kicking against the pricks', *The Independent*, 27 August.

Sturges, Fiona (2019), 'Carry On films celebrated the working class in its heyday', *Guardian: The Journal*, 4 July.

Wardle, Irving (1962), 'Wesker in Sheffield', *The Observer*, 6 May.

Weatherby, W. J. (1960), 'Breakfast with Wesker', *The Guardian*, 18 January.

Wesker, Arnold (1963), *Chips with Everything*, New English Dramatists: 7, Harmondsworth: Penguin, pp. 15–72.

——— (1976), *Three Plays*, Harmondsworth: Penguin.

——— (1994), *As Much as I Dare: An Autobiography 1932–1959*, London: Century.

Wesker, Arnold Papers (AW2) (1960a), Original hand-written manuscript and character sketch, n.d., Austin, Texas: Harry Ransom Center, Box 2.4.

——— (1960b), First draft, 15 September–3 December, Austin, Texas: Harry Ransom Center, Box 2.4.

Wesker, Arnold Papers (AW3) (1997), Review by Roy Shaw, *The Tablet*, 27 September, Austin, Texas: Harry Ransom Center, Box 42.

FIGURE 6: Arnold Wesker on the stage of the Roundhouse, *c*.1966. Photo by William Glenesk.

5

Wesker's Flawed Diamond:
Their Very Own and Golden City

Chris Megson

A story I'm fond of retelling is the one Doris Lessing wrote – I forget its title – but it's about a diamond merchant who is going to get married and decides himself to cut the diamond for his wife's ring. He purchases a raw, uncut diamond, places it in the middle of a table, and walks round and round it for three days looking at it, contemplating it, trying to understand its nature. At the end of three days he knows exactly how it must be cut. The material has dictated to him the way it must be handled. I think in the same way most writers approach their material – perhaps that's what Doris Lessing was writing her story about.

(Wesker 1996: n.pag.)

The short story by Doris Lessing that prompted Arnold Wesker to reflect on the process of writing is titled 'Out of the Fountain', first published in her anthology *The Story of a Non-Marrying Man and Other Stories* in 1972. Although Wesker misremembers details of the plot (the diamond cutter is not, in fact, preparing the jewel for his wife, but for the daughter of a wealthy Alexandrian merchant), his description of the way Lessing conceives the forensic work of a diamond cutter as a metaphor for creative writing reveals much about Wesker's own approach as a dramatist, where the primary material of the play – the subject matter – sets terms for (or 'dictates') how it will be shaped ('handled') theatrically. It is typical of Wesker to emphasize the time, craft and material labour involved in writing and – albeit implicitly – to acknowledge that the form of his plays (the 'cut' of the diamond) is drawn from the 'raw' material, or experience, of life.

In *Their Very Own and Golden City* (1965), Wesker cuts his diamond invent-ively: the play interweaves topical debate on pressing social issues with moments of utopic reverie as the main characters endeavour to verbalize and then implement a new social vision.[1] The idealism of this premise is countered by Wesker's exca-vation of the link between compromise and self-deception in the (partial) realiza-tion of that vision, and the tension between idealism and compromise in the play is closely aligned with the turbulent social and political landscape of the post-war years. The ambitious structure of *Golden City*, with its expansive historical sweep and fluid, rapid-fire progression of action, undergirds the thematic preoccupation with social transformation and new designs for living.

The opening scene of the play is set in Durham Cathedral in 1926. A group of four young adults wanders in with sketchbooks at the ready, awed by their surroundings. Amongst them is an aspiring architect called Andrew Cobham, Wesker's Master Builder, who dreams of building new cities that will be owned co-operatively by the people. Through the course of the play, Andy becomes increas-ingly disillusioned as his ambitions are frustrated and he is forced to scale down his plans and settle for an eviscerated version of his project (in the end, only one city is built). On the one hand, Wesker's play shows the progressive potential of cities to improve quality of life and unlock new social imaginaries; on the other, he traces the containment and neutralization of radical vision by the familiar forces of conservatism in English public life, which include the Labour Party, trade unions and industry. In performance, the cathedral setting in 1926 remains a constant presence that frames the entire piece. The subsequent scenes, which shuttle the action from 1926 to the mid-1980s, track the attempts by Andy and his friends Jessie, Paul and Stoney to win support for their city-building initiative; these scenes set in the future take place on an interior revolve stage behind two mock-gothic ecclesiastical screens that part to reveal each new episode. *Golden City* thus takes the form of a play-within-a-play, a reverie of the future, in which scenes featuring the adult versions of the four characters are counterpointed by intermittent sequences, set in 1926 in the cathedral, where their younger selves share their dreamy aspirations for the future.

As I will demonstrate, *Golden City* looks back despairingly on the piecemeal reforms of post-war governments and is informed by Wesker's own bitter experi-ences with Centre 42 (C42) – his purposeful attempt to create, with trade union sup-port, a variety of new opportunities to maximize cultural participation in Britain's working-class communities. However, although the play is clearly of its time, its concerns remain urgent: the demand for radical ambition in politics (especially on the Left), the desire for a mode of public discourse that will inspire people and the importance of urban renewal, house building and public architecture in liberating the potential of ordinary people. In other words, Wesker uses the conceit of the golden city as a way of critiquing the post-war social structure and confronting the difficulty of mapping an ideal society in language as well as bricks and mortar.

To date, theatre scholars have attended only sporadically to this play, and often in passing. There are two notable exceptions: in an article in *Modern Drama* published in 1986, Heinz Zimmerman offers a thoughtful anatomization of the play's utopic impulses, while Anne Etienne's article for *Studies in Theatre and Performance*, published in 2016, explores C42 in detail and traces its impact on Wesker's career and playwriting (including *Golden City*). In this chapter, I will take a more expansive view, documenting the composition and production history of *Golden City*, before evaluating its theatrical and political significance – particularly in regard to its ambivalent conclusion and strategic rupture of naturalism – as well as its mixed critical reception. In so doing, I aim to illuminate the ongoing resonance of the play's social critique.

'It does work'

> To cut a diamond perfectly is an act like a samurai's sword-thrust, or a master archer's centred arrow. When an important diamond is shaped a man may spend a week, or even weeks, studying it, accumulating powers of attention, memory, intuition, till he has reached that moment when he finally knows that a tap, no more, at just *that* point of tension in the stone will split it exactly *so*.
>
> (Lessing 1975: 13)

Wesker began writing *Golden City* on 27 April 1963 and completed the first draft on 5 November that year. His initial working title, *Congress*, was meant to indicate the play's focus on trade unions, but Wesker dispensed with this given the association of the word 'congress' with sexual intercourse in the *Kama Sutra*, which was made legally available in English translation for the first time in 1962 (Wesker 2000). Three months passed before Wesker commenced work on the second draft; by that time, in early 1964, he was experiencing problems with C42 and 'personal relationships' (his relationship with Beba Lavrin, his assistant at C42, led her husband, the painter John Lavrin, to file for divorce, naming his friend Arnold Wesker in the process): as he noted in his diary on 9 February 1964,

> I sit in my room staring at the first draft of 'Golden City' and I cannot raise my pen to write a single word. For almost twenty-four hours now I have not been able to tear my thoughts away from all that is happening.
>
> (Wesker 2000: n.pag.)

Despite these debilitating distractions, Wesker nonetheless persevered and wrote seven drafts up to November 1965 (Wesker 2000).[2] During this period, he showed the script to 'a well known architect and town planner', who gave him two pieces of feedback: first, he advised Wesker not to include 'huge architect drawings' in the play as this would likely distract the audience, leading them to question the plans on display rather than consider the play's main theme of compromise (this explains why the building of the city is evoked in speech, sound and abstract lighting in performance, rather than via physical or diagrammatic representation); and, second, 'You portray Andy Cobham as a man who has compromised and failed, but, he said, you have no idea how much it takes to build one city. For Andy to have done that is a huge achievement' (Wesker 2000: n.pag.). Wesker accepted this advice and sought to create a sense of uncertainty and – as I will discuss later in the chapter – strategic ambivalence about the elderly Andy's situation at the end of the play.

Golden City was entered for, and won, the Marzotto Prize in 1964, which was adjudicated by an international jury that included the theatre critics Martin Esslin and Ossia Trilling, the Greek film and stage actress Katina Paxinou and the directors Erwin Piscator and Jean Vilar; Wesker was awarded £3,000 in prize money. According to a contemporary report in *The Times*, Wesker wanted his play to be staged by C42, but the timing was problematic; he hoped, instead, that a London management would stage the play, with Jocelyn Herbert as designer (AW 1964a).[3] A news item in *The Observer*, published later that year in October, reported that a '[y]oung manager' called Bob Swash intends to stage the play in London in early 1965, but this did not materialize (AW 1964b).[4]

In addition to the prize money, the Marzotto award guaranteed the winner a staging of their play at the Belgian National Theatre in Brussels. Accordingly, the first production of *Golden City* took place in that venue, in the French language, on 13 August 1965; it was, as Etienne notes, 'well-received' (Etienne 2016: 139). However, William Gaskill, the then Artistic Director of the Royal Court Theatre in London, turned down the play, as did his colleague, the Court director John Dexter, who had established a strong creative partnership with Wesker directing his early plays. Wesker was bewildered by the rejection of his play by the Court's management:

> It seems as though I write plays which people cannot understand by just reading them. They first need to hear them, see them. It's only when the play is on stage that they can see how it works and where its power lies. But this time I cared so much about the play and, after all, it had won an important prize awarded by a jury of international theatre luminaries, and there had already been one successful production of the play [in Brussels], so there was evidence to suggest

that the play had merit. So I fought for it. I argued with William Gaskill that The Royal Court Theatre owed me a production of this play, and I urged him to read it again. He did and finally agreed to mount it himself.

(Wesker 2000: n.pag.)

Consequently, *Golden City* opened at the Royal Court on 19 May 1966, directed by Gaskill, designed by Christopher Morley and starring Ian McKellen as Andy and Gillian Martell as Jessie, with David Leland and Kenneth Cranham cast in minor roles. The production was programmed in repertory with a revival of *The Voysey Inheritance*, Harley Granville-Barker's forensic dissection of Edwardian double standards, which was first performed at the Royal Court 60 years previously (the coupling of Wesker with Granville-Barker is intriguing, and points to their shared preoccupation in writing plays that critique an ossified social structure).

The appointment of Gaskill as director of *Golden City* proved to be controversial. Some reviewers of the production, such as Simon Trussler, appreciated the honed and characteristic Brechtian economy he brought to the staging:

> Gaskill's direction was, significantly, at its best in those scenes – the majority – which least cluttered the stage with scenery or props: simple projections, odd tables and chairs, and a pair of flats were sufficient to evoke a setting as it emerged out of the last.
>
> (Trussler 1966b: n.pag.)[5]

However, many years later in 2000, when reflecting on the Royal Court production, Wesker insisted that Gaskill 'was the wrong director for the play': 'He was an expert in directing Brecht and Edward Bond, and I think he was uncomfortable with the emotion of the relationships in *Golden City*' (Wesker 2000: n.pag).

Wesker was especially vexed by Gaskill's approach to casting the play. After ten days of rehearsal, Gaskill invited John Dexter to watch a run-through and Dexter advised that, rather than having two groups of actors play the four main characters in their youthful and older incarnations, there should only be one group of actors playing the characters throughout the performance. In his preface, dated December 1980 and included in the 1990 edition of the play, Wesker condemned this decision as 'mistaken and crippling' (121); his exasperation was still apparent in a speech given in 2000:

> It was so obviously important to have two groups playing side by side so that the contrast between the dream and the reality could be seen. I do not understand how I allowed the structure of the play to be changed so radically.
>
> (Wesker 2000: n.pag.)[6]

In Wesker's view, two groups of actors are prerequisite: the first group play the young characters in the cathedral; the second group play the adults moving forward in time. Without this doubled approach, the echoes and overlaps in the dialogue between present and future, and the poignancy of the final scene – in which the old Andy speaks the lines of his younger self in the cathedral – are theatrically unrealizable. The use of two groups enables the play to return the audience continually back to the future, contrasting the white-hot idealism of the youths in the cathedral with the increasingly embittered experience of their adult counterparts, whose attempts to build six new cities meet with withering institutional indifference or outright hostility. Wesker also made the practical observation that, in the Royal Court production, the single cast of actors 'had to make very quick changes of costume back and forth which disturbed their performances, and of course the rhythm of the play was lost' (Wesker 2000: n.pag.); Etienne underlines this point, arguing that 'the structure and rhythm of the play were altered, which in turn affected the reception of the performance' (Etienne 2016: 139). It is notable that several reviews of the production do indeed draw attention to problems that derive from the use of a single cast: '[Ian McKellen's] age transitions, admittedly difficult in any circumstances, were too sudden and not always consistent' (Trussler 1966b).

Aside from casting, there were also disagreements about the script and scenography. Gaskill wanted to cut the card-playing scene near the end of the play, but Wesker felt this sequence was vital because it showed Andy at ease with people he would formerly have loathed. Wesker threatened legal action on this point, stating that – if necessary – he had a lawyer standing by to apply for an injunction to stop the performance taking place. The scene was kept in, although Wesker admitted (much later) that the legal injunction was a 'bluff' (Wesker 2000: n.pag.). As for the scenography, Wesker wanted a fluid production style, but, as he put it, 'This could not happen in the London production. The play moved forward like a tired old machine. Clunk, clunk, clunk!' (Wesker 2000: n.pag.).

A conspicuous feature of the published play-text is that it conveys a sense of Wesker's residual anxiety about the decisions made by Gaskill in 1966. It is impossible to ignore the extent of Wesker's authorial interpolations: there is a dedication, preface, excerpted quotes from William Morris, an author's 'Note' on both the play and 'The Set', and a list of scenes with further commentary. At one point, Wesker seems to grow weary of his own presence in the text, commenting in a footnote that he will refrain from giving further stage directions on the way that transitions between scenes are meant to be orchestrated (142). The play-text, then, is disposed to inhibit future compromises with the play's casting, design and structural ambition.

Although Wesker was disappointed by the Royal Court production, he had a much more satisfying experience when the play was revived and revised eight years later, in May 1974, at the Aarhus Theatre in Denmark. The Aarhus Theatre was led by Henryk Bering Liisberg, who is acknowledged in Wesker's preface to the play, which includes the textual changes made for this production. The staging at Aarhus, much to Wesker's delight, used two groups of actors:

> I was able to see the play as I had originally written it – with two sets of actors. I had as my designer a brilliant young man from The National Theatre called Hayden Griffin. Hayden designed a set which gave me just the fluidity I wanted. Using both a revolve and the device of flying scenery up and down he made one scene appear just before the previous scene was ending. His sets were so perfect that I made changes in my stage directions to fit them.
>
> (Wesker 2000: n.pag.)

Wesker's comment indicates – with due regard to the creative ingenuity of Hayden Griffin – the importance of dynamic scenography to the impact and meaning of the play: Wesker states in his preface – with tangible relief – that the Danish production proved that 'though it attempts too much, [the play] is not *irretrievably* flawed. It *does* work' (121, original emphasis).

Golden City has been largely neglected by British theatre directors since its fractious 1966 production at the Royal Court.[7] Thirty years later, in 1996, Wesker tried to persuade the Royal Shakespeare Company to stage it (Wesker 1996), and, in 2003, he advocated that Nicholas Hytner should revive the play at the National Theatre: 'It's only the National who can really do it justice' (Wesker 2003: n.pag.).[8] These sporadic attempts to revive the play proved fruitless, perhaps because of the intensive resources required to stage it, perhaps because of the difficult circumstances of its original production at the Royal Court, and perhaps because the play was perceived to be too close to Wesker's experience with C42. Nonetheless, *Golden City* – irrespective of its heady ambition, arguable flaws and chequered performance history – is a deeply significant play in post-war British theatre precisely because it captures the febrile theatrical and political tensions of its time.

Antecedents and influences

Before examining *Golden City* in more detail, it is useful to note that the play refracts a broad range of antecedents and influences from both theatre and film, which in turn indicates Wesker's immersion in the wider cultural field. Wesker's interest in film – he wrote his early play, *Chicken Soup with Barley* (1958), while completing 'a short course at the London School of Film Technique' – is often neglected in studies of his work, but the influence of cinema is palpable in *Golden*

City (Taylor 1969: 148). In an interview with Wesker in 1966, Simon Trussler observes that the sequencing of scenes in the play resembles the film technique of cross-cutting: in his reply, Wesker acknowledges that the play is cinematic in scope and that he would like to see a film adaptation (Wesker 1966: 200). He elaborates this point in his preface to the published play-text – 'the theme belongs to the cinema, it stretches across more time and action than the theatre properly should handle' (121) – and, in a speech in 1985, he acknowledges 'a very strong influence of cinema on my work, stronger than theatre' and claims it was the 'epic quality of film' that 'gave me the courage' to cover such a broad historical span of time in *Golden City* (Wesker 1986: 368). The influence of film is perhaps most apparent in Act II, scene 5 – one of the lengthiest scenes in post-war British playwriting. This 'continuous' scene is comprised of fifteen parts, which trace the action from 1948 to 1985 '*or thereabouts*' (175, original emphasis). In his 'Special Note' in the play-text, Wesker asserts that this scene 'must appear as one continuous movement, slowly and inexorably unfolding – rather like watching the painting of Dorian Gray slowly change from a young man into an old and evil man – as in the film' (174).

Aside from its cinematic structuring of the passage of time, and its curious nod to the atmospherics of Albert Lewin's film *The Picture of Dorian Gray* (1945), *Golden City* also has a variegated theatrical genealogy with roots in the socially engaged theatre of Galsworthy, Granville-Barker and Bernard Shaw. Ronald Bryden notes that – with *Golden City* – Wesker 'moves unmistakably into the line of English popularizer-prophets with Priestley, Laski, Charles Morgan and Colin Wilson'; for him, the play – at least in part – recalls 'a sentimental commercial play of the forties [...] essentially it's an old-fashioned chronicle of compromised ideals' (Bryden 1966: n.pag.). However, if certain thematic aspects of the play resurrect staple theatrical fare of the 1940s – which is questionable – *Golden City* is also closely aligned with the 'New Wave' drama of the 1950s, notably in its dubious figuration of sexual politics: Andy Cobham – volatile, alienated, charismatic – is a latter-day iteration of the iconic 'angry young man'. Indeed, Andy's 'substitution' of Jessie for the upper-class Kate bears a striking resemblance to Jimmy Porter's 'substitution' of Alison for the upper-class Helena in John Osborne's *Look Back in Anger* (1956).

As with many of Wesker's plays, *Golden City* is semi-autobiographical, and, as Etienne observes, it shares the ongoing preoccupation in his theatre with '[deconstructing] the manners in which the rebel can be absorbed into, belittled and finally rejected by English society' (Etienne 2016: 140–41). Robert Wilcher, meanwhile, notes the common ground between *Golden City* and Wesker's other plays written around this time, making the perceptive observation that *Chips with Everything* (1962), *Golden City* and *The Friends* (1970) are, respectively, 'a prologue, an allegorical counterpart, and an epilogue' to Wesker's 'task of transforming the cultural landscape of the materially affluent Britain of the 1960s' (Wilcher 1991: 55).

Yet, *Golden City* also signals a distinctive shift in tone from Wesker's previous work. Given its focus on an increasingly disillusioned protagonist whose actions are played out against a panorama of recent social history, its tracing of the agonized shift from idealism to despair, and its ferocious indictment of English political institutions, *Golden City* might feasibly be regarded as a foundational state-of-the-nation play – a genre of political playwriting that came to prominence in the 1970s. After all, Act I concludes with a curtain line of unmistakable force as Andy lambasts English public life – 'A cheapskate dreariness, a dull caution that kills the spirit of all movements and betrays us all – from plumber to poet' (163); in contrast, at the end of the play, Andy sits in isolation and cannot even unclench his teeth because he fears that he might howl. The sense of betrayal and embittered incandescence exemplified in such moments is carried forward into state-of-the-nation plays of the 1970s such as David Hare's searing testament of post-war disillusionment, *Plenty* (1978).

'Patchwork' politics

One of the most compelling features of *Golden City* is its arbitration of the large-scale and long-term project of national renewal in the aftermath of the Second World War; more specifically, the play was written and staged at the historical apex of the 'new town' movement. This movement had its origins in the campaign for garden cities in the nineteenth century, which proselytized for the construction of new and healthier towns outside congested and insanitary inner-city environments. The impetus for building new towns accelerated in the immediate post-war period, with the election to government of Clement Atlee's Labour Party by a landslide vote in 1945: Atlee's government passed two monumental pieces of legislation, the New Towns Act in 1946 and the Town and Country Planning Act the following year. More than thirty 'new towns' were built in total: the first wave in the late 1940s, the second in the early 1960s and the third in the late 1960s (Alexander 2009: 4). These towns 'were intended to showcase the work of a new generation of architects, as well as the pioneering new profession of town planner' (Alexander 2009: 8). Welwyn Garden City was the second garden city in Britain (founded in 1920) and was designated one of the first 'new towns' in 1948; the jewel in the crown of the 'new towns' programme, Milton Keynes, was famously designated in 1967 – the year following the Royal Court production of *Golden City*. In this context, the play's provocative premise – the viability of constructing six new cities – is contentious but not beyond the bounds of real-world possibility.[9]

Wesker negotiates the competing and paradoxical political energies involved in the 'golden city' project: the driving optimism associated with youth, emblemized by Andy's desire to build new cities, is tempered by an escalating distrust of politicians and trade unions in blocking the Left's ambitions (both the theatre programme for the Royal Court production and Wesker's revised play-text include an excerpt from a lecture on 'Socialism' given by William Morris at Victoria Hall, Norwich, in March 1886, in which he attacks the complicity of trade unions in enabling capitalist managerialism). The word 'patchwork' circulates in the play as the derogatory term for piecemeal, not structural, reform: as early as Act I, scene 8, which is set in 1935, Andy's faith in the Labour movement begins to erode – 'they do nothing but patchwork' (148). There is a seam of argument running through the entire play about what constitutes 'patchwork' reform. For Andy, it is Labour's programme of slum clearances bereft of a wider vision of social change; for the brusque Chairman of the local town planning committee, it is Andy's idea of new cities: 'Bits of oasis in the desert that the sun dries up, that's all' (163). It is worth noting that Wesker himself made a concerted effort to ensure the production of *Golden City* was seen by those he held responsible for tepid 'patchwork' politics: on the morning of 27 May 1966, a special performance of the play was organized for an audience of high-profile political and trade union leaders – Wesker invited every Member of Parliament and Trade Union general secretary ' "because these people are always making excuses that they are too busy in the evening to see plays" ' (AW 1966: n.pag.). The union leaders Clive Jenkins, Jack Jones and Ron Smith, and the politician and diplomat Sir Geoffrey de Freitas were amongst those reported to be present.

At the heart of the play is a ferocious debate about the value of principle versus compromise. The argument between Andy and the veteran trade union organizer Jake Latham in Act I, scene 5 echoes the real-life confrontation between the political titans Ernest Bevin and the then Labour leader George Lansbury in the 1930s on the issue of appeasement and pacifism at the time of fascist ascendancy in Europe. As D. A. N. Jones asserts in his review of the production in the *New Statesman*: '[Wesker has] made something new out of the old tale of Lansbury's defeat' (Jones 1966). Jake, with his dogged attachment to pacifism, argues that principles matter because it is important that future generations have examples in history of people who have stuck to their ideals. In the subsequent debate between Andy and Jake in Act I, scene 11, the latter repeats his argument that the prospect of defeat comes secondary to setting a principled example for future generations; Andy responds, as did Bevin to Lansbury, that you cannot hook national destiny to the equivocations of individual conscience.

However, in Act II, scene 5, Andy acknowledges that the golden cities project is an example of self-deception in practice: 'Six Golden Cities could lay the foundation of a new way of life for all society – that's a half-truth, one that we're going to perpetrate, with our fingers crossed' (170). In Act II, scene 4, set in 1948, Andy's speech to the Trade Union Congress (TUC) recalls William Morris's speech quoted at the start of the published play-text. Andy attacks the paucity of ambition on the Left, celebrates vision as the quality that holds a community together and defends the right to dream: 'The dull and dreary men, beware – beware the dull and dreary men' (174). However, later in the play, a posse of trade union leaders asks Andy to drop five of his six cities and build just one. The TUC General Council advises Congress 'not to vote in favour of financing industry in the six cities', and, of course, without industry finance, the cities will stagnate with unemployment (185). In effect, Andy has no choice but to compromise. At the end of the play, in a mordant image of political co-option, a banquet is held in the prestigious Guildhall in London to celebrate Andy's knighthood. The city has now been built: Andy describes it ruefully as 'a hint, if nothing else, of what might be' (195).

In this context, it is telling that the word Wesker employs to describe his experience of C42 is 'patchwork': he acknowledges the 'parallels' between the attempt in the play to build six golden cities and his own experience at the helm of C42 (Wesker 1966: 199). In an interview published in 1966, he discloses that the play emerged from the sense of 'constipation' he felt from abandoning writing to work on this project (Wesker 1966: 198). Several reviewers of the Royal Court production of *Golden City*, including J. W. Lambert, were quick to identify C42 as the autobiographical catalyst for the play: 'this tale of vision and disillusion is clearly a projection of Mr Wesker's work for Centre 42' (Lambert 1966: n.pag.). On the day of the opening of *Golden City* at the Royal Court, Irving Wardle wrote a piece in *New Society* surveying the parlous state of popular theatre in Britain and noted that 'Centre 42 [...] is the latest and grandest of a series of causes [Wesker] has taken up along the route to the golden city' (Wardle 1966: n.pag).

Under Wesker's leadership, C42 raised enough money to tour an arts festival to six towns and cities – Bristol, Birmingham, Hayes, Leicester, Nottingham and Wellingborough (there is an obvious corollary between the six festivals and the six golden cities in the play). But the project ran up debts, and, while it managed to secure a permanent base – the Roundhouse in London – '[t]he building came to be used as a space for hire. It was not the same as the original dream. We had compromised' (Wesker 2000: n. pag).

C42 attracted criticism for its perceived top-down approach to working-class culture. For example, the socialist director and playwright John McGrath, despite being one of the founders of C42, described Wesker sardonically as 'the laureate of Wilsonian politics' (McGrath cited in Patterson 2003: 31) and later condemned C42 in unequivocal terms: 'The idea, which [Wesker] shares with Roger Planchon in France, that culture is a product to be sold by culturally-conscious (therefore superior) artists and intellectuals to culturally-starved (therefore inferior) workers, is based on a bourgeois concept of culture' (McGrath cited in Patterson 2003: 31–32). However, despite his disillusionment and the 'patchwork' results of the initiative, Wesker deserves some credit for his attempt to broaden working-class participation in, and access to, culture: as Etienne affirms, 'no other politically committed playwright had carried his opinions beyond the stage into long-term cultural action' (Etienne 2016: 140).[10]

'Poet [of] committed theatre'

> *Their Very Own and Golden City* never seems quite to decide what it is about, triumphant idealism or compromise. Of course, in a way it is about both; its architect hero is gradually led astray from his original purpose of building six co-operatively owned golden cities, but he does manage to build one. [...] The trouble is that the play, by trying to be simultaneously about the failure of socialist ideals and their continuing validity, takes on too much at once: the defeat is real, the triumph only a hopeful dream, and though the play could culminate with either, it really cannot workably culminate with both. [...] If [...] he can discipline his uneven talents (which is a big if), Arnold Wesker, hitherto by choice and on principle the most prosaic of our young dramatists, may turn out after all to be the poet the committed theatre in this country has so long awaited.
>
> (Taylor 1969: 169, 170)

The critic John Russell Taylor's comments on *Golden City* exemplify wider concerns that were expressed about the play's seemingly mixed political messages. He is dissatisfied with Wesker's breach of the aesthetic conventions of naturalism – admonishing the playwright for the lack of 'detailed notation' of significant events – and is troubled by the lack of definitive closure (Taylor 1969: 169). It is as if *Golden City* somehow exceeds or overflows itself, not only in language – Taylor is critical of 'heavy verbiage' – but also in form and meaning (1966: 169). His view is that Wesker cannot be a 'poet' unless he disciplines his 'uneven talents' – thus, both play and playwright are indicted for their perceived excess.

What is overlooked by Taylor, however, is that the play's subject matter necessitates the 'excessive' rupture of naturalism. In his review, Esslin notes the rationale for the play's 'expressionistic technique': 'a large social complex is being compressed into a relatively short span of time, which means that it must be reduced to its essentials' (Esslin 1966: 12, 57).[11] The form of the play is designed to encapsulate the 'essentials' of an intractable personal and political impasse involving painful compromise and an embryonic but unrealized vision of a new society. Crucially, the expressionist features of *Golden City* are most apparent in the way the construction of cities is represented in the fast-moving second half of the play:

> *The first of the 'building-site sounds' is heard: a pneumatic drill* [...] *added to by other building-site sounds as the play progresses. These sounds, each different and real, should pulsate rhythmically, like a musical background.*
>
> (181)

And, later,

> *The light grows and the scene becomes a magnificent abstract set of a building site.* [...] *Till now, we've built an image of the Golden City through words – now, visually, for the first time we must see and feel the magic and excitement of a city growing.*
>
> (192)

The influence of Hayden Griffin on the conceptualization of these moments is apparent: the scenography becomes abstract, even magical, when the play is at its most visionary. Critics of the play tended to neglect this point – Malcolm Page, for example, criticizes Wesker's lack of specificity about the form the cities will take: 'Presumably Wesker does not want us to think of them as variants on Welwyn Garden City or the post-war New Towns, but as any splendid dream' (Page 1968: 324). There is indeed an oneiric rather than documentary or social realist quality to these theatrical sequences, as the new city is evoked elementally in light and sound.

The play's evocative abstractions also intersect with some of the criticisms of the New Left in the early 1960s that placed a strong emphasis on culture. Dan Rebellato points out that many theatre practitioners associated with the Royal Court were involved in the New Left and that 'the New Left shared with the New Wave that frustrating vagueness as they groped towards new definitions of socialism' (Rebellato 1999: 20); Rebellato also shows that Wesker's plays give persistent expression to 'a cluster of terms that are distributed equally through the works of the New Left and the New Wave' (Rebellato 1999: 21). Given these observations, it should be noted that the text of *Golden City* is dedicated to Tom Maschler, the publisher and writer who was editor of *Declaration* (1957), 'the manifesto of the angry young men' (Rebellato 1999: 11).

The perceived 'vagueness', rhetorical excess and scenic abstraction of the play constitute an aesthetic of indeterminacy in performance that can be linked to the ambiguous New Left politics of hope geared towards a putative envisioning of a future socialist society. Hope manifests in the theme of commitment, and we might recall that Taylor sees in Wesker the potential to be the 'poet' of 'committed theatre'. Simon Trussler, with characteristic perspicacity, offers a deeper elaboration of Wesker's 'commitment':

> Arnold Wesker has never completely severed the umbilical cord which links him to the fifties. Commitment was the cultural key-word of that decade – an over-intellectualised commitment, perhaps, more talked about in Partisan basements and in the leading articles of *New Left Review* and *Encore* than acted out in Labour Party committee rooms.
>
> (Trussler 1966a: n.pag.)

For Trussler, C42 is the principal example of Wesker's commitment in practice: 'a tradition of committed drama needs to be kept alive, to *relate* the private pain and the neuroses to their causes, to establish that there can even be some kind of community, and therefore of hope, in despair' (Trussler 1966a: n.pag., original emphasis).

Hope in despair is, of course, the image crystallized at the end of the play: Wesker stipulates that 'Old Andrew Cobham must be left on stage after the bridge scene. The last cathedral scene revolves round him as he says young Andy's lines – thus creating a dreamlike effect; the "flash-forward" will have become "flash-back"' (199). As we have seen, the casting of the Royal Court production made this simultaneous appearance of Old and Young Andy impossible to achieve on stage. Wesker wanted two endings to unfold simultaneously: 'Andrew Cobham alone and defeated in his armchair, and the defiant young people in the cathedral still full of hope' (Wesker 2000: n.pag.). This image proved unsettling for the critic Malcolm Page: is the audience meant to understand the final scene as a 'flash-forward', suggesting therefore that the future may be alterable, or as flash-back, in which case the play 'shows near-defeat' (Page 1968: 322).

Wesker's mother echoed these concerns when she read a draft of the play. The image of the elderly Andy slumped in his armchair recalled the memory of her husband, Wesker's father, sitting defeated in his chair when he was ill. In her diary entry of 14 November 1964, Leah Wesker wrote a response to her son's draft conclusion:

> Do you think all old people finish up in an armchair, or all disappointed politicians end up ill like your Daddy? [...] the end should have been that even if Andy could not achieve what he wanted by the time he is old and disappointed nevertheless the play should implying [sic] that Andy's work was not in vain, and that the youth of the future will carry on. And so at the end a young man should

spring up from the audience and say 'I will continue to build the six Golden
cities and more, for the whole world!' And old Andy should ask him – 'what is
your name young man?' and he should say, 'My name is Andy Cobham' and
then – bring down the curtains.

(Wesker 2000: n.pag.)

This note, with its chastening maternal tone, is endearing but also invigorating,
not least because her suggested revisions to the play's concluding moments wholly
eradicate the 'fourth wall' of the naturalist stage, thus bestowing on the audience
a measure of agency and responsibility. The imagined declamation of the young
man in the audience – 'My name is Andy Cobham' – also, perhaps, carries an echo
of the famous scene of doomed solidarity in the film *Spartacus* (released in 1960,
just four years before the date of this letter) when the army of defeated slaves,
one by one, identify themselves as Spartacus. The implication is clear: although
Andy Cobham has failed, everyone – anyone – has the potential to stand up and
fill his shoes.

'So much better than Serjeant Musgrave, darling!'

Some theatre reviewers reacted negatively to the play's perceived ambivalence.
J. W. Lambert, for example, argued that it

> falls between two stools. The poetic force is lacking in his language [...] and the
> details he does offer awake the dormant town-planner in us all, whose mounting
> scepticism must edge us to the side of the thick-headed trade unionists and bland
> upper-class politicians.

(Lambert 1966a: n.pag.)

Other critics, such as B. A. Young, wanted to hear more detail about the cities: 'Who
were the contractors who built this city of 60,000 population, including all muni-
cipal and amenity buildings and factories? How did they avoid any suggestion of
labour disputes?' (Young 1966: n.pag.). Such comments registered unease with
the play's refusal to render the factual or quotidian specificities associated with
naturalism. In similar vein, Ronald Bryden criticized what he perceived to be
the 'generalised vagueness' in Wesker's characterization of Andy, especially in
respect of his opaque personal and domestic life (Bryden 1966). There was also
scepticism about the play's autobiographical content: as the indefatigably testy
Lambert put it, 'I have often found myself wishing that Mr Wesker and, indeed,
most of our younger dramatists [...] could be put through a rigorous course in

sublimation' (Lambert 1966a: n.pag.). One or two reviewers criticized the perfunctory role of women in the play but did so in sexist language: 'It's good to see a
girl so dominating in a Wesker play but, despite Ann Firbank's crisp performance,
she confuses the story and ought to be docked' (Jones 1966: n.pag.); Esslin, meanwhile, unwittingly pointed to the lack of sophistication in the play's female characters even while praising the actresses' performances: 'Gillian Martell and Ann
Firbank are a splendid pair of contrasting female archetypes' (Esslin 1966: 57).

Esslin was, of course, on the jury that awarded Wesker the Marzotto prize (a
fact he disclosed at the start of his review); predictably, he offered a strong defence
of the play, dismissing its flaws as unimportant: 'Surely, that Wesker has a vision,
proclaims it and is even positively fighting for it in the real world as well as in the
theatre, surely that can't be held against him' (Esslin 1966: 12). However, he was
also critical of the play's final scene because of its inference – as we have seen – that
the aged Andy may be merely dreaming about the optimism of his youth; thus,
the final melancholy image of Andy in his chair seemed to assert, 'What fools we
were to take up the struggle which has led to this!' (Esslin 1966: 12). In Esslin's
view, it was more apposite and effective to interpret the play as 'a projection of the
future as seen by Andy Cobham in 1926 in Durham Cathedral' (Esslin 1966: 12).

Some reviewers offered brief but tantalizing glimpses of audience responses to
the performance, although these were inconsistent. Herbert Kretzmer discerned
'a somewhat chilly and faintly affronted audience' (Kretzmer 1966: n.pag.), while
Bryden observed that 'the play radiates a concern to which the audience warmed
eagerly' (Bryden 1966: n.pag.). In a humorous comment at the expense of the
playwright John Arden, Esslin reported that he overheard at least one glowing
endorsement from an audience member: ' "So much better than *Serjeant Musgrave*,
darling!" said that rather toothy lady to her companion as we trudged up those
narrow steps towards Sloane Square […] I couldn't agree more!' (Esslin 1966: 57).

Conclusion

For all the difficulties that attended its production at the Royal Court, and despite its limited performance history, *Golden City* remains an important and
undeservedly neglected play that gives an insight into the heated debates on the
Left about idealistic principle and pragmatic compromise in the 1950s and early
1960s – debates that are encapsulated in Wesker's troubled experience with C42.
As I have shown, the play also invites reflection on the post-war boom in 'new
towns' and the kind of society that new towns and cities should give expression to.

The play also resonates in the context of contemporary experience and speaks
to current issues such as the paucity of affordable housing for young people,

the pressure on successive governments to build new homes and the scandalous poor standards of safety in social housing. In respect of the latter issue, Andy's denunciation of the local council in Act I, scene 13 – 'when I told this council years ago that Floral Houses should come down or they'd fall down, the reply was "Nonsense! We've got schools to build, can't afford it." Well they fell and the new school was missing ten children' – is especially poignant in the context of the Grenfell Tower fire in 2017 (162). Wesker also anticipates the current pre-occupation in politics with press management and 'spin' – the earnest chanting of 'New Labour' by Andy and his friends early in the play carries an irony that could not have been foreseen (148) – and the various disputations in the play raise timely questions about the embattled status of facts in public discourse (in his debate with Andy, Jake argues that it was emotion, not facts, that swung the audience in his favour [159]).

For all these reasons, *Golden City* remains dynamic and acute in its political analysis of social history. The form of the play, while indebted to theatrical antecedents, also anticipates the large-scale state-of-the-nation drama of the 1970s; the moments of expressionist abstraction conjugate the nebulous politics of the New Left but also charge the audience to take responsibility for envisioning a new and better world. To borrow Doris Lessing's analogy, *Golden City* may be a flawed diamond in Wesker's canon, but its imperfections are intrinsic to its ongoing lustre.

NOTES

1. To avoid repeated citations, subsequent quotations from the play-text are taken from the revised second volume of Wesker's collected plays (Wesker 1990). Page references for quotations are provided in parentheses.
2. Michael Patterson states that the play 'was released only after nine drafts' but gives no evidence for this assertion (Patterson 2003: 34).
3. The article contains some inaccuracies, such as the claim that *Golden City* is about 'the rise and fall of a trade union leader' and that the plot covers the years 1909–90.
4. Swash was later to become an eminent theatrical producer.
5. More recently, David Pattie describes *Golden City* as 'Brechtian, episodic' in his assessment of Wesker's drama (Pattie 2012: 247).
6. The Royal Court director Lindsay Anderson also criticized the draft of the play but for a different reason: Anderson felt the early draft was unclear about the attitude of the central character to the golden cities project – was the protagonist an idealist or a pragmatist? Wesker 'accepted this criticism': '[Andy Cobham] must at some point recognize that it's patchwork, but recognize then that there is no alternative, and this recognition would reflect the state of the Left in this country' (Wesker 1966: 199).

7. There have been several international productions of *Golden City*, including at Malmö Stadsteater in 1968, the Deutsches Theater in East Berlin in 1971 and the Staatstheater Braunschweig in 1985; the Genesian Theatre company staged the play in Sydney in 1973.
8. In 2003, I wrote a short piece calling for a revival of *Golden City*, which was published on the now-defunct but pioneering theatre blog *Encore*. Dan Rebellato, who founded and curated the *Encore* website, sent a copy of my article to Wesker using the pseudonym 'Theatre Worker' (all contributions to *Encore* were published anonymously to encourage open dialogue and spirited provocation). Wesker sent a reply – 'Thank you. It helped warm the chill winds' – and this quote is taken from his email.
9. Wesker's interest in new towns surfaces again in his 1988 community play *Beorhtel's Hill*, commissioned to mark the fortieth anniversary of the new town of Basildon and discussed by Robert Wilcher in this book.
10. For further detail on the achievements, travails and legacy of C42, see Coppieters (1975) and Etienne (2016), as well as Lawrence Black's chapter in this volume.
11. In Wesker's 'Notes for 1st day rehearsal Golden City' in Aarhus, he observes: 'All the elements and all the scenes together will have created the *impression* of what it was like for a man to try to realize an ideal and why he failed. So it's an impressionistic play' (AW 1974: n.pag., original emphasis). This suggests the style of the play is designed, at least in part, to convey the mutable affective experience of its protagonist.

REFERENCES

Alexander, Anthony (2009), *Britain's New Towns: Garden Cities to Sustainable Communities*, Abingdon: Routledge.

Bryden, Ronald (1966), 'A breeze of inspiration', *The Observer*, 22 May.

Coppieters, Frank (1975), 'Arnold Wesker's Centre fortytwo: A cultural revolution betrayed', *Theatre Quarterly*, 5:18, pp. 37–54.

Etienne, Anne (2016), '"Visions don't work"? The role of Wesker's theatre and Centre 42 in 1960s' British culture', *Studies in Theatre and Performance*, 36:2, pp. 130–44.

Esslin, Martin (1966), 'Wesker's visionary', *Plays and Players* (July), pp. 12–13, 57.

Jones, D. A. N. (1966), 'Arnold and the unions', *New Statesman*, 27 May.

Kretzmer, Herbert (1966), 'Royal Court – *Their Very Own and Golden City*', *Daily Express*, 20 May.

Lambert, J. W. (1966a), 'An idealist at bay', *Sunday Times*, 22 May.

Lessing, Doris (1975; 1972), 'Out of the fountain', in *'The Story of a Non-Marrying Man' and Other Stories*, London: Penguin Books, pp. 11–28.

Page, Malcolm (1968), 'Whatever happened to Arnold Wesker? His recent plays', *Modern Drama*, 11:3, pp. 317–25.

Patterson, Michael (2003), *Strategies of Political Theatre: Post-War British Playwrights*, Cambridge: CUP.

Pattie, David (2012), *Modern British Playwriting: the 1950s: Voices, Documents, New Interpretations*, London: Bloomsbury Methuen Drama.

Rebellato, Dan (1999), *1956 and All That: The Making of Modern British Drama*, London: Routledge.

Taylor, John Russell (1969), *Anger and After: A Guide to the New British Drama*, rev. ed., London: Methuen Drama.

Trussler, Simon (1966a), 'I'm talking about Arnold Wesker … and his new play …', *Tribune*, 20 May.

——— (1966b), 'Portrait of a reformer', *Tribune*, 27 May.

Wardle, Irving (1966), 'A theatre for the People', *New Society*, 19 May.

Wesker, Arnold (1966), 'His very own and golden city: An interview with Arnold Wesker', Interview with Simon Trussler, *The Tulane Drama Review*, 11:2, pp. 192–202.

——— (1986), 'The nature of theatre dialogue', *New Theatre Quarterly*, 2:8, pp. 364–68.

——— (1990), *Volume Two: The Kitchen and Other Plays*, London: Penguin.

——— (1996), Letter to Chris Megson, 16 August.

——— (2000), 'For Osaka', speech delivered in Osaka on the occasion of a new production of *Their Very Own and Golden City*. Unpublished (copy of speech obtained courtesy of Anne Etienne).

——— (2003), Email to 'Theatre Worker', 21 July.

Wesker, Arnold Papers (AW) (1964a), 'Wesker on rise and fall of a trade union leader', *The Times*, 13 May, Austin, Texas: Harry Ransom Center, Box 109.2.

——— (1964b), 'Wesker win', *The Observer*, 25 October, Austin, Texas: Harry Ransom Center, Box 109.2.

——— (1966), 'Invited to Court', *The Observer*, 29 May, Austin, Texas: Harry Ransom Center, Box 109.2.

——— (1974), Handwritten notes for 1st day of rehearsal in Aarhus, n.d., Austin, Texas: Harry Ransom Center, Box 88.4.

Wilcher, Robert (1991), *Understanding Arnold Wesker*, Columbia: University of South Carolina Press.

Young, B. A. (1966), 'Their very own and golden city', *Financial Times*, 20 May.

Zimmerman, Heinz (1986), 'Wesker and utopia in the sixties', *Modern Drama*, 29:2, pp. 185–06.

PART 2

UNIFYING FRAGMENTS

FIGURE 7: Arnold Wesker, with production poster of *The Friends* at the Roundhouse, Bishop's Road, 1970. Photo by Dusty Wesker.

6

'Let Battle Commence!': The Wesker Controversies

Harry Derbyshire

Arnold Wesker had a lifelong knack for initiating, and being drawn into, controversies. The title of Wesker's first published piece of non-fiction, for *Encore* magazine in 1958, was 'Let Battle Commence!' (Wesker 1965: n.pag.). His Centre 42 (C42) project in the 1960s was increasingly characterized, as is shown elsewhere in this book, by argument and acrimony. In 1966, a suggestion that the CND yearly Easter March should be abandoned generated months of heated debate in *Challenge* (the Young Communist League's periodical) under the heading 'THE WESKER CONTROVERSY'[1] (AW 1966: n.pag.). In 1972, Wesker's short letter declining to participate on the theatre activist Ed Berman's 'Fun Art Bus' children's project was printed in the resulting book alongside a highly critical response from Berman: 'for you [art] is a matter of money and pretence' (Berman cited in Wesker 1985: 70).[2] The playwright's outsider status, which he sometimes regretted and sometimes enjoyed, informed and was further entrenched by his participation in controversies that often began as responses to perceived personal attacks but grew into strongly felt assertions of general principle.

Wesker's contentious interventions related both to the world of the theatre and to the wider sphere of cultural and political debate. In lectures, articles, reviews, memoirs, letters to newspapers and pieces posted online, the dramatist addressed a range of sensitive topics, often relating to his own career, and steadily consolidated a reputation for argumentativeness. The flyleaf of the 1985 collection *Distinctions*, which contains a wealth of evidence of this, describes its author as 'outspoken, prolific [and] uncompromising', and in his Preface, Wesker himself writes that 'Re-reading these fragments from the past even, [*sic*] I feel how they might irritate' (Wesker 1985: xi). John O'Mahony refers to the idea of 'Wesker the splenetic malcontent' as a 'myth', but this is a myth with some basis in truth (O'Mahony 1994: n.pag.). In this chapter, I'll consider a representative (though far from comprehensive) selection of skirmishes and campaigns dating from the 1970s to the 2000s. The first three sections – Wesker versus reviewers, Wesker versus directors and Wesker versus his fellow playwrights – concern the world of the theatre. The last – Wesker and global politics – considers the playwright's public comments on a cluster of contemporary issues which relate in complex ways to his cultural identity as a Jew.

Whether professional or political, these interventions were also personal, reflecting the same beliefs, opinions and preoccupations that informed Wesker's celebrated plays. Surveying his varied non-fictional output, including many interventions which are receiving scholarly consideration for the first time, I will argue that as well as shedding light on the values and priorities which inform Wesker's drama, they also offer – because they so frequently broke them – a rare opportunity to discern some of the unspoken but implicit rules of British cultural and political discourse. A working-class Jew elevated to prominence at a very specific moment in British cultural history, Wesker became a canonical playwright and, eventually, a knight of the realm, but always felt, or was made to feel, to some degree, an interloper. His frequent breaches of etiquette, moreover, were not necessarily accidental: as he admitted, 'Part of me relishes being an outsider' (Wesker cited in O'Mahony 2002: n.pag.). In this context, his outspoken interjections throw into relief the insularity and homogeneity of a cultural establishment that accepts social mobility on very specific terms. Time spent with Wesker the public commentator is time spent raising one's eyebrows, shaking one's head and occasionally having to reset one's jaw, responding to a writer who saw the initiation of debate as an absolute good.

'Critic as Censor': Wesker versus reviewers

Wesker's early hopes of bringing about wholesale change in British culture via his work with C42 may have been dashed, but this did not stop him in his later years from calling out and confronting what he saw as endemic and fundamental problems with the way British theatre functions as an industry and a cultural institution. Reviewers and the journalistic culture that informed their assessments were the first to feel his wrath, something Wesker looked back on in a 1995 *Guardian* piece prompted by Tony Slattery's expletive-filled tirade against reviewers at that year's Olivier Awards and Stephen Fry's disappearance following bad reviews of his performance in Simon Gray's play *Cell Mates* (1995). These incidents reminded Wesker of an experience of his own, some twenty-five years earlier:

> In 1970 I received a mixed bag of reviews for a difficult and ambitious play called *The Friends* […] Like Tony Slattery and Stephen Fry, I was hurt and angry but

instinct and temperament drove me in a different direction from them. 'Let's sit down and reason with one another', I said to myself, believing in the rational nature of mankind. And I sat me down to work for months, yes months, on a major essay provocatively entitled Casual Condemnation [*sic*] – A Study of the Critic as Censor. It was published in the most serious of journals – Theatre Quarterly. I waited for the debate to begin. Silence, from that day to this – though I suspect the essay coloured certain subsequent reviews of later plays.

(Wesker 1995c: n.pag.)

If 'Casual Condemnations' was intended to promote reasoned debate, its opening gambit was perhaps ill-judged, with Wesker comparing 'the styles and judgements of critics' to 'those strange, facial distortions [which] distinguish mongoloid children' (Wesker 1971: 16).[3]

In the piece, Wesker takes especial issue with Ronald Bryden, whose review of *The Friends* was indeed sharply critical. Bryden writes, at least ostensibly, more in sorrow than anger, telling his readers, 'I wish I could say the play was as impressive as the intention which churns woolily beneath its almost total lack of action' before concluding that a hardworking cast 'can't make the characters more than automata, puppets woodenly mouthing the windy generalities of a playwright whose real betrayal has been to abandon the role of our most precise social realist for that of a cloudy prophet of uplift' (Bryden 1970). In 'Casual Condemnations', Wesker ascribes the hostile reception of *The Friends* – a play in which he controversially declares via the character of Manfred, 'I despise the Englishman' (97) – to 'the English temperament, [...] suspicious of feeling and intellect'(Wesker 1971: 20). Because *The Friends*, he writes, 'contains both', critics were plunged into a state of 'rage, or irritation, or embarrassment', their various criticisms of his play serving as unconvincing rationalizations of an irrational response determined by national character (Wesker 1971: 20).

Behind Wesker's vengeful wrath lies a painful context that may not justify his rhetorical choices but certainly informs his impassioned response. *The Friends* was the first play he directed in the United Kingdom, and it was on the stage of the venue he had founded, the Roundhouse; this was meant, following his successful direction of the play in Stockholm in January 1970, to be his return home. Unfortunately, the circumstances of the rehearsals proved agonizing when Wesker was openly and repeatedly challenged by actor Victor Henry (see O'Connor 1971). A negative review appeared in *Black Dwarf* on 12 June 1970, written by playwright John McGrath, a co-founder of C42, asserting that what Wesker 'must do is not to confuse anybody including himself into thinking that he is in any way socialist, or that this play relates in any way to any possible form of socialist theatre' (AW 1970: n.pag.). This, and their ensuing heated correspondence, further conspired to render this professional experience a personal wound.

Nonetheless, the critique of reviewers which Wesker set down in a number of essays was general and comprehensive, including but not limited to

> an ignorance of the theatre's language; laziness [...]; imagining their early opin-
> ions had applauded when in fact they had been derisive or indifferent; making
> the playwright victim of private hates and thus distorting meaning; sacrificing
> fact to feeble humour; disarming through self-abasement; criticizing on the
> basis of misquotation; boldly stating opinions without attempting to substan-
> tiate them; and failing to listen to the play.
>
> (Wesker 1971: 16)

Of course, Wesker is not the first theatre worker to take issue with a critic or indeed to extrapolate endemic failings from particular reviews. Anybody who has ever had a bad notice will recognize the temptation to engage in a phrase-by-phrase rebuttal, but most refrain from doing so, at least publicly, because they know their rejoinder will be seen as a subjective expression of hurt feelings rather than a reliable indicator of critical ineptitude. They also know that taking issue with a critic will inevitably draw new attention to the fact that their work has been panned.

Wesker was not oblivious to such considerations and made no attempt to disguise his personal stake in the debate he was hoping to provoke. He admitted that his response arose from distress, but emphasized that such a reaction reflected the possibility of real damage to his reputation and livelihood. In a charged open letter to Harold Hobson following a critical review of *The Old Ones* in 1972, in which Wesker memorably urged the ageing critic to 'Retire!' (Wesker 1985: 343), he unapologetically asserted that 'Terror at being destroyed is my right' (Wesker 1985: 342). As we shall see, Wesker had already weathered a battle over the play's production, but, even so, he did not feel that he was agitating purely on his own behalf: he believed it was fundamentally unjust and undemocratic that reviewers could affect the artist's ability to reach an audience and, correspondingly, the public's access to work that might speak to its values and concerns. This is what lay behind his description of the 'Critic as Censor', as he explains in his letter to Hobson:

> It is generally believed that opinion is what [the reviewer] deals in. I disagree.
> He traffics in censorship. [...] Audiences are not permitted to see a play and
> judge its merit for themselves because you can fold it. If you do not like the defi-
> ance in an artist's spirit you have the power to cripple his career and hence his
> growth. [...] I consider this an awful power.
>
> (Wesker 1985: 341–42)

For Wesker, the really formidable adversary is not the critic in and of him/herself but the media providers which make reviews 'individual opinions magnified out of proportion by print' (Wesker 1985: 352). As he says of James Fenton, whose anthology of theatre reviews Wesker is (both fittingly and ironically) giving a critical review, 'Behind his anger, his enthusiasm [...] is the *Sunday Times*' (Wesker 1985: 353). Incidentally, it was in the offices of that same newspaper for eight weeks in 1971 that Wesker researched the background material for his play *The Journalists*. Not only did the play create a unique case of censorship, as discussed below, but the diary version of his visit, published as *Journey into Journalism*, was also vetoed for five years by a few *Sunday Times* journalists before being publicly permitted in 1976 by editor Harry Evans when pointedly interviewed by Melvyn Bragg on TV (AW 1976).

The fact that Wesker identifies 'defiance' as a quality disliked by reviewers, coupled with his highlighting of the power of the established media to magnify such dislikes so that they take on the function of censorship, allows us to infer a larger critique of the British cultural establishment and its resistance to the broadening of its demographic make-up. It is easy to see how Wesker may have felt dismayed if not betrayed as critical enthusiasm for his work drained away over time, and it would be understandable if he came to feel rejected by or excluded from a monolithic culture working to reinscribe its boundaries. Such an understanding of the situation might be supported by reference to the work of Pierre Bourdieu, who argued in *Distinction* that judgments of taste relate to social position and that critics function as a 'corporation [...] mandated by the [social] group to produce legitimate classifications' (Bourdieu 2010: 20). For Bourdieu, critics' judgments will be informed by the criteria accepted as 'legitimate' and made with a view to maintaining their own status as legitimate judges. Following Bourdieu, Yael Zarhy-Levo has written specifically about British theatre reviewers, defining them (in her book's title) as 'cultural agents', 'active participants [...] endow[ed] with the authority to "give value" to a theatrical product and/or a playwright' (Zarhy-Levo 2001: 4–7). Wesker, I think, would immediately have recognized these ideas: his animosity towards reviewers may have begun as something personal, but his critique of their individual and collective failings evolved to become as piercing as it was comprehensive.

'One of us is mad': Wesker versus directors

Alongside these hostilities with the critics, Wesker entered into conflict on a second front, taking aim at another group of cultural agents whose acceptance of his work was vital to his prosperity: directors and, more particularly, the Artistic Directors of prestigious theatres. As with the critics, his attacks were motivated at least partly by personal affront, but in challenging what he saw as 'the disproportionate power of the director' (Wesker 1994a: 9–10), Wesker believed he was aligning himself with the views of other significant theatre people, including his fellow playwright John Osborne and even prominent directors such as Peter Hall and Nicholas Hytner. Whereas from the critics Wesker had wanted approbation or at least conscientious consideration, from the Artistic Directors of the Royal Shakespeare Company (RSC) and the National Theatre (NT) he required the respect he felt his past achievements had earned him. Specifically, he demanded that they produce his new plays, even if their merits were debatable. Again, Wesker was responding to a series of deeply felt personal disappointments while at the same time campaigning against what he saw as the closed and self-reflective nature of a cultural establishment which restricted access to its resources to a privileged minority.

The trouble began when the NT reneged on a commitment to produce *The Old Ones* in 1972. The play was to be directed by John Dexter, whose close and lengthy relationship with Wesker was eventually to break down in 1976 over *Shylock* (as documented in *The Birth of Shylock and the Death of Zero Mostel*), arguably inaugurating a pattern of conflict between the playwright and directors. NT Artistic Director Laurence Olivier gave 'the continuing critical situation with our finances' as his reason for scheduling the commercially dependable *School for Scandal* instead of *The Old Ones* (cited in Rosenthal 2013: 173). Wesker, however, recalled that 'while Dexter was abroad, Ken Tynan […] threw *The Old Ones* out of the scheduled programme due, I think, to an internal quarrel between the two men' (Wesker 1997: xii), and Tynan had indeed admitted that the play wasn't 'his dish' (AW 1971: n.pag.), though he had also assured Wesker 'how he pleased he was' to have him at the National (AW 1972a: n.pag.). In any case, Wesker was outraged and, upon the advice of Lord Goodman, took initial steps to legally contest the decision on 10 January. Within two weeks, the NT offered to reprogramme the production in July to fit Dexter's schedule, but on the same day the National was 'saved from its predicament by the Royal Court's request to do *The Old Ones*' (AW 1972b: n.pag.). The statement officially released, 'to prevent the press making a fool of either of us', cites casting difficulties (AW 1972c).

Worse was to come. A planned RSC production of Wesker's next play *The Journalists* – a study of 'the poisonous human need to cut better men down to our size' (AW 1975a: n.pag.) – was prevented by the actors' collective refusal to perform in it – a unique event in the history of the company (Chambers 2004: 184–85). Wesker was understandably distraught, as he recalled in emphatic terms in a 1981 piece for the *Sunday Times*:

> The delivery of a play to a theatre that has contracted for it is a commitment of faith of such delicacy that to abuse it in any way is a kind of rape. Once a

116

play is accepted, the theatre is trusted guardian. The solemnity of such a trust
cannot be over-emphasized. Break it, scorn it, and the rage 'hath no bounds'.

(Wesker 1985: 56)

Wesker quotes the actors' stated reason for their revolt: their 'great lack of faith
in the play' (Wesker 1985: 60). As with the cancellation of *The Old Ones*, however, Wesker had an alternative theory, which he would consistently articulate in
later years (Wesker 1997: xii, AW3 1999: 2):

> I believe it was due to a collective anger, perhaps in some cases unconscious,
> with what [the actors] imagined to be the play's politics. It was, remember, a
> time when the influence of the Workers' Revolutionary Party was at its height
> among actors, and my play would seem to have committed the cardinal sin of
> having four Tory cabinet ministers who were intelligent.

(Wesker 1985: 65–66)[4]

Whatever its cause, the revolt placed the RSC's Artistic Director, Trevor Nunn, in
a difficult position, since the RSC had commissioned, contracted and announced
the play. Accepting that a production had been planned, he denied that one was
legally guaranteed and offered Wesker a commission to rewrite *The Journalists* for
The Other Place, the RSC's third auditorium. For the playwright, these compromi-
ises were unsatisfactory: not only did he feel that a promise had been broken, but
his income and wider reputation had been materially affected, not least because
the RSC's insistence that their production be the world premiere – similarly to
the National's planned staging of *The Old Ones* – had obliged Wesker to refuse
permission for performances elsewhere. As he later wrote, 'I was angry and felt
insulted and betrayed [...] their suggestion of the third auditorium seemed not the
best setting for the play and smacked of perfunctory treatment [...] I filed a law
suit claiming £25,000 damages' (Wesker 1985: 64–65).

Though Wesker's account of the affair was only published later, his issuing of
a lawsuit against the RSC (a move he came to regret) made public a serious dis-
agreement with one of the bastions of the British subsidized theatre. For Wesker the
eventual result was a Pyrrhic victory, as after seven years he won less than a fifth of
the damages he'd claimed. Wesker's controversial exchanges with the RSC briefly
resumed in 1996, when he commented in *The Guardian* on Artistic Director Adrian
Noble's views about the importance of the visual in contemporary productions of
Shakespeare. For Wesker, Noble's was a 'Theatre of Gawping', but he nonetheless
added, 'I'd let you do my plays on a stage that wasn't empty. I would. I'd let you do
them with a zing a bing a bang and drums galore' (Wesker 1996: n.pag.). Perhaps
this letter was intended as an attempt at reconciliation, inviting new collaboration

despite acknowledged artistic differences, but if so, its combination of flippancy, mockery and apparent desperation was probably counterproductive.

After *The Journalists*, Wesker's disappointments continued. In 1975, the NT rejected *Shylock*. Wesker's first response on hearing the bad news from Lord Birkett, the National's Deputy Director, was unequivocal, as he later recalled: ' "You're all potty", I exploded. "Absolutely potty" ' (Wesker 1997: 15). In retrospect, Wesker acknowledges that this was not the most diplomatic reaction, especially when Artistic Director Peter Hall had taken pains to stress that '[e]verybody has an affection for Arnold and a great desire to present the best of his work' (AW 1975b). Yet, it remained essentially his position when he wrote to Birkett a couple of weeks later, following detailed discussion between the two, to insist that 'one of us is mad' (Wesker 1997: 23). In his response to Hall, Wesker is careful to avoid personal attacks, casting himself instead as speaking for playwrights in general:

> Here's what I think. That twenty years in the theatre [...] gives me an authority equal to anyone of you sitting on the artistic direction of the National. [...] Time and again I've been vindicated, and I'm still not trusted. [...] Can't you under-stand how I, we, resent no machinery existing through which our authority can operate? [...] [T]here operates a tyranny of directors that is unhealthy for the creative life of the theatre in this country.
>
> (Wesker 1997: 25–27)

The correspondence continues, the emollient Hall conceding many of Wesker's points, but this butters no parsnips with the playwright. The missives grow shorter until they cease altogether, leaving Wesker in a state of 'fear' and 'rage', defeated once again by the establishment (Wesker 1997: 31).

Wesker's views about the institutional marginality of playwrights at the National were publicly stated in a 1978 piece for *The Listener* entitled 'Look! No playwrights' (Wesker 1978: n.pag.), though his ire perhaps faded in the wake of two NT productions of new plays, *Love Letters on Blue Paper* (1978) and *Caritas* (1981). Under Hall's successor Richard Eyre there was collegiate correspondence with Wesker, but no productions until *Chips with Everything* (discussed in John Bull's chapter) in 1997.[5] Afterwards, Wesker would find himself at a further dis-advantage, when Nunn – to whom he hadn't spoken for 25 years following the *Journalists* debacle – became NT Artistic Director. Despite a dinner at the Ivy, Nunn soon ceased contact, which, along with unreturned production photos of *Golden City*, and Nunn's production of *The Merchant of Venice* at the NT, drove Wesker to publish an 'Open Letter to Trevor Nunn in Two Acts' on his website in November 1999. In the letter, Wesker characterizes Nunn's silence as ' "passive aggression" [...] symptomatic of a rudeness permeating theatre in general' (AW3

1999: 1) and says of Nunn's disinclination to mount a production of *Shylock* to run alongside his *Merchant of Venice*: 'to suppress an original play for an interpretation was an abuse of power' (AW3 1999: 7). That he was once again burning his bridges was not lost on Wesker:

> I'm aware this letter may ensure you never present a play of mine during your reign as artistic director of The Royal National Theatre but as our exchanges over the last three and a half years suggest this is unlikely anyway I have nothing to lose. [...] perhaps I have a duty to blow the whistle on behalf of younger generations who follow and will surely become victims of the opportunism which seems rife in this 'unholy trade'.
>
> (AW3 1999: 2)

Wesker's intervention attracted comment in the media, with the *Daily Telegraph* reporting on 'a dramatic feud [...] being fought out on the Internet', an inaccurate description since Nunn, predictably, never replied (Reynolds 1999: n.pag.).[6]

Three dominant themes can be traced through Wesker's charged and often public interactions with the leaders of the RSC and the NT. There is the pain of the spurned artist, or 'The Disinherited Playwright' (Wesker 1985: 360–64); there is the conviction that this spurning, rather than resulting from any inadequacy in Wesker's writing, indicated that (as he had expressed it to Hall) 'something *is* wrong in the theatre' (Wesker 1997: 27, original emphasis); and there is the determination to argue for change not only in order to improve his own situation but 'on behalf of younger generations' and 'all established playwrights' (Wesker 2003a (Reynolds 1999)). Ultimately, Wesker argues for a theatre in which the playwright, rather than the director, is the central figure, in which new plays by established dramatists are 'performed simply because we'd *earned the right*' (Wesker 1997: 27, original emphasis). It might be noted that this ideal bears a close resemblance to the ethos of the Royal Court during its early years under George Devine – the years of Wesker's greatest success (see Little and McLaughlin 2007: 62–63). Although Wesker complained about 'the Court's retreats and hesitations' during this period, he encountered a model of theatre-making there against which the practice of the director-led institutions of the later twentieth century fell decidedly short (Wesker 1985: 6).

Taken together, Wesker's impolitic engagements with directors and reviewers consistently demonstrate a stubborn belief in the validity of his point of view and a consequent refusal to be silent. This was neither the anticipated nor the advisable response. The way to earn critical rehabilitation and renewed preferment – if either was ever a realistic prospect – was not to protest but to defer, because in both cases the power lay in the hands of an establishment that those who hope for approval are expected to respect.

'However admirable they may be': Wesker versus other playwrights

Wesker's battles with critics and artistic directors were, as we have seen, waged on behalf of playwrights everywhere, but their status as fellow sufferers did not necessarily make them safe from friendly fire. The relationship between Wesker and Harold Pinter is discussed elsewhere in this volume: the similarity of the two writers' backgrounds coupled with Pinter's much greater eminence making him a particular touchstone; David Hare and Tom Stoppard were also regularly cited as points of comparison:

> However admirable they may be, Stoppard, Pinter, Hare – they're comfort-
> able. Harold by now gives you what you expect. I don't. David Hare, who is a
> very intelligent writer, is quite predictable. Of course, they are more successful
> than I am.
>
> (Wesker cited in Brandreth 2001: n.pag.)

Talking down the work of more successful peers while attributing his own relative obscurity to his greater artistic range, Wesker clearly risks appearing arrogant or conceited – but this seems to be a chance knowingly taken. A more inadvertent controversy was created when Wesker published a recollection of John Osborne that drew the wrath of his widow. 'An entertainer's farewell' appeared in *The Guardian* in January 1995, describing a reception for theatre people at Buck-ingham Palace, which he and Osborne had attended along with Pinter and many others the previous summer. Wesker's vivid pen portrait is affectionate and respectful, but also unsparing. As the evening's events are recounted, Osborne is described variously as 'already quite drunk', 'so drunk!', 'drunk – he kept looking for more champagne' and 'desperately unsteady on his legs'. Osborne 'talks slightly nasally', Wesker tells us, and 'when he's drunk, becomes maudlin'; he complains 'pitifully' about his finances, and his 'hearty, theatrical crudeness makes me wince' (Wesker 1995a: n.pag.).

If Wesker had not thought these words about his recently deceased peer might offend, he was to be disabused. A letter from Osborne's widow Helen was printed two days later, insisting that rather than being drunk her husband had in fact been 'gravely ill, unto death as it turns out' and declaring that Wesker 'would not have dreamt or dared of [sic] publishing such a piece if John were alive' (Osborne 1995: n.pag.). The same issue contains a letter from Pinter and his wife Antonia Fraser confirming that in their opinion, 'Osborne did not appear to be in the least drunk', suggesting behind-the-scenes communications and a degree of solidarity that might be thought a surprise (Pinter and Fraser 1995: n.pag.). These admonishments prompted a response from Wesker the following day, in which he said that 'My intention was to record an affectionate encounter with a man I deeply admired, and if I caused distress I apologise without reservation' (Wesker 1995b: n.pag.).

Wesker's decision not to argue his corner against the combined might of a grieving widow and Britain's foremost dramatist was wise, though two days later Greville Poke, President of the English Stage Company, wrote to defend 'An entertainer's farewell' as 'a charming, loving, humorous tribute to a man [Wesker] obviously greatly admired' (Poke 1995: n.pag.). The last word, however, belonged to the Osborne camp, when Wesker was expressly banned, along with Peter Hall, actor Albert Finney and critic Nicholas de Jongh, from attending the playwright's memorial service a few months later.[7] A handwritten note displayed by the church door, believed to be the work of Helen Osborne, listed those to be excluded, referring to Wesker as 'the BARD of HAY ON WYE'. Asked about his exclusion, Wesker expressed disingenuous puzzlement, saying, 'I know John couldn't possibly have done that [...] I hadn't had a falling out with him at all' (cited in Jury 1995: n.pag.).

These occasional and (sometimes) inadvertent skirmishes with fellow dramatists lack the principled edge of Wesker's battles with critics and directors and may be ascribed to professional rivalry. What they have in common with those other disputes is that they reflect the playwright's drive to assert his presence within the scheme of things and his lack of deference to commonly accepted pieties – which can also be seen in Wesker's political interventions during the same period.

'Stand up and be counted': Wesker and global politics

The working conditions of playwrights was far from being the only issue on which Wesker expressed a view in the latter part of his career. In particular, between the late 1980s and the mid-2000s, he made a series of often-outspoken public comments and statements on Israel, the Salman Rushdie affair and 9/11. The running thread is the playwright's understanding of himself as a 'Jew by upbringing and temperament', and, characteristically, Wesker's interest in international and domestic affairs was both political and personal (cited in Brandreth 2001: n.pag.). This is not to suggest that he spoke from a fixed and predictable perspective, however, and in fact a significant progression can be identified by tracing these interconnected narratives.

As a left-wing Jew, Wesker – like many – was often torn as violent incidents and controversial policies in Israel pulled either on his liberal conscience or his ethnic and cultural loyalties, or both at the same time. The complexity of his position – and the difficulty of ensuring its accurate representation – is illustrated by a 1988 *Observer* piece reporting on an exchange of letters between Wesker and Shimon Peres, then Israel's foreign minister, concerning his handling of the then current crisis in Gaza and on the West Bank. The article tells readers that Wesker has 'attacked the "unimaginative crassness", the "utter oblivious-ness to world opinion", the "callous disregard for human concern", and the "sheer political or diplomatic ineptitude" of Israel's response' (Anon. 1988: n.pag.). This chimes well with the editorial leanings of the left-wing *Observer*, but for Wesker this was misleading reporting. He wrote to the paper quoting other parts of his letter to Peres, which express admiration for the Israeli project both in principle and practice, and stressed that 'This is the context in which my criticism of Israel's presentation of its policy towards the Palestinians should be seen' (Wesker 1988: n.pag.).

A comparable degree of balance is attempted in a letter Wesker wrote to *The Guardian* in the wake of the 1994 Cave of the Patriarchs massacre in Hebron and the retaliatory murder of three Jewish students in New York. Responsi-bility for revenge attacks, he wrote, should be placed with those whose acts had inspired them:

> There should be no doubt that the man responsible for the murder of the three Jewish students in Brooklyn was their fellow Jew, Baruch Goldstein; just as those responsible for the carnage of the praying Muslims worshipping at the Tomb of the Patriarchs in Hebron are their fellow Muslims who have murdered inno-cent Israelis; just as every innocent murdered Catholic in Northern Ireland was murdered by the IRA and every Protestant by a Protestant terrorist.
>
> (Wesker 1994b: n.pag.)

This is a thought-provoking way to assert the moral equivalence of all terrorist activity whatever the stated cause, and it is interesting to consider how far Wesker's thinking here anticipates Sarah Kane's presentation of a never-ending spiral of revenge and counter-revenge in *Blasted* (1995) and debbie tucker green's con-sideration of the densely interconnected networks of responsibility underlying human rights violations in *truth and reconciliation* (2011). Wesker wants to be seen issuing a non-partisan condemnation of violent action on both sides: 'as a Jew I would like to state publicly that I mourn the innocent dead of Hebron'; yet, his suggested reversal of responsibility makes Goldstein responsible for just three deaths – while the 29 deaths and hundreds of injuries he in fact caused become the responsibility of Muslims (Wesker 1994b: n.pag.).

The Hebron letter can be interestingly compared to another written in response to the assassination of Israeli president Yitzhak Rabin by an Israeli extremist. Where previously Wesker had urged readers to place the blame for Jewish deaths – metaphorically speaking – with a Jewish murderer, now, talking of the actual murder of a Jew by a Jew, he counselled them to discount the assassin's Jewishness:

> Jewish distress for the murder of President Rabin is natural. Expression of this
> distress 'that a Jew has murdered a Jew' is irrational. [...] An age-old and rec-
> ognisable mutant, found in all cultures, races, religions, who this time happens
> to be a Jew, has murdered Israel's prime minister.
>
> (Wesker 1995d: n.pag.)

Wesker's aim seems twofold: to counsel against collective self-blaming on the part
of Jewish people and to discourage antisemitism in the wider population. While
both aims reflect Wesker's identification with Jewishness and, by extension, with
the state of Israel, both are also compatible with his humanist principles and neither is controversial, in that few would disagree that it is wrong to associate an
entire cultural or ethnic group with the violent actions of one individual.

In the 2000s, however, there is an apparent turn towards a more robust stance.
Wesker argues against the view that criticism of Israel should not be thought to
imply or demonstrate anti-Jewish prejudice. In a discussion that resonates strongly
with the controversy in which the British Labour Party became embroiled in 2016,
Wesker writes that the acceptance of such a principle would mean that

> we can't suggest someone is being anti-semitic in the manner and tone with
> which they are being anti-Israeli, though we know in our bones that is the case.
> [...] There are many Jews, like myself, who are critical of aspects of Israeli
> policy; we also know there is, there most definitely, identifiably *is* a molten flow
> of anti-semitism burning the air of reason and screened unreachably behind
> smoky anti-Zionism, complaining comfortably that to say otherwise is obscene.
>
> (Wesker 2003b: n.pag.)

It is doubtless true that antisemitism lies behind some non-Jewish criticism of
Israel, and Wesker states the case for this strongly and eloquently; what he does
not do is suggest how a Gentile critic of Israeli policy could ever demonstrate that
his or her views were not underpinned by prejudice. One potential inference is that
only Jewish people can criticize Israel without fear of being thought anti-Semitic.

This new forcefulness is still more pronounced in a 2005 letter prompted by the
Israeli disengagement from Gaza, which saw the dismantling of all Israeli settle-
ments inside the Gaza strip. Wesker combines a caustic tone with a stark argument:

> The sight of Jews ethnically cleansing Jews out of Gaza is shocking. [...] now,
> like the Germans had wanted, Gaza is ethnically pure. At last they've got rid of
> those nasty, clever, hardworking Jews who made more money than was good
> for them and had a bad habit of making everyone else seem an idiot. Enough
> already! [...] There is one important lesson we can all learn from these events: if

you have a cause needing the support of the international community, make
sure your enemy is a Jew.

(Wesker 2005: n.pag.)

Wesker's stance here cannot be described as pro-Israeli since it is Israeli government policy that he is criticizing, but neither can it be considered non-partisan.
Gone is the careful balance of previous years, and in its place are extreme and
potentially divisive comparisons with the genocides of the 1990s (through the
phrase 'ethnic cleansing') and with the Holocaust. This is an early instance of a
hardening of Wesker's tone and stance which can be discerned between 1988 and
2005, which I suggest can be best understood in connection with his comments
during the same period on the Salman Rushdie affair and the terrorist attack on
New York of 11 September 2001.

When a *fatwā* calling for the death of British novelist Salman Rushdie was
issued in 1989, Wesker was prominent among the group of leading writers who
declared their support for him. In a letter to *The Independent*, the playwright
entered the debate with characteristic boldness:

> When the Nazis forced the Jews of Denmark to wear a yellow star, the Danish
> king and many of his subjects wore one too. If the Ayatollah Khomeini is
> declaring this absurd death sentence upon Salman Rushdie for daring to ques-
> tion the notion of divinity, and naming him an enemy of Allah, then the mil-
> lions of us who also question such notions should declare ourselves similarly
> enemies of Allah. I for one do.

(Wesker 1989a: n.pag.)

The comparison to Nazi persecution immediately establishes a personal identification between Rushdie and Wesker, via the latter's Jewishness, and this has possibly influenced his judgement. Underlying the declaration of himself as an enemy
of Allah seems to be a belief or assertion that the Ayatollah's statements could be
taken to represent the common view of the world's entire Muslim population, placing Wesker in a position of antagonism to over one billion believers with whom
he had previously had no quarrel. The urge to show solidarity and stand up to
those who seek to stifle artistic expression is laudable, but the position Wesker
articulates goes further than was necessary, perhaps suggesting a pre-existing or
underlying hostility either to religious authority in general or to Islamic authority
in particular.

Wesker may have regretted the impetuosity of his opening salvo, because a few
months later he was making an explicit distinction between Muslims who supported Khomeni and Muslims who did not. Now writing in the formal capacity

124

of a member of the International Committee for the Defence of Salman Rushdie and his Publishers, Wesker states:

> I have many friends who are Muslims and they are very ashamed of the furore their brethren have created. They fear that the community is in the hands of immature minds who are using the Rushdie book as a means of gaining power over the community. I would ask the silent majority in the Muslim community to stand up and be counted among those who reject fanatical fundamentalism.
>
> (Wesker 1989b: n.pag.)

This makes a sensible and important distinction. However, in calling on 'the silent majority in the Muslim community to stand up and be counted', Wesker was arguably placing on all Muslims the onus to demonstrate that they were not extremists, as if this was the default expectation. The concern about Islamist terrorism in the years following 9/11 would see widespread pressure on British Muslims to disassociate themselves from, speak out against and even somehow prevent violence carried out in the name of Islamism, pressure which would increasingly come to be seen as unfair and counter-productive (see Dearden 2017).

The shocking attack of 9/11 prompted Wesker to write an unusually short letter to the *Guardian*, which reads in full: 'What monstrous concept of God sanctioned such massive, violent cruelty? And what mentality dances upon the ashes?' (Wesker 2001a: n.pag.). Wesker's instinct once again is to home in immediately on the issue of faith, although there is an ambiguity to his phrasing which leaves open how far the attack should be considered a legitimate expression of Muslim belief.[8] In a subsequent letter, Wesker makes explicit comparison between the violent extremism of Al-Qaeda and the *fatwā* against Rushdie, suggesting that Khomeini had been a direct inspiration to Osama bin Laden (Wesker 2001b). This was one of many comparisons Wesker publicly drew in relation to 9/11:

> We knew how inferiority complexes lashed out murderously on a local scale – the bully at school, the raging car-driver seeking manhood behind the wheel, the second-rate mind rubbishing the star, but Bin Laden's psychotic mind has tapped into infantile ignorance on a global scale. [...] He is not a man of God, he is a type that was there in the Inquisition, when the guillotine fell, when the gulags were opened, the gas chambers built, the little red book waved, and Satanic Verses burned.
>
> (Wesker cited in Addley et al. 2001: n.pag.)

As before there appears to be a reconsideration of a potentially divisive opening position, with Wesker now explicitly stating that bin Laden was not acting legitimately on behalf of his religion. The historical parallels he cites range across different religious and political contexts, echoing some of Wesker's statements about violence carried out by Israelis and Palestinians, but include more than one situation with which the playwright will have felt a personal connection either in cultural or political terms. Perhaps the strongest association of all, however, is with 'the bully at school', because in a scripted film sequence that begins his last published drama *Joy and Tyranny* (2011), Wesker was to make the same comparison in a startlingly concrete way. The sequence is set in a school playground:

> BULLY *smashes a straight-from-the-shoulder fist into* BOY 2's *eye.*
>
> NOTE: *It is important that the offending arm is filmed moving horizontally to its target because the arm must mix and morph – filmically – into the aeroplane crashing into the* TWIN TOWERS [...]
>
> *Our images link the* BULLY's *spiteful action to the murderous spiteful action of the* TWIN TOWER DESTROYERS, *suggesting that both actions spring from an adolescent-like inferiority complex.*
>
> (Wesker 2011: 15)

This dramatized playground incident, the book's back cover tells us, is autobiographical, drawn from a formative experience whereby the young Wesker had been hit by a boy whose liquorice stick he had refused to try. The sudden jump from individual to global history, recognizably in the tradition of Kane's *Blasted*, suggests a very personal response on Wesker's part to the 9/11 attack and the threat of Islamist terrorism more generally.

Similarly, in an open letter to Tony Blair published in *The Times*, he stated his belief that

> [i]t is not the corrupt West that bin Laden hates, it is the colourful West that he hates, colour as an image of joy, energy and creativity. There is something about other people's happiness and sense of free spirit that irrationally rouses the wrath of certain mentalities, whether in the school playground or the religious/political arena.
>
> (Wesker 2006: n.pag.)

That Wesker is again making a personal identification is indicated both by another reference to the playground and by the similarity of these comments to remarks made elsewhere about the hostility that he himself seemed to arouse: in 2002, for instance, he told an interviewer that 'I seem to be someone that people want to put down [...] It seems to be a sense of hostility to my joy and ebullience. I detected it early' (cited in O'Mahony 2002: n.pag.). In Wesker's mind, then, the reasons why

Islamist terrorists wanted to destroy the West were fundamentally the same as the reasons why some people didn't like him. It follows from this that the defeat of bin Laden would be, for Wesker, a symbolic defeat of the playground bully and all those others who had reacted negatively to his very particular energy. These feelings are likely to have contributed to Wesker's support for the 2003 US-led invasion of Iraq, which placed him further at odds with the left-wing consensus of the time and was in striking contrast to the position adopted by Harold Pinter.

The public statements on world affairs that Wesker periodically made between the late 1980s and the mid-2000s reveal a position that discernibly developed, while at the same time relating consistently to a densely entwined knot of personal and political preoccupations. The changing climate of opinion during those years, whereby fierce criticism both of Israel and of the United States's 'war on terror' became the dominant left-wing standpoint, would seem to have pushed Wesker towards a less diplomatic, more combative stance. Though he repeatedly retreats from divisive statements made in the heat of the moment, the general tenor of his interventions grows less moderate and more committed, reflecting his own subject position more and more decisively. Although public positions are often, if not always, informed by personal concerns, the transparency with which Wesker makes plain the connections is unusual, showing up how commonly such factors are downplayed, if not actively hidden.

Conclusion: 'Perhaps I don't play the game'

In later years, Wesker often had cause to reflect on his disputatious behaviour and its consequences for his career. He accounted for it in a range of ways, the first being his Jewish heritage: 'I think it's very Jewish to argue. Somebody says something you think is silly, you don't sit back. You say something. It's not very wise especially in the theatre' (cited in O'Mahony 1994: n.pag.). Elsewhere he spoke about the temperamental difference between himself and many of his professional peers:

> I don't think that I am a quintessentially English writer, though whenever I'm abroad I feel very English. And perhaps I don't play the game. I'm not really a theatre man, I'm not a theatre personality. I don't mix with actors and directors. I just happen to write plays.
>
> (Wesker cited in Brandreth 2001: n.pag.)

Finally, he brought social class into the equation:

> Harold Hobson once advised me in a roundabout way to keep my mouth shut because that would be the sensible, almost gentlemanly thing to do. It's part

of public-school upbringing to take your punishment. But I never felt I had a choice. Part of me relishes being an outsider.

(Wesker cited in O'Mahony 2002: n.pag.)

As a working-class, state-educated Jew 'by upbringing and temperament', a person who had never felt completely accepted in the world of the theatre, and someone who didn't fully identify with his own nationality, Wesker felt himself an 'outsider' who was both unable and unwilling to 'play the game' (cited in Brandreth 2001: n.pag.). As we have seen, he found himself time and again taking issue with the discourse and practice of the cultural establishment, but this was something he felt he had to do, something which brought him professional disadvantage but also personal satisfaction.

Wesker was surely correct in identifying a mismatch between his approach to professional and public debate and the approach taken by the majority of his peers. He was no doubt right to think of this as resulting from his own individual character, though equally the positions he adopted were more or less exactly those that a person of his background and circumstances could have been expected to adopt. At the same time, it can be argued that 'the Wesker controversies' reveal something more fundamental about the conduct of cultural and political discourse in post-war and modern Britain. Put in plain terms, Wesker is the exception that proves the rule: his refusal to take the usual or approved approach allows us to perceive an unspoken and near-universal consensus that such an approach exists and should normally be followed. Contrary to accepted practice, Wesker did not accept negative criticism, defer to the authority of cultural gatekeepers, speak politely about rivals or take pains to seem dispassionate about global issues that bore a personal relation to him. Instead he spoke his mind and wore his heart on his sleeve. This led to his ever greater marginalization, attesting powerfully to the dominant role played by shared codes of discourse and behaviour within a cultural establishment that had at first opened its arms to Wesker as an 'angry young man' but ultimately could not find a space for him as an eminent, mature dramatist.

In speaking up as he did, Wesker did not advance his career, but the eloquent public record he made of his trials helpfully exposes the workings of a self-perpetuating cultural establishment that excludes those with insufficient social and cultural capital and, as a result, maintains the soft boundaries that keep high cultural products such as theatre out of the reach of large swathes of the population. In this way, he remained true all his life to the insights that he had famously expressed through the character of Beatie Bryant in *Roots*.

NOTES

1. Asked if he would send a message of greetings to that year's CND Easter March, Wesker replied that he felt the march 'should be abandoned as a form of protest which has, for the moment, outworn its usefulness'. Five hostile responses to this suggestion were printed over the next two issues, followed by an article headed 'WESKER REPLIES', in which he addresses 'the series of abusive, soap-box screaming letters my observations [...] have provoked' (AW 1966: n.pag.). Incidentally, 20,000 people marched in 1966: compared to the 150,000 who had marched in 1961 and 1962, it does indeed look as if the protest was dwindling, as Wesker had suggested.

2. Wesker in turn wrote his own reply to Fun Art Bus co-ordinator Ed Berman, re-publishing the correspondence to give himself the last word in his collection *Distinctions* (see Wesker 1985: 69–73; Wintle 1973: 21–22).

3. Any reviewers reading in 1971 would have found it difficult not to feel insulted by Wesker's comparison between people of their profession and people suffering from a genetic disorder that typically causes learning disabilities; and of course the implied criticism through comparison is equally, if not more, offensive from the point of view of people living with Down's syndrome. A similar effect is achieved in Wesker's 1972 reference to 'the imbecilities of a cretinue of critics' (Wesker 1985: 343). Cretinism is a now-outmoded term for congenital iodine deficiency syndrome, a variation on which Wesker is using pejoratively. Imbecility is another outmoded term for what would now be referred to as intellectual disability.

4. Only Wesker appears to have connected the contemporary popularity of socialist politics among actors with the debacle of *The Journalists*: Terry Hands, in 1972, an RSC Associate Director, dismissed the suggestion, saying 'there was no conspiracy, no brandishing of wooden spoons in the canteen' (cited in O'Mahony 1994: n.pag.), and an examination of the RSC archives revealed 'no convincing evidence' to support Wesker's contention (Sweet 2012: n.pag.).

5. As Wesker wrote in his autobiography, '[Eyre] has promptly and unstintingly read and said no to six new plays [...] He never fails to sign off in the most friendly manner' (Wesker 1994: 8).

6. A previous open letter to a prominent artistic director, Stephen Daldry, was prompted in 1994 by the failure to transfer the RCT's *Kitchen* production to the West End and by Daldry's subsequent and lengthy silence (AW 1994).

7. According to Dan Conaghan of the *Daily Telegraph*, relations between Osborne and Hall were 'often good-natured but sometimes strained'; Finney had 'incurred Osborne's wrath after a row about the film of Tom Jones, for which Osborne had written the script'; and de Jongh 'is thought to have angered Osborne's family when he wrote an account of the playwright's sexuality' (Conaghan 1995: n.pag.).

8. Wesker's phrasing also echoes the famous last lines of W. B. Yeats's apocalyptic poem 'The Second Coming'.

REFERENCES

Addley, Esther, Libby Brooks, Oliver Burkeman, Amy Fleming, David Gow, Simon Hattenstone, Ian Katz, Merope Mills and Stephen Moss (2001), 'Has the world changed? – Part two', *The Guardian*, 11 October.

Anon. (1988), 'Wesker talks tough about Jerusalem', *The Observer*, 20 March.

AW3 (1999), 'Theatre-cheats: An open letter to Trevor Nunn in two acts', Box 24.

Bourdieu, Pierre (2010), *Distinction*, trans. Richard Nice, Routledge Classics, London: Routledge.

Brandreth, Gyles (2001), 'The angry old man of the theatre', *Sunday Telegraph*, 4 February.

Bryden, Ronald (1970), 'Wesker's ritual of atonement', *The Observer*, 24 May.

Chambers, Colin (2004), *Inside the Royal Shakespeare Company: Creativity and the Institution*, London: Routledge.

Conaghan, Dan (1995), 'Vengeful Osborne has final word', *Daily Telegraph*, 3 June.

Dearden, Lizzie (2017), 'Government risks "alienating" Muslims', *The Independent*, 27 July.

Jury, Louise (1995), 'Locked out in anger, the celebrities John Osborne didn't want at his memorial', *Daily Mail*, 3 June.

Little, Ruth, and McLaughlin, Emily (2007), *The Royal Court Theatre Inside Out*, London: Oberon.

O'Connor, Garry (1971), 'Production casebook no. 2: Arnold Wesker's *The Friends*', *Theatre Quarterly*, 1:2, pp. 78–92.

O'Mahony, John (1994), 'Frozen in time', *The Guardian*, 11 February.

—— (2002), 'Piques and Troughs', *The Guardian*, 25 May.

Osborne, Helen (1995), 'Letter: Playwrights at the palace', *The Guardian*, 13 January.

Pinter, Harold, and Fraser, Antonia (1995), 'Letter: Playwrights at the palace', *The Guardian*, 13 January.

Poke, Greville (1995), 'Letter: Angry men', *The Guardian*, 16 January.

Reynolds, Nigel (1999), 'Playwright uses open letter to attack Nunn', *Daily Telegraph*, 20 November.

Rosenthal, Daniel (2013), *The National Theatre Story*, London: Oberon.

Sweet, Matthew (2012), 'Arnold Wesker: Did Trotskyists kill off the best seventies play?', *Daily Telegraph*, 16 May.

Wesker, Arnold (1965), 'Let Battle Commence!', in C. Marowitz, T. Milne and O. Hale (eds), *The Encore Reader: A Chronicle of the New Drama*, London: Methuen, pp. 96–103.

—— (1971), 'Casual condemnations: A brief study of the critic as censor', *Theatre Quarterly*, 1:2, pp. 16–30.

—— (1978), 'Look! No playwrights', *The Listener*, pp. 500–1.

—— (1985), *Distinctions*, London: Jonathan Cape.

—— (1988), 'Letter: A speech for Jerusalem', *The Observer*, 10 April.

—— (1989a), 'Letter: Time for the rest of Allah's enemies to stand up', *The Independent*, 17 February.

—— (1989b), 'Letter: Muslims and the freedom to question beliefs', *The Independent*, 29 May.

—— (1994a), *As Much as I Dare*, London: Century.

—— (1994b), 'Letter: Time to stop aid to Israel', *The Guardian*, 5 March.

—— (1995a), 'An entertainer's farewell', *The Guardian*, 11 January.

—— (1995b), 'Letter: Fond farewell', *The Guardian*, 14 January.

—— (1995c), 'Cursing the critics as the curtain falls', *The Guardian*, 4 April.

—— (1995d), 'Letter: Death of a statesman', *The Guardian*, 7 November.

—— (1996), 'Letter: Realising a dream', *The Guardian*, 6 January.

—— (1997), *The Birth of Shylock and the Death of Zero Mostel*, London: Quartet.

—— (2001a), 'Letter: Attack on America: March to destruction', *The Guardian*, 13 September.

—— (2001b), 'Letter: Attack on Afghanistan: Faith school', *The Guardian*, 11 October.

—— (2003a), 'What about the writers?', *The Independent*, 3 April.

—— (2003b), 'Letter: Anti-semitism in the air', *The Guardian*, 6 December.

—— (2005), 'Letter: The leaving of Gaza', *The Guardian*, 20 August.

—— (2006), 'On waking, we think about life. Bin Laden thinks of slaughter', *The Times*, 16 September.

—— (2011), *Joy and Tyranny: Arias and Variations on the Theme of Violence*, London: Oberon.

Wesker, Arnold Papers (AW) (1966), 'The Wesker Controversy', clippings, 1st accession, Austin, Texas: Harry Ransom Center, Box 109.6.

—— (1970), Correspondence with John McGrath re. *The Friends*, Austin, Texas: Harry Ransom Center, Box 38.8.

—— (1971), Letter from Tynan to Dexter, 23 December, Austin, Texas: Harry Ransom Center, Box 65.4.

—— (1972a), Letter from Wesker to Olivier, 5 January, Austin, Texas: Harry Ransom Center, Box 65.3.

—— (1972b), Letter from Wesker to Olivier, 25 January, Austin, Texas: Harry Ransom Center, Box 65.3.

—— (1972c), Letter from Wesker to Olivier, 29 January, Austin, Texas: Harry Ransom Center, Box 65.3.

—— (1975a), Introduction note to rehearsed reading, Jacksons Lane Community Centre, 24 January, Austin, Texas: Harry Ransom Center, Box 42.7.

—— (1975b), Peter Hall to Wesker's agent Robin Dalton, 24 October, Austin, Texas: Harry Ransom Center, Box 79.8.

—— (1976), Transcript of interview between Bragg and Evans, Austin, Texas: Harry Ransom Center, Box 44.8.

—— (1994), Open letter to Stephen Daldry, 3 September, Austin, Texas: Harry Ransom Center, Box 48.7.

Wintle, Justin (1973), *Fun Art Bus*, London: Eyre Methuen.

Zarhy-Levo, Yael (2001), 'The theatrical critic as cultural agent: Constructing Pinter, Orton and Stoppard as absurdist playwrights', *Artists and Issues in the Theatre*, Vol. 12, New York: Peter Lang.

FIGURE 8: Production photograph of *Badenheim 1939* by the Guildhall School of Music and Drama at the Silk Street Theatre, London, November 2010. Photo by Clive Barda/ArenaPAL.

7

Representing Jewishness and Antisemitism in Arnold Wesker's Work: *Shylock, Badenheim 1939* and *Blood Libel*

Sue Vice

It is notoriously hard to define literary Jewishness. In attempting to do so, critics have hesitated between drawing on biographical, plot-related or other more implicit aspects of a particular work or writer's oeuvre, as well as making efforts to discern a hybrid of British and Jewish elements in such writing (see Sorin 2010; Gilbert 2013). The example of Arnold Wesker might seem more clear-cut: the critic David Jays identifies him as one of a small group of British playwrights, along with Bernard Kops and Julia Pascal, 'who centre their work in Jewish stories' (Jays 2019: n.pag.). These stories are of two kinds in Wesker's case. The first category consists of those plays whose domestic settings are characterized by elements of Jewish life and history, often forming the context for other concerns. Wesker claims this was the case for his *Trilogy*'s focus on working-class life and its elements of idealism and self-discovery. It is equally apparent in his later work, as the playwright says of *The Old Ones* (1970), almost all the characters 'happen to be Jewish; nevertheless, this play is essentially about defiant old age' (Wesker 1980: 128).

By contrast, the focus of the second category in Wesker's oeuvre is on Jewish-gentile relations, often taking the form of plays about historical episodes of persecution. The playwright subjects antisemitic occurrences of this kind, and the texts which voice them, to revision and re-enactment in specifically theatrical ways. However, it is not always possible to distinguish definitively between the two. Thus, in his play *When God Wanted a Son* (1997), antisemitism exists within the family itself, as we learn that it is partly the Jewishness of her ex-husband Joshua which turned the 'Protestant and pragmatic' Martha against him (Wesker 1990a: 171). In Wesker's unpublished *Breakfast* (1981), a 30-minute play for television, the genocidal past unexpectedly intrudes into the scene of the eponymous meal at a German hotel. The British protagonist Mark Bell is an 'unconventional Jewish businessman', confronted in comfortable post-war Munich by an Israeli, also called Mark, who demands why he has not ever visited that country. Mark replies:

MARK: I love England.
MARK TWO: But does England love you?

(Wesker 1981: 17)

Although there is a wry humour to this exchange, the play's denouement, in which Mark suddenly breaks down in tears at the memory of an inhumanity that haunts even the welcoming and contrite-seeming contemporary Germany, gives it the status of a chilling warning against complacency.

Throughout his career, Wesker addressed the question of his work's Jewishness in articles and interviews and was equally subject to expectations and responses that assumed its particular meaning. He described his own relation to Judaism as one of agnosticism and one which also drew upon his upbringing in London's East End, including the history, politics and everyday lives of his parents, both immigrants from Eastern Europe (Bigsby 2001: 255). The three plays discussed in this chapter centre on what could be called case studies of antisemitism in different national and historical contexts. For *Shylock* (1976), the setting is sixteenth-century Venice in the days of the original ghetto; *Blood Libel* (1996) concerns the eponymous myth's origins on its first occurrence in medieval England; *Badenheim 1939* (2010) is set in the early years of Nazi rule in Europe. However, while taking for granted any kind of documentary transparency in these plays is to overlook their dramatic form and ethical interests, assuming their Jewish content only to be a metaphor for broader questions is equally to simplify them.

Shylock

Wesker's play *Shylock*, which premiered in Stockholm in 1976 under the title of *The Merchant*, is a revisioning of Shakespeare's *The Merchant of Venice* (c.1596) and is the best known of the three works analysed here. Wesker's engagement with such a canonical text offers an alternative to what he considers a tendentious representation of a Jewish figure whose very name has become an 'ominous epithet', in Efraim Sicher's phrasing (Sicher 1991: 57). *Shylock* is a crucial early step in Wesker's concern with antisemitic discourse since, perhaps unsurprisingly, his attack on the Shakespearean version of a Jewish character is also the first play he devoted to the question of antisemitism. However, the play's renown is not the result of its being widely staged. After Zero Mostel, who was due to take the central role, died on the first night of a pre-Broadway premiere in Philadelphia in 1977, the play's Broadway run was limited and followed by a brief production in Britain at the Birmingham Repertory Theatre a year later (Wesker 1997: 347). Apart from a reading directed by Wesker in London in 1989 and a radio version broadcast by the BBC in 2008, it has not since been professionally performed. In a late interview, Wesker described his life's wishes as a peaceful conclusion to the Israel-Palestine conflict and a London staging of *Shylock* (Billington 2012).

At the time of its pre-Broadway run, Wesker attributed the short stage-life of his play to its lukewarm critical reception, particularly a review by Richard Eder in the *New York Times*, which criticized its dramatic structure and concluded that 'Mr Wesker's language lives, but sporadically: the evening is stimulating but only sometimes successful' (Leeming 1985: 39). Looking back some forty years later at his entire oeuvre, including this play, Wesker claimed that the lack of exposure given to almost all of his 44 works, apart from those of the 1950s and 1960s which made his name, was because 'the plays are not English and do not sit well on the English scene' (Bigsby 2001: 255). Such a clash of cultural expectations is typified by the playwright's response to what Graham Saunders calls the 'myth of Shylock' (2017: 130) and equally to '*the* canonical figure of the Jew in Britain' (Malkin and Voigts-Virchow 2018: 175, original emphasis). The Shylock myth is at once the creation of Shakespeare, the 'universal genius' and 'the greatest English writer', yet it has exerted an influence that Wesker judges to be a means of normalizing antisemitism (Prior 1981: 479; Main 2018: 178). It was Wesker's experience of seeing Jonathan Miller's National Theatre production of 1973, in which Shylock was played by Laurence Olivier, that prompted his decision to write a new version in order to redress what he calls the play's 'lie about the Jewish character' (Wesker 1990b: 178). The fact that 'character' here refers both to the individual on stage and to a much wider sense of the cultural and ethical nature of Jewish subjectivity underlies Wesker's project of radical revision.

Wesker is not alone in reappropriating Shakespeare's *The Merchant of Venice* – with its plot drawn from three folk tales – about a Jewish usurer whose loan of money to the Venetian Antonio is underwritten by the bond of 'a pound of flesh' should the merchant be unable to repay the debt. Writers ranging from Julia Pascal to Charles Marowitz and Philip Roth have styled revisionary drama and fiction after Shakespeare's Shylock, as a means of addressing the character's construction as a Jewish figure (see Saunders 2017: 127–49; Brauner 2018: 45). As Efraim Sicher argues is the case for Wesker, this phenomenon constitutes a revisionary writer's own projection of a Jewishness at odds with the 'libellous' Shakespearean image (Sicher 1991: 67). Like each of these other writers (Kiehl 2014: 9), Wesker has produced an 'original' work, not an adaptation (Wesker and Pascal 2014:

n.pag.). As Sicher's use of the term 'libel' suggests, the very one used to describe a murderous fantasy in *Blood Libel* and implicit in *Badenheim 1939*, there are clear links between the three plays under discussion here. Each is a dramatic 'answering back', in Sicher's term, to an earlier text that represents the perfidy and blood-thirstiness on the Christ-killing Jews' part, as well as, particularly in the case of *Badenheim*, their diasporic vulnerability.

The opening of Wesker's *Shylock* reveals its great distance from the original. Although critics have noted the didactic effect of his play's first act, situated in a historically precise Venice of 1563 far from Shakespeare's mythical city, such a sense of deliberate difference is a crucial one. Wesker's Shylock Kolner is a Jew of German origin living in Venice in the year in which Hebrew book-production was allowed to resume and where between him and Antonio there exists a loving friend-ship. The relationship between the two men is introduced in the style of a double-act, indebted to comic stand-up routines, of the kind with which Mostel began his career in New York's Café Society and Paramount Theatre, where Antonio has the role of straight-man:

ANTONIO: Until I met you, old Jew –
SHYLOCK: Not so old *then*, old man, only just past fifty –
ANTONIO: – and I became caught up in your – your passion, your hoardings, your –
            your vices!
SHYLOCK: Is he complaining, or thanking me?
ANTONIO: You've poisoned me, old Shylock, with restlessness and discontent, and
            at so late a time.
SHYLOCK: He's complaining.

(Wesker 1990b: 191, original emphasis)

Wesker argues that an actor's portrayal of the original Shylock, even one imbuing him with 'heavy tragedy', cannot disguise the play's 'inescapabl[e]' message that 'the Jew is mercenary and revengeful, sadistic, without pity' (Wesker 1990b: 178). Wesker's changes are established to redress such an effect: 'The challenge for me was to write a play which explored how [Shylock] was involved in a contract that he didn't want to sign' (Wesker 2014: 208). In this way, Wesker's Shylock, by con-trast to Shakespeare's, is subject to the legal requirement that every interaction between a Jew and a non-Jew in Renaissance Venice take the form of a contract. Acknowledging that it is established in protest at this, Shylock calls the stake of the pound of flesh 'A lovely, loving nonsense bond' (Wesker 1990: 213). The audience is encouraged to see the bond both beyond the horror of its original and in a redoubled form, since its agreement is followed by a moment of affectionate horseplay drawing attention to Antonio's body:

ANTONIO [*pinching himself*]: Do I have a pound of flesh? I don't even have a pound of flesh.

SHYLOCK [*pinching him*]: Here, and here, and here, one, two, three pounds of flesh! [*He's tickling him* [...] *Like children they're goosing each other.*]

(Wesker 1990b: 213)

The demand of a contract shows, as Iska Alter argues, the antagonist in the play is not personal but institutional, one that is 'woven into the social fabric' of imperial Venice (Alter 1988: 537). Such a foe takes the place of the original's construction of 'racial antagonism' between Shylock and Antonio, and the play's central conflict is one that lies instead within Shylock (Saunders 2017: 126). Like Sophocles' Antigone, faced with a choice between loyalty to her brother, whose corpse she wants to bury, and the state's laws which forbid such burial for a rebel, Shylock is made by the contract to choose between killing his friend or betraying his community. His sister Rivka, a character added by Wesker, points out to Shylock that if he begs to be relieved of his bond, the reliability of the law will be compromised: 'we'll live in greater uncertainties than before [...] Who to save – your poor people or your poor friend?' (Wesker 1990b: 239).

Yet, such an identification of a structural antagonist does not mean that bigotry is the norm in the social world of the play. In this way, Bassanio and Lorenzo's voicing Renaissance-era versions of contemporary racist slurs stands out for the audience to jarring effect. While Bassanio is amazed to learn that there are only fourteen hundred Jews in Venice – 'Really? As few as that? Well, they seem more' – Lorenzo tries to distance himself from Shylock, his fellow countryman:

LORENZO: You were born here, of course.
SHYLOCK: Yes, I was born here, of course.
LORENZO: I ask because so many of you come from here and there and everywhere.
SHYLOCK: I know why you ask.

(Wesker 1990b: 223)

Such moments mark the presence of struggle and debate with the original, so that we 'must constantly think of Shakespeare as we watch', as Alter argues (1988: 537). The process of dramatic revision extends to the 'few [...] original lines' Wesker has retained from *The Merchant of Venice* (Wesker 2014: 208). This is most striking in the transfer of the speech about the Jew's humanity from Shylock, in Shakespeare's original, to Lorenzo in Wesker's version, the prospective son-in-law who Shylock describes as a 'sour, silly young man' (Wesker 1990b: 241).

Wesker has argued eloquently against viewing the original Shylock as a tragic figure, or that his plight is feelingly represented, as a letter to *The Guardian* attests: 'Shakespeare's Shylock enables [audiences] to indulge their cherished image of the Jew as a grasping monster while those whitewashing, patronising lines "Hath not a Jew eyes …" etc. lets them off the hook of antisemitism into sympathy' (Wesker 2002b: n.pag.). In Wesker's version, Shylock answers back to such patronage. Thus, Shakespeare's lines are defamiliarized and subverted, not only by their reallocation to Lorenzo but also by the fragmentation of interruption:

LORENZO: No one doubts the Jew is human. After all, has not a Jew eyes?
SHYLOCK: What is *that* fool attempting now? [...]
LORENZO: If you prick him, does he not bleed?
SHYLOCK: No, no, NO! I will not have it!

(Wesker 1990b: 254, original emphasis)

Shylock's indignation culminates in his final dismissal of Lorenzo: 'My humanity is my right, not your bestowed and gracious privilege' (Wesker 1990b: 255). As Saunders argues of this exchange, Lorenzo's words are not simply an assertion of 'moral superiority' but also a revelation of his hypocrisy, in attempting to present himself as an honest and rational spokesperson (Saunders 2017: 127). By this symbolic and dramatic means, Wesker has returned the voice of condescension to what he sees as its origin in the non-Jewish hegemony.

Wesker's revisionary drama emerged from his conviction that 'When Portia suddenly gets to the bit about having a pound of flesh but no blood, it flashed on me that the kind of Jew I know would stand up and say, "Thank god!"' (Wilcher 1991: 110). The playwright's invocation of 'the kind of Jew I know' is not based on anecdotal evidence but refers to a cultural construct or potential. Wesker explains that he did not recognize any

> Jew that [I] know in Shakespeare. The Jew of my knowledge was Isaiah Berlin, George Steiner, Lord Robert Gavron, Jonathan Miller: these were the Jews that I knew. And so I created a Shylock who was a mixture of all these people and a bit of myself thrown in to create this new version of the character of Shylock.
> (Wesker 2014: 209)

Wesker's Shylock is established to fulfil the image of an enlightened, free-spirited individual. In this way, Wesker's Shylock is a projection of an ideal kind of Jew, yet one who is not without personal flaws even as he utters some of the playwright's own views. The play exists to enact this moment of relief at not having to fulfil the bond, and it is as if Shylock is directly voicing Wesker's insight when Portia points out that the contract 'is not binding because – impossible': 'SHYLOCK [*stunned, moves first to embrace ANTONIO*]: Thank God! Thank God! Of course! Idiots! Cut flesh draws blood. No blood, no flesh' (Wesker 1990b: 256). Significantly, and in contrast to Mark Bell in *Breakfast* a decade later, the location for which this Shylock leaves Venice is that of Jerusalem.

Badenheim 1939

Wesker's version of Aharon Appelfeld's allegorical and even Kafkaesque novel (Budick 1999: 224) is thoroughly theatrical, requiring at least 35 actors, as well as the presence of musicians and the composition of original music. This is one reason for the long gap between the play's composition in 1987 and its world premiere in 2010 at London's Barbican Centre. It was performed at the Silk Street Theatre by students from London's Guildhall School of Music and Drama, who constituted an 'entire company of final year actors with Guildhall musicians performing together in a large ensemble' (Anon. 2010: n.pag.).

Indeed, as the Guildhall's director of drama Christian Burgess has claimed, it was these very elements of Wesker's play as a 'massive undertaking' that attracted him to the project (Burgess 2010: n.pag.). His memories of Wesker's first ensemble play *The Kitchen* (1959), which also puts 'vast social groups on stage' (Billington 2010: 10), led Burgess to the then-unperformed *Badenheim 1939* as a project suitable for final-year Guildhall students, since mounting it meant that 'actors and musicians need to be on stage together' (Thomson 2011: n.pag.). Even the instruction on the script's title page, 'with music needing to be composed', was an asset for Burgess, and the score was written by the Guildhall's head of composition, Julian Phillips, in a style that echoed the work of 'composers contemporary to the events such as Kurt Weill' (Burgess 2010: n.pag.).

The play, like Appelfeld's novel, is set in the eponymous Austrian spa town of Badenheim during its annual summer music festival. The patrons, performers and the organizer Dr Pappenheim become aware that changes are taking place, the ominous nature of which they attempt to downplay. The town is patrolled by 'sanitation inspectors', who record the inhabitants' details; it becomes isolated from the outside world and experiences an influx of displaced strangers (Wesker 1994: 9). The novel's central characters are for the most part 'middle-class [...] Jews' (Wesker 1994: 4), ranging from Professor Rainer Fussholdt and his young wife Mitzi, the local chemist Martin and his wife Trude, to Princess Milbaum, who has married into the gentry. These individuals are gradually reconciled to the need for emigration to Poland that is being urged upon them, trying to view it as a holiday, and, at the conclusion, they board a train to that destination.

Although Wesker was not familiar with Appelfeld's novel before the invitation to write the play, he observes acutely that it is 'so full of visual images that my task was simply to organise the existing images into a theatrical framework' (Carrier 2010: n.pag.). The play's locations include the *Mitteleuropa* settings of town square, café, telegraph-office, station and grand hotel. The Barbican production thus emphasized the novel's visual signification in the staging, as well as in such elements as costume, so that, in ominous fashion, 'the sanitation officers wear white boiler suits with masks' (Burgess 2010: n.pag.). Similarly, visual projections were used 'to create an atmosphere a bit like *The Sound of Music* at the start, when everything still seems wholesome', thus emphasizing the ephemeral nature of this wholesomeness (Burgess 2010: n.pag.).

The play's final, bitterly ironic moments equally draw directly on Appelfeld's novel and its bleak conclusion. On their arrival at the local station, the Badenheim Jews see that the train to Poland is composed not of passenger carriages but freight wagons, at which Pappenheim self-deludingly declares, 'Well! If the coaches are so dirty, it must mean that we have not far to go' (Wesker 1994: 92). Wesker was uncertain about how best to represent the crucial final image of the train, as the tentative stage directions reveal:

> *The sound of an engine shunting into the platform. [...]*
> *Do we see the freight wagons?*
> *Are they projected on huge screens?*
> *Do we guess what is there from their faces peering out at us?*
> (Wesker 1994: 92)

In the event, as the filmmaker and musician Benjamin Till, a former collaborator of Wesker's, recounts, the Barbican production used an expressionist device with clear historical resonance to convey the train's unsettling presence. He describes the emotional shock for an audience member, exaggerated by the youth of the Guildhall actors, of seeing 'thirty young people carrying suitcases and musical instruments rushing into a cloud of white smoke' (Till 2010: n.pag.). Such an effect not only conveyed the characters' journey but their destination, meaning that it was as if the audience were seeing 'the gas chambers turning them instantly into silhouettes' (Till 2010: n.pag.).

Critics have long debated what Appelfeld's vision, to which Wesker declares fidelity, consists of, and the playwright himself came to see the novel as 'controversial' (Carrier 2010: n.pag.). Its setting has in common with many of Appelfeld's other works a focus on 'the pre-crisis and the brink-of-crisis world', rather than the details of the Holocaust experience that followed (Shacham 2004: 109). The novel, and Wesker's play, therefore shows the characters attempting to adjust to their increasingly threatening circumstances up to the moment of deportation. As his words at the sight of the freight-train to Poland suggest, the festival impresario, Dr Pappenheim, is the locus of such efforts, although we witness the nostalgia for Poland on the part of other characters, which underlies their willingness to entertain the idea of return. This is so much the case for the chemist's wife Trude that Wesker added a speech in which she tries out her childhood Polish. While Till describes this as 'blind optimism in the face of adversity', other critics have seen a more disquieting significance in Appelfeld's allegory (Till 2010). In *Foregone Conclusions*, his study of literary works which depend on historical hindsight, Michael André Bernstein claims that Appelfeld

> treat[s] his characters as marionettes whose futile gestures on an absurd stage we watch, half in horror, half in anxiously bemused melancholy at their foolish-ness. We know they are doomed; they stubbornly refuse to know it [...] [Thus] a fable of willed self-delusion unfolds.
>
> (Bernstein 1996: 58)

However, the 'stage' on which the characters of Wesker's play appear does not expose them to the tendentious 'ideological determinism' that Bernstein detects in the novel (Budick 1999: 223) but to an ontological gulf that the playwright discusses in an interview as 'haunting' him (Carrier 2010: n.pag.):

> While the audience watching the play has the knowledge that a dark cloud is forming over Europe, the people on stage, the characters in the play, are bliss-fully unaware of what is to come. [...] It is very chilling to watch these relation-ships played out by these people who do not know what is going to happen, but you do.
>
> (Wesker, cited in Carrier 2010: n.pag.)

Indeed, the very nature of dramatization allows us to see clearly that the other characters blame Pappenheim, 'this bohemian second-rater', as the hotel guest Dr Langman describes him, in a meta-theatrical warning against our falling into such a trap (Wesker 1994: 38).

The form of Wesker's theatrical adaptation, as well as the play's focus on the 'doubly privileged' nature of the audience, rather than the blindness of the charac-ters, entails the removal of what often appear as victim-blaming narratorial nudges in Appelfeld's original (Harrison 2006: 103). Wesker's play makes increasingly ambivalent this notion of what Ruth Wisse describes as Appelfeld's novel being 'more damning of the victims than of the crime perpetrated against them' (Wisse 1983: 76). In the play, the ominous details of the Jews' impending fate appear in

the form of staging and dialogue, rather than the characters' mistaken consciousness, as is the case when Professor Fussholdt is interrogated by the sanitation
inspectors on the subject of his new book:

1ST SANITATION INSPECTOR:	It is about?
PROFESSOR FUSSHOLDT:	[…] I've lectured about Karl Kraus, now *there* was a great Jew – though he didn't like Jews if the truth be known but – he revived satire! Very important! How can a society be healthy without satire? It could be a book about that.

(Wesker 1994: 26, original emphasis)

The equivocation about the precise topic of Fussholdt's book becomes in
Wesker's drama a refusal to answer the inspector's questions, thereby giving
the Professor's speech greater defiance. The detail of the Catholic convert Kraus's
distaste for the Jews who were formerly his co-religionists is Wesker's own inclusion, to make clear that Fussholdt himself, and not just the audience, is aware
of this irony.[1]

As Burgess points out of the Barbican production, although the Nazis 'are not
explicitly identified' here or elsewhere in the play, so that their 'strange' flags do
not bear swastikas but invented devices, 'there is no doubt about what it's about'
(quoted in Thomson 2011: n.pag.). Yet, there is doubt and misinterpretation on
the characters' part, taking the form of dialogue between a musician, Samitzky
and Frau Zauberblit, by contrast to Appelfeld's novel, in which the speakers are
not identified:

SAMITZKY:	If you ask me, the Sanitation Department is going to all this trouble because the festival's going to be a big affair this year.
FRAU ZAUBERBLIT:	Our dear Dr Pappenheim is making a name for himself at last.
SAMITZKY:	There'll be more fun and games this year than ever.
MITZI:	How can you be so sure?

(Wesker 1994: 27–28)

The final warning question from Fussholdt's wife Mitzi is Wesker's addition and has
an uncertain reference. It is not clear if Mitzi is asking about the festival's success,
Pappenheim's reputation or what the Sanitation Department's 'trouble' is for, as if
she embodies a sense of the uncertain future on all these counts that is, to the audience, only too clear in retrospect. Ultimately, the characters' taking the spa activities
more seriously than their own future turns in Wesker's stage version into dramatic
irony rather than condemnation by the very means of his theatrical revisioning.

Blood Libel

Wesker was invited to write *Blood Libel* in the late 1980s for the inauguration of a new theatre, the Norwich Playhouse. The one-act drama was completed in 1991, and its premiere took place in early 1996. The artistic director Henry Burke suggested to Wesker the idea of a play about 'William, the Norwich boy-saint' and sent the playwright an article on the subject from V. D. Lipman's historical study *The Jews of Medieval Norwich* (1967), its influence clear in the play's final version. Both the invitation and Wesker's positive response – 'Yes, William of Norwich as the cause of one of the Jewish pogroms based on the old calumny of blood libel does interest me' – emphasize the centrality of Jewishness in his work, since the play explores the notorious case of the murder of William, an 11-year-old boy, which took place in Norwich in 1144 and was blamed on the local Jewish population (AW 1989: n.pag.). Magda Russell describes the eponymous blood libel, in an interview with the playwright, as 'A terrible "first" for Norwich, but a natural "story" for Wesker' (Russell 1992: 18). This comment risks confusing the two categories of the playwright's Jewish-related writing, those with Jewish domestic settings and those which centre on antisemitic atrocity. It implies that Wesker's well-known works such as the *Trilogy*, with their stagings of twentieth-century Jewish family life, automatically suit him to write on persecutory events that occurred a millennium earlier. Yet, it is the absence from *Blood Libel* of any Jewish characters, whose unmistakeable presence in Wesker's other work was the very reason for his commission, that is one of its most striking features. Given its subject-matter, Wesker became concerned that 'a gentile director would develop a resistance to the play', leading him to consider approaching such individuals as Nicholas Hytner, Karel Reisz or David Mamet for the role after Deborah Warner and Peter Hall had declined the offer to direct (AW 1993a).[2] In the event, it was directed by the Russian-born Irina Brown, who had been 'brought up in the Soviet system as an atheist' but began 'to make connections between this play and her own Jewish origins' when 'half-way through the rehearsal period' (Lyndon 1996: 57).

In *Blood Libel*, the elements of the antisemitic myth of the title are presented as part of the historical narrative about events in medieval Norwich. The libel rests on the claim that Jews habitually abduct and ritually murder Christian children, their blood to be used for religious purposes at Passover. As is the case for William, such a child is said to have been murdered in a way that imitates the Crucifixion, in a taunting acknowledgement by the Jews of their role in the original event. Wesker drew on Thomas of Monmouth's twelfth-century account of the so-called martyrdom of William, and that monk is one of the play's two central characters. The other is Thomas's opponent, Prior Elias, whose rationality and wish to protect the church's integrity cause him, at least at first, to defy the monk's insistence on William's meriting canonization.

The play opens by immediately revealing the two colliding elements of antisemitic religious discourse and the unrelieved materiality of the murder. First, in the form of a prologue, we hear Herbert de Losinga's words, based on a historical sermon given by this real-life Bishop of Norwich. The sermon establishes the era's atmosphere of anti-Jewish sentiment, as well as flashing forward to twentieth-century genocide, by means of its account of another child victim. That boy's death was followed by an act of 'most just' Christian vengeance, taking the form of the Jews being burnt 'in a furnace' (Wesker 1994: 296). This sermon is immediately followed by a stylized representation of the murder of William, who is shown to have been killed in the woods by a stranger. Wesker, following Lipman's account, interprets the murder of William as a sexual rather than a ritual crime: 'The rape is my view of what happened' (Wesker cited in Russell 1992: n.pag.).

In a review of the Norwich production, David Self describes Losinga's sermon as undramatically 'long [and] static' for an opening (1996). However, the pairing of scenes in this stylized prologue shows that the play's multi-voicedness is not just a dramatic technique, allowing the characters to listen to each other on stage in their guise as 'witnesses and jury' (Wesker 1994: 289). It is also a compositional procedure, by means of which materials from different documentary sources are juxtaposed. In this way, Thomas's account vies with Lipman's interpretation that William was the victim of a sexual killing. The dramatizing of William's murder is, as the stage directions have it, accompanied by *an intensely bright, ethereal light* alongside *a swelling sound of mob voices*': 'The Jews! The Jews! [...] THE JEWS!' (Wesker 1994: 297). In what might be called an example of historical expressionism, both the impulse to sanctify William after his death and the blaming of the murder on the Jews are enacted in this scene, the precise details of the fantasized relation between the two events to be presented and contested over the rest of the play's extent.

As is the case in each of the three cases examined here, Wesker's historical research is the substratum of the play. In *Blood Libel*, this is part of an attempt 'to piece together the story of a crime about which there are only a few inconclusive facts' (Wesker 1994: 289). Wesker describes drawing on 'selected moments from [Thomas's] records which shape the story', so that the play's constituent parts follow the original narrative (Russell 1992: 19). Yet, such apparent fidelity to the source is of course a dramatic stratagem, and the audience are prompted throughout to judge for themselves. We first encounter Thomas writing 'at his table' in a monastery cell, 28 years after the events of William's death. This conceit shows the occasion for his published account but also allows us to experience the enactment of his 'testimony', consisting as it does of 'all that I know to be true and will prove to be true' (Wesker 1994: 298). What Thomas claims to be 'true' is both William's martyrdom and the Jews' culpability, since the two are interdependent. As the historian Gavin Langmuir argues, 'confidence in William's sanctity depended entirely on certainty as to who had killed young William and how they had killed him' (Langmuir 1984: 821). Within the play, as another of Prior Elias's antagonists, Don Aimar, insists, for William to be sanctified he must have died 'for his religion': 'prove it was the Jews, and you prove a martyr' (Wesker 1994: 325). The drama is thus shaped by Wesker's decision 'in recreating history as drama, […] to select from Thomas's record and comment on its veracity' (AW 1991b: n.pag.). In this way, *Blood Libel* follows the shape of Thomas's text in order to challenge it, with a focus on the rape scene, Prior Elias and the unreliability of witnesses.

The impression of a 'dissenting voice' throughout the play's presentation of Thomas's view is not only evident in Elias's counterarguments but in the form of the dramaturgy itself. Individuals claiming to testify to the guilt of the Jews give self-subverting accounts and 'betray themselves', in Wesker's phrase (Russell 1992: 18). For instance, in the moment of professing to have had a dream 'about Jews', William's aunt Hethel reminds her husband Godwin: 'An' *you* know I can't never remember my dreams, only the sensation o' them' (Wesker 1994: 311, original emphasis). Yet, each time Hethel recounts her dream, it gains in details that implicate the Jews, culminating in her describing it at the synod hearing as a 'vision' in which the Jews 'tear off' her leg: 'They ran off wi' me leg like they run off wi' me nephew' (Wesker 1994: 320–21). Alongside the increasingly obvious false nature of the testimony presented to the audience, the repeated scene representing William's rape and murder equally acts as a commentary on the plot's progress. We are presented with the distressing image of this crime three times after its first appearance at the play's opening. On each repetition, the characters 'turn their backs' on this, the 'only scene they do not watch' (Wesker 1994: 289). This entails the characters' looking outwards to the audience in their incantation of blame, as well as dramatizing a disinclination to face the crime for what it was. The scene of murder – 'The sound of William's scream. The light. "The Jews! The Jews!" The light dies' (Wesker 1994: 353) – appears again as the very last one of the play, where it follows a 'hymn of praise' (Wesker 1994: 350), while William's coffin is transferred to Norwich Cathedral's Chapel of Martyrs, ensuring, in Wesker's words, 'that the nagging truth is not "out-beautified"' by the spectacle and music (AW 1995: n.pag.).

For its production in Norwich in 1996, a location for this particular play that Wesker describes as potentially 'explosive' (AW 1994: n.pag.), *Blood Libel* was staged in the form of a 'succession of images' (Shuttleworth 1996: n.pag.). This presentation was said by critics to resemble the paintings of Bosch or Brueghel, in a set over which 'a curtain of chains' dangled from the ceiling (Kingston 1996:

n.pag.). Such a staging offers its own commentary on Thomas's narrative, in its allusions to the 'base reality' of peasant life, while the narrative form is that of a crime drama. In this use of an investigative pattern, in which witnesses give their testimony, the tables are turned on Thomas. In a model that seems uncannily up-to-date, the superstitions of local people about the Jews are exploited by church officials for reasons of prestige and profit. Indeed, Wesker's original name for the play was *Martyrs for Sale*, changed to the present and more symbolic title at Burke's suggestion (AW 1992).[3] After the ecclesiastical hearing to investigate the responsibility for William's murder, a crucial dialogue takes place between Elias and Don Aimar, the Bishop of St Pancras, who has participated in the enquiry. Don Aimar urges the Prior to take William's death seriously: 'Think on it. A precious treasure on your doorstep, Elias. I would guard it most diligently' (Wesker 1994: 327). Don Aimar's phrase 'precious treasure' has a revealing ambiguity, referring both to a spiritual and a monetary asset. The argument proceeds by means of each speaker antagonistically repeating each other's phrasing:

ELIAS: 'It'll bring pilgrims!', [my bishop] cries.
DON AIMAR: He cries wisely.
ELIAS: He cries shamelessly.

(Wesker 1994: 325)

Not only do the two men talk at loggerheads, but the stage direction emphasizes that even after the Prior's long speech decrying the 'ignorance and stupidity of the simple flock', along with the 'fevered intoxications of illiterate monks', Don Aimar '*ignores Elias's words*' (Wesker 1994: 326). The unresolved dialogue here points towards a series of historical events in England which the audience knows will follow, including the 'blood libel' massacre of Jews after the death of Hugh of Lincoln a century later in 1255 and the Jews' eventual expulsion in 1290. The origins of these eruptions of violent anti-Jewish action in gullibility and irrational thinking are dramatized in *Blood Libel*. Their extremity notwithstanding, these events establish a continuity with Wesker's other works, as explicit instances of the ambivalence about British responses to Jewish life as it appears onstage even in Wesker's plays with contemporary settings, *Breakfast* and *When God Wanted a Son*.

Despite its focus on the antisemitic 'blood libel', Wesker's play does not include any Jewish characters, allegedly 'to extend the subject to embrace all forms of prejudice' (AW 1993b: n.pag.). Michael Billington expressed regret in a review at this absence, arguing that it leaves the audience with 'no idea of [the Jews'] learning, financial structures or religious rituals, nor indeed of how they reacted to their widespread victimisation' (Billington 1996: n.pag.). Billington's plea for social detail is to ask for a different, more naturalistic drama, harking back, once more, to memories of Wesker's earlier plays, where the 'learning' and 'rituals' of the Jewish families in *The Trilogy* or in *The Old Ones* are indeed centre stage. Although Wesker describes the omission of Jewish characters from *Blood Libel* as his 'first' decision in the process of composition (Russell 1992: 18), he did sketch out an early possible alternative when his play had the original title *Martyrs for Sale* as a two-act version in which the Jews are present in the first half (AW 1991a).

In Wesker's early draft outline, some of the same events as those in the staged play take place, but with a different emphasis. In the draft, after they have been accused of murder, Wesker's notes make clear that the 'Jews go to Sheriff John who says the Bishop has no right over Jews' (AW 1991a: n.pag.), while in the final version, by contrast, the Sheriff appears unannounced to declare that 'The Jews are the property of King Stephen and I'm King Stephen's man [...] There'll be no blood-letting while I'm Sheriff of Norwich' (Wesker 1994: 316). John's efforts come to nothing, since he dies after a bout of 'internal haemorrhage', a fate that is interpreted by Thomas as 'the vengeance of God' for the Sheriff's attempts to protect the Jews (Wesker 1994: 316). The final version of the play emphasizes the Jews' lack of agency in the historical and theatrical plots, which gathers momentum even though they are not present. In the early draft, by contrast, the presence of Jewish figures amounts simply to a series of failed endeavours: they 'refuse to attend' the synod hearing, at which their 'request [for] time' to consider the threatened 'trial by ordeal' is itself 'denied' (AW 1991a: n.pag.). Their physical absence from the staged play is more compelling in dramatic terms. Even in this draft version, the risk is clear of personifying any individual in this story that is not about identifiable Jewish characters.

In its second act, the draft version of the play turns to the church's hasty declaration of William as a martyr 'even before all the facts are known' and to the motives of the church officials in supporting the 'persecution' of the Jews (AW 1991a: n.pag.). Such a shape to the drama in this draft places greater emphasis on the historical chronology and detail of the action. It lacks the dramatic collisions of personality as they take place in the staged version between Thomas and Elias, the role of William's employer and family, and, most crucially, does not possess its reliance on expressionism and ritual to represent the boy's murder as a very secular type of crime.

Wesker's artistic choice to omit Jewish characters is thus inextricable from ethical ones, as he claims: 'The story of William is a Christian problem' (Russell 1992: 18). Their absence shows that the Jews are figures of fantasy in every respect, a sense that is dramatized in a self-defeating statement in the staged version in which Maude, a 'maidservant for the Jews', relates to Thomas a long and detailed narrative. Maude claims to have seen the ritual murder of William taking place in

147

the house of a Jew, about which she concludes, 'I see all I need to see. In that small second. Through the chink in the door. All what I tell you' (Wesker 1994: 334). The conceit of the 'chink in the door' economically conveys the idea that invention can substitute for eyewitness where there is nothing to be seen.

Perhaps unexpectedly, the invisible nature of the victims of persecution makes them both clearly Jewish, in the play's historical setting, yet also reveals the contemporary nature of the victimizers' psychology. It allows *Blood Libel*'s concern with more general questions of fanaticism and intolerance to come across even more starkly. Responding to this sense, in an article on ways of staging the play in the new millennium, Eric Binnie argues for its relevance to 'Holocaust study' as well as 'contemporary social issues' such as Black Lives Matter (Binnie 2017: 175). Wesker's claim that 'the blood libel is a metaphor for all religious fanaticism and bigotry' allows us to see connections between the play and his wider political concerns at the time of its composition (Wesker 2002a). It seems likely that Wesker was inspired by his experience of campaigning on behalf of Salman Rushdie, against whom a *fatwā* had been issued in 1989 after the publication of his novel *The Satanic Verses*. In an article in the *New Humanist*, Wesker's phrasing on the subject of Rushdie's antagonists could equally be a description of the church officials in *Blood Libel*, as 'bigoted priests [who] stirred up the religious mud used long ago to build simple spiritual comforts for simple minds' (Wesker 2002a: n.pag.).

Conclusion

It might seem an essentialist fallacy to expect that cultural works about Jewish life and culture be produced only by Jewish-identified artists, or that such figures have a particular responsibility to do so. On the other hand, in Wesker's case, his upbringing and adult relationship to his Jewish heritage are indeed often the lens through which he views and dramatizes both existential questions about individual life stages and the injustices of class and other forms of social hierarchy. This is the case for both categories of his Jewish-related plays, those set within the family and those dramatizing Jewish-gentile conflict. Julia Pascal convincingly argues that Wesker's 'distinctive achievement lay in reminding audiences that Jews are an essential part of British history', as is clear in his revisiting cultural myths in *Blood Libel* and *Shylock*, as well as in the terms of social realism in the *Trilogy* (Pascal 2016: n.pag.). At the same time, Wesker's rhetorical question in his article 'The Jewish Artist and the Jewish Community', 'have I the right to be sectarian in my subject matter when any issue worth writing about at all concerns all nations, all peoples?', suggests that Jewish detail exists on its own account but also to convey wider political questions (Wesker 1959: 21).

Such a paradox is clear in an article by Dan Carrier about the playwright's commission to write *Badenheim 1939*, in which the journalist quotes Wesker on the play: ' "Its themes fit into the canon of my work well," says the playwright, whose previous productions include *Chicken Soup With Barley*, *Shylock* and *Blood Libel*' (Carrier 2010: n.pag.). Carrier's naming of these particular examples from the catalogue of Wesker's plays relies on the presence in each of Jewish characters. Yet, these are in such widely divergent theatrical styles and social contexts – a social-realist dramatization of working-class London life, a sixteenth-century reimagining of Shakespeare's *The Merchant of Venice* and an expressionist treatment of the 'blood libel' myth in twelfth-century Norwich – that the very act of linking them draws attention to the fact that Jewish content is notable as an exception in British theatre. Other writers, including Pascal, place Wesker's works in a European rather than a British tradition, by reason of their combination of the everyday with the political and equally because of their Jewish imagery (Pascal 2016; Patterson 1995: 33). Wesker's remark in the interview with Carrier about the suitability of *Badenheim 1939*'s themes in light of his *oeuvre* might, by contrast, be taken to refer to the plays' political commonalities. While each of the plays discussed centres on anti-Jewish slurs, all based in Christian myths, they equally constitute cautionary dramas about not falling prey to manipulation or self-delusion. The more specific is Wesker's representation of a particular historical moment, the more widely applicable are its ethical implications.

In interviews and his own writings, Wesker invariably insists on his cultural rather than religious Jewish allegiance, placing himself on the side of what he calls the 'rationalists' rather than the 'ritualists', since, for him, God is simply the projection of what he calls humanity's best self (Wesker 1985: 253). In his essay 'The Two Roots of Judaism', Wesker describes such an influence in terms of the importance placed on 'ethical considerations' (Wesker 1985: 221). Each of the plays explored here makes an episode in Jewish history the setting for ethical questions of this kind. These include the importance of having to decide between allegiance to community or to an individual, the relationship between a collective and its minority members and the dispelling of illusion. The context in each case is inseparable from the posing of these questions, while evading them has serious consequences, as the respective plays' denouements show. *Shylock*, as suggested by the change of title from the original *The Merchant*, is distinctive in this triad of plays in centring on an individual. In this play, the ideal of the 'supremacy of the individual over authority', an insight Wesker claims that he takes from his Jewish background, is mooted but defeated (Wesker 1995: 59). *Badenheim 1939*, where the protagonists cannot see the extent to which they risk being made responsible for their own fates, not least in the eyes of the audience, contrasts with *Blood Libel*, where the emphasis falls upon the instigators of fantasied intolerance and cynical greed.

Wesker's longstanding concern with antisemitic discourse prompted some of his starkest commentary as well as forming the impetus for his dramatic writing. His conviction that 'antisemitism, like stupidity, is deep in the blood-stream of humanity, and here to stay' was repeated in various contexts, including a letter to *The Guardian* (Wesker 2002: n.pag.). He even came to feel that a particular 'English' variant of such discriminatory thinking was directed at him, especially late in his career when it seemed that none but his earliest plays found favour. This is the message of Wesker's pamphlet *Dark Suspicions* of 1991, in which he claimed that reluctance on the part of the British theatre establishment to stage *Shylock* was an expression of 'subconscious antisemitism' (Pascal 2016: n.pag.). Indeed, despite his declaration to Magda Russell that there is something 'fundamentally just' about 'the English', two of the examples here revisit specifically British manifestations of antisemitic prejudice (Russell 1992: n.pag.). As Wesker claimed of *The Merchant of Venice*, likening himself to Shakespeare's character in so doing, 'I seek no pound of flesh but, like Shylock, I'm unforgiving, unforgiving of the play's contribution to the world's astigmatic view and murderous hatred of the Jew' (1981: n.pag.). The implication is that both the figure of Shylock and the blood libel slur have had regrettable effects in contexts far more recent than medieval Norwich or Shakespeare's London.

In all three plays, the shadow of the Holocaust is apparent, not only in their shared imagery of burning and murder but in a less tangible form as warnings about the terrible consequences of self-seeking actions. The playwright's temperament, that of a 'melancholy optimist' (cited in Rabey 2003: 36), is apparent in the fact that both Shylock and Antonio from their different positions see hope in the next generation, embodied by Portia, who, 'blossoming with purpose', in Antonio's phrase, has what Shylock calls a 'great future' (Wesker 1990b: 260, 258). Such a view could be seen as an expression of a Jewish optimism which recognizes neither tragedy nor the punishment of hell. Instead, Judaism's influence on Wesker takes the form of what Malkin and Voigts-Virchow call a 'cultural inscription', underlying the value of political and moral education by means of dramatic warning in each of these plays (2018: 176).

NOTES

1. Wesker's nonetheless high regard for Kraus's satire is evident in his using the writer's comments as the epigraphs for his play *The Journalists* (1981).
2. It must be noted nonetheless that his list of directors for *Blood Libel* was primarily led by the fame and theatrical sensitivities of the directors.
3. The working title between *Martyrs for Sale* and *Blood Libel* was simply *William of Norwich*.

REFERENCES

Alter, Iska (1988), '"Barbaric laws, barbaric bonds": Arnold Wesker's *The Merchant*', *Modern Drama*, 31:4, pp. 536–47.

Anon. (2010), 'World premiere of *Badenheim 1939* presented by Guildhall actors and musicians', *Guildhall Publicity Bulletin*, 10 November 2010, https://www.gsmd.ac.uk/about_the_school/news/view/article/world_premiere_of_badenheim_1939_presented_by_guildhall_actors_and_musicians/. Accessed 4 May 2019.

Appelfeld, Aharon (1981 [1978]), *Badenheim 1939*, trans. Dalya Bilu, New York: Washington Square Press.

Bernstein, Michael André (1996), *Foregone Conclusions: Against Apocalyptic History*, Berkeley: University of California Press.

Bigsby, Christopher (2001), *Writers in Conversation with Christopher Bigsby*, London: Pen & Inc.

Billington, Michael (1996), 'Lies of the saint', *The Guardian*, 5 February.

—— (2010), 'Introduction to Arnold Wesker', *Wesker's Political Plays*, London: Oberon, pp. 7–10.

—— (2012), 'Arnold Wesker: Food for thought', *The Guardian*, 21 May, https://www.theguardian.com/stage/2012/may/21/arnold-wesker-food-for-thought. Accessed 9 April 2020.

Binnie, Eric Alexander G. (2017), 'The Norwich Blood Libel Mounted Once Again: A Pedagogy for Tolerance in Arnold Wesker's *Blood Libel* (1991)', in M. Krummel and T. Pugh (eds), *Jews in Medieval England: Teaching Representations of the Other*, London: Macmillan, pp. 171–87.

Brauner, David (2018), '*Shylock Must Die*', review, *Jewish Renaissance*, July, p. 45.

Budick, Emily Miller (1999), 'Literature, ideology, and the measure of moral freedom: The case of Aharon Appelfeld's *Badenhaim 'Ir Nofesh*', *Modern Language Quarterly*, 60:62, pp. 223–49.

Burgess, Christian, (2010), Interview, https://soundcloud.com/guildhallschool/2010-11-22-christian-burgess. Accessed 4 May 2019.

Carrier, Dan (2010), 'Theatre feature: *Badenheim 1939*', *Camden New Journal* 4 November, http://archive.camdennewjournal.com/feature-theatre-based-aharon-appelfelds-allegorical-holocaust-play-badenheim-1939-sir-arnold-weskers. Accessed 4 May 2019.

Harrison, Bernard (2006), 'Aharon Appelfeld and the problem of holocaust fiction', *Partial Answers*, 4:1, pp. 79–106.

Jays, David (2019), '"We've been ashamed of our voice": The secret history of UK Jewish theatre', *The Guardian*, 13 March, https://www.theguardian.com/stage/2019/mar/13/uk-jewish-theatre-voice-secret-history. Accessed 5 May 2019.

Kiehl, Christine, and Torti-Alcayaga, Agathe (eds) (2014), 'Introduction', in *Variations Contemporaines Autour de Shylock 2, Coup de Théâtre*, 28, pp. 7–16.

Kingston, Jeremy (1996), 'Catch in his martyr's voice', review of *Blood Libel*, *The Times*, 5 February.

Langmuir, Gavin (1984), 'Thomas of Monmouth: Detector of ritual murder', *Speculum*, 59:4, pp. 820–46.

Leeming, Glenda (1985), *Wesker on File*, London & New York: Methuen.

Lipman, V. D. (1967), *The Jews of Medieval Norwich*, London: Jewish Historical Society of England.

Lyndon, Sonja (1996), 'Blood libel: A Norwich scenario', *Jewish Quarterly*, 43:1, pp. 55–57.

Main, Vesna (2018), 'Shakespeare on the buses', in *Temptation: A User's Guide*, London: Salt.

Malkin, Jeanette, and Voigts-Virchow, Eckart (2018), 'Wrestling with Shylock: Contemporary British Jewish theatre and Shakespeare's *The Merchant of Venice*', *European Judaism*, 51:2, pp. 175–85.

Pascal, Julia (2016), 'Obituary of Sir Arnold Wesker', *The Guardian*, 13 April, https://www.theguardian.com/stage/2016/apr/13/sir-arnold-wesker-obituary. Accessed 9 April 2020.

Patterson, Michael (1995), 'The reception of Arnold Wesker's plays in Europe', *History of European Ideas*, 1:3, pp. 31–34.

Prior, Moody E. (1981), 'Which is the Jew that Shakespeare drew? Shylock among the critics', *The American Scholar*, 50:4, pp. 479–98.

Rabey, David Ian (2003), *English Drama Since 1940*, London: Longman.

Russell, Magda (1992), 'One to one', interview with Arnold Wesker, *Arteast*, June, pp. 18–19.

Saunders, Graham (2017), *Elizabethan and Jacobean Reappropriation in Contemporary English Drama: 'Upstart Crows'*, London: Palgrave.

Self, David (1996), 'Review of *Blood Libel*', *The Stage*, 15 February.

Shacham, Chaya (2004), 'Language on the verge of death: On language and language criticism in *Badenheim 1939* by Aharon Appelfeld', *Orbis Litterarum*, 59, pp. 108–20.

Shuttleworth, Ian (1996), 'Review of *Blood Libel*', *Financial Times*, 2 February, http://www.cix.co.uk/~shutters/reviews/96006.htm. Accessed 5 May 2019.

Sicher, Efraim (1991), 'The Jewing of Shylock: Wesker's *The Merchant*', *Modern Language Studies*, 21:2, pp. 57–69.

Thomson, Peter (2011), 'Waltzing into the abyss', *Times Higher Education Supplement*, 31:1, November 25, https://www.timeshighereducation.com/features/culture/the-pick-waltzing-into-the-abyss/414409.article. Accessed 9 April 2020.

Till, Benjamin (2010), 'He meets us at the lift waving a walking-stick', 30 November 2010, http://pepysmotet.blogspot.com/2010/11/he-meets-us-at-lift-waving-his-walking.html. Accessed 4 May 2019.

Wesker, Arnold (1959), 'The Jewish artist and the Jewish community', *AJA Quarterly*, June, pp. 20–24.

——— (1980), *The Old Ones, Chips with Everything and Other Plays*, Harmondsworth: Penguin.

——— (1981), 'Why I fleshed out Shylock', *The Guardian*, 29 August.

—— (1985), *Distinctions*, London: Jonathan Cape.

—— (1990a), *Lady Othello and Other Plays*, London: Penguin.

—— (1990b), *Shylock and Other Plays*, London: Penguin.

—— (1994), *Wild Spring and Other Plays*, London: Penguin.

—— (1995 [1994]), *As Much as I Dare: An Autobiography*, London: Arrow Books.

—— (1997), *The Birth of Shylock and the Death of Zero Mostel: The Diary of a Play*, London: Quartet.

—— (2002a), 'The fundamental right to blaspheme', *New Humanist*, https://newhumanist.org.uk/articles/502/the-fundamental-right-to-blaspheme Accessed 4 May 2019.

—— (2002b), Letter to *The Guardian*, 28 February.

Wesker, Arnold and Pascal, Julia (2014), Interviewed by Anne Etienne, in A. Etienne and A. Alcagaya (eds), *Variations Contemporaines Autour de Shylock*, *Coup de Théâtre*, HS4, pp. 207–30.

Wesker, Arnold Papers (AW) (1989), Correspondence with Henry Burke, 30 June and 5 July, Austin, Texas: Harry Ransom Center, Box 19.3.

—— (1991a), *Martyrs for Sale*, possible sequence of events, n.d., Austin, Texas: Harry Ransom Center, Box 18.5.

—— (1991b), Notes on *William of Norwich*, 23 October, Austin, Texas: Harry Ransom Center, Box 19.8.

—— (1992), Letter to Henry Burke, 23 January, Austin, Texas: Harry Ransom Center, Box 19.3.

—— (1993a), Fax to Henry Burke, 3 May, Austin, Texas: Harry Ransom Center, Box 19.3.

—— (1993b), Henry Burke to Stephen Daldry, 6 December, Austin, Texas: Harry Ransom Center, Box 19.3.

—— (1994), Letter to Stephen Daldry, 11 May, Austin, Texas: Harry Ransom Center, Box 19.4.

—— (1995), Letter to Henry Burke, 1 December, Austin, Texas: Harry Ransom Center, Box 19.5.

—— (1996), Programme for *Blood Libel*, Austin, Texas: Harry Ransom Center, Box 19.8.

Wilcher, Robert (1991), *Understanding Arnold Wesker*, Columbia: University of South Carolina Press.

Wisse, Ruth (1983), 'Aharon Appelfeld, survivor', *Commentary*, 76, pp. 74–76.

FIGURE 9: Production photograph of *Je parle de Jérusalem*, directed by Jean-Claude Bastos at the Grenier de Toulouse, with Josée Lefèvre (Sarah) – Philippe Cointin (Ronnie) – Dominique Lagier (Ada) – Alain Rothstein (Dave). Photo by Michel Stuck.

8

Wesker's French Connections

Anne Etienne

'If it weren't for the foreigners, I should be in despair' (Cleave 1981: 35). So spoke Arnold Wesker as *Caritas* (1981) was about to premiere at the National Theatre. The claim cannot be interpreted as an empty complaint since commentators regularly brought up Wesker's lack of popularity in the United Kingdom, especially on the main stages of the capital. However, abroad it was a different matter. *Their Very Own and Golden City* (1965) premiered in French at the National Theatre of Belgium. *The Friends* (1970) was successfully staged at the Stadsteater, Stockholm, prior to its infamous Roundhouse production the same year, and *The Journalists* (1977)[1] was first professionally presented on 15 June 1978 on France Culture radio. *The Wedding Feast* (1974) premiered in Stockholm, again, three years before its British opening in Leeds. *The Merchant* (1976, later retitled *Shylock*) opened at the Royal Dramatenteater in Stockholm a year before its New York debut and two years before its Birmingham premiere. *Annie Wobbler* (1983) opened in Stuttgart six months before Wesker directed it at the Birmingham Repertory Theatre Studio. *Four Portraits – of Mothers* (1982), a Japanese commission, opened in Tokyo five years before its London run at the now defunct Man in the Moon. *Whatever Happened to Betty Lemon* (1986, [hereafter *Betty Lemon*]) premiered at the Théâtre du Rond-Point in Paris before Wesker directed the play in a double bill with *Yardsale* at the Lyric Theatre Studio, London, in 1987. The world premiere of *The Mistress* (1991) took place in Rome, and the play then opened in Cardiff in 1997. *Letter to a Daughter* (1992) premiered in Seoul and was broadcast on Norwegian television six years before a British production at the Edinburgh Festival in 1998. *Men Die Women Survive* (1992) was produced at the Northlight Theatre, Chicago. Following its Tokyo premiere, *Wild Spring* (1994) enjoyed a three-year run in Budapest.

One may draw tentative conclusions from this list of United Kingdom and foreign premieres. Despite his concern for a London premiere, Wesker's priority was to have the plays performed; if nothing else the list confirms Wesker's international career; it suggests that his poor reputation in Britain as a 'troublemaker with directors' and a dramatist 'at war with critics' was confined to home (Wesker cited in Billington 1977: n.pag.). Beyond these considerations, the endurance of Wesker's appeal abroad against a lack of popularity in the United Kingdom is a predicament shared by other British dramatists of the same generation such as Edward Bond, John Arden and Peter Nichols.

Bearing in mind Wesker's large body of dramatic work (46 plays), one observes another difference between the British stage and its international counterparts in the production of his first play, *The Kitchen* (1959): 'a play not professionally seen on the London stage for thirty-three years' before Stephen Daldry's production, whereas 'it has been performed constantly throughout the world in over sixty cities, twenty-five countries, and sixteen languages' (AW 1994a: n.pag.). Although Wesker mused in his letter to Daldry that '[t]he play must be in the air' (AW 1994a), *The Kitchen* clearly defies temporal and geographic limits since it has been constantly produced around the world, thereby generating Wesker's only continuous source of income. The unique case of *The Kitchen*'s international appeal warrants a study in itself, but two factors have dictated why this chapter has approached the question of the international reach of Wesker's plays through the national lens of France. Beyond the linguistic considerations, Wesker's working experience in Paris, at the restaurant Le Rallye, bore a pivotal influence on his career: 'I would not have begun to write about people I met in the Paris kitchen if I hadn't sensed they embodied a theme that could cross time and frontiers' (AW 1994b: n.pag.). Although his plays were performed in French in Belgium, Switzerland and Canada, only French productions will be considered here as the texts were often further adapted for specific national audiences. For example, Jacques Huisman (director of the National Theatre of Belgium) explained to Wesker that 'we have often had problems with Parisian translations because there are marked local nuances and different verbal expressions in Belgium [my translation]' (AW 1981a: n.pag.).

This chapter will question whether Wesker's 'works do "speak"' in France by observing which plays were produced and then by examining the directors' motives and approaches through archival material and interviews (Wesker 1977–78: 5). Finally, focusing first on two significant productions of *The Kitchen*, the chapter will go on to explore the critical reception of subsequent work by Wesker in this country.

From Racines to Souvenirs fantômes

Between 1967 and 2005, eleven of Wesker's plays were professionally produced in France, on 22 occasions. If *The Kitchen* (*La Cuisine*), unsurprisingly, prompted six productions, the five productions of *The Four Seasons* (1965, *Les Quatre saisons*) – a play that notably received neither critical nor commercial acclaim in the United Kingdom – indicate that French *metteurs-en-scène* had a different sensibility to Wesker's oeuvre than their British colleagues. His only commercial success in the United Kingdom, *Chips with Everything* (*Des Frites, des frites, des frites!*), albeit 'because they heard it was a comedy', divided critics at the prestigious and politically tainted Théâtre National Populaire (TNP)[2], which further confirms discrepancies in reception each side of the Channel (Wesker cited in Pierre 1972: n.pag.). Not only were plays that had been critically disparaged in the United Kingdom successfully produced in France – *The Four Seasons*, *The Friends* (1970, *Les Amis*) – but later plays were well represented on the French stages, from three of Wesker's one-woman plays – *Betty Lemon*'s world premiere and *Annie Wobbler* (1984) in 1986, as well as *Four Portraits – of Mothers* (*Mères, portraits*) produced with *Yardsale* (*Souvenirs à vendre*) in 1990–1991 – to *Denial* (2000, *Souvenirs fantômes*) in 2004. Chronologically, while Wesker was regularly performed from the mid-1960s to the end of the 1980s (with five to seven productions per decade), the 1990s and 2000s each saw only three productions, which included three revivals of *The Kitchen* but only one new play, *Denial*.

A seminal theatre event which revealed Ariane Mnouchkine's company and collaborative practice, the Théâtre du Soleil's production of *The Kitchen* in April 1967 is widely regarded as 'the first play of Wesker's to be performed in France' (Bradby 1984: 192). However, Edmond Tamiz's *Roots* (1959, *Racines*), performed at the Comédie de Bourges between 17 February and 18 March 1967, predated Mnouchkine's discovery of Wesker, as did the Malmö Stadtsteater production of *Chips with Everything* directed by Stig Nelson, presented by the Théâtre des Nations in Swedish – a linguistic factor that explained the play's limited impact at the time according to critics (*Le Masque et la plume* 1967).

The year 1968 stands as the *annus mirabilis* abroad for Wesker: not only was he invited in Japan for Wesker 68 – a festival dedicated to his work – but he also directed the world premiere of *The Four Seasons* in Havana (Cuba), *The Kitchen* was performed in Bogota (Colombia) and he had three plays on in Paris: Mnouchkine's *The Kitchen* toured in Europe and performed in factories on strike in and around Paris, Tamiz's *Roots* was revived in Paris and Claude Régy's *The Four Seasons* opened at the Théâtre Montparnasse on 4 October 1968, making Wesker 'THE English author of the year' (Schifres 1968: 98).

The 1970s saw the first and last French production of *Chips with Everything*, directed by Gérard Vergez, in 1972 (a prominent actor-director who trod the boards at Avignon and the Comédie Française) at the TNP, which offered that year an anglicized programme. This and Mnouchkine's revival of *The Kitchen* in 1970 were the only Parisian productions. Though this period proved quantitatively fertile, the plays failed to generate the kind of enthusiasm that would prompt more than a one-month run or a transfer to Paris, where they could hope to earn recognition on par with Mnouchkine's 1967 success. *The Four Seasons* elicited two new provincial productions, both translated by Claude Régy and Pierre Roudy: in Villiers-le-Bel, directed by Serge Lascar in February 1976, and in April 1978 by the Théâtre Populaire d'Eté in Nantes, directed by Jacques Schiltz. *I'm Talking about Jerusalem* (1960, *Je parle de Jérusalem*) was first directed in May 1974 by Pierre della Torre at the Théâtre Populaire du Val-de-Marne. In March 1979, directed by Jean-Claude Bastos, it was programmed by the Centre Dramatique National (CDN)[3] of the Grenier de Toulouse. Directed by Gilles Chavassieux in March 1979 at the Théâtre Les Ateliers (Lyons), *Roots* toured the region and was revived in January 1980.

In the 1980s, Chavassieux also directed *Annie Wobbler* for Les Ateliers in November 1986. It was revived in 1987, with another actress, Edith Scob, and transferred to the Athénée Théâtre Louis-Jouvet from 17 March 1987, before running again at Les Ateliers in April 1988. One might suggest that the 1980s offer snapshots of an eclectic Wesker. The early plays are present: *Roots'* provincial 1979–80 run is joined by *The Kitchen*, directed by Maurice Sarrazin for the Grenier de Toulouse at the Théâtre Sorano in February 1982, and revived in Montauban in November 1983. Two plays reflecting his Centre 42 (C42) experience emerge, sharing poetic and tragic overtones: *The Four Seasons* was directed by Jean-Louis Merarzob at the Théâtre Présent in 1981 and in 1989 at the Dix-Huit Théâtre by Jean Macqueron in a new translation by Keith Gore, while *The Friends* was directed by Yves Gasc (of the Comédie-Française) at the Lucernaire in May 1981. These Parisian productions of *The Four Seasons* remain obscure, partly due to lukewarm reception; whereas Gasc's *Friends*, adapted by Pascale de Boysson and Jill Nizard and produced by Laurent Terzieff's company, was critically acclaimed – despite being disliked by Wesker. Finally, a few days before *Annie Wobbler* opened in Lyons, *Betty Lemon* received its world premiere at Paris's Théâtre du Rond-Point, suggesting, to borrow Wesker's phrasing in *Annie Wobbler*, that 'there's something about' woman solo plays in the 1980s that resonated in France more than in England.

Of his cycle of six one-woman plays, *Mothers* and *Yardsale* (directed by Patrice Kerbrat) were presented together at the Festival of Sète; the show was then produced at the Théâtre de Nice in 1990 and briefly at another Parisian venue the following year. But the Wesker event of the 1990s, though it failed to generate the success he yearned for, was the repertory run of the *Trilogy* in six theatres located in the Parisian suburbs between May 1994 and February 1995. This was a mammoth production directed by Jean-Pierre Loriol[4]: not only was this the first occasion French audiences got to see *Chicken Soup with Barley* (1958, *Soupe de poulet à l'orge*), but they were actually served chicken soup prepared by Dusty Wesker (AW 1994c). In December 1998, *The Kitchen* was directed in France for the third time, by Jean Maisonnave, in suburban Paris (Centre Culturel Jean-Houdremont, La Courneuve).

This was rapidly followed by another two productions of *The Kitchen* in 2002–3 and 2004: the production at the Studio-Théâtre of Asnières directed by Jean-Louis Martin-Barbaz in May 2002 transferred to the Théâtre Sylvia Montfort between 25 April and 15 June 2003; directed by Claudia Stavisky with the assistance of a hip-hop choreographer, a second production opened at the Théâtre Les Célestins in Lyons and toured regionally between 28 October and 31 December, 2004. Also that year, Wesker's friend Jacques Rosner opted for a more recent play when he directed *Denial* at the Théâtre 14 in March–May 2004.

This brief chronology paints a performance history that both shadows and departs from its English counterpart. Wesker wrote sixteen plays in the 1990s and 2000s,[5] spanning intimate short dramas for women[6] (*Letter to a Daughter* [1992], *Wild Spring* [1994], *The Confession* [1997]) to more ambitious historic plays (*Blood Libel* [1996] and *Longitude* [2005]). Most were produced in the United Kingdom, either on stage, television or radio, but they did not achieve the popular impact of his earlier work. One cannot expect all foreign plays to be adapted (Vigouroux-Frey 2000: 137); yet out of the sixteen plays written in that time only one, *Denial*, graced the French stage, running for a month and a half in Paris. In the same period, three productions of *The Kitchen* and the disappointing first production of the *Trilogy* indicate that, following the one-woman plays, French taste favoured the timeless vision of the world offered in his first play.

At the same time in the United Kingdom, a return to early successes is notable: these included Stephen Daldry's 1994 production of *The Kitchen* at the Royal Court followed in 2011 by Bijan Sheibani's at the National, Dominic Cooke's *Chicken Soup with Barley* 2011, also at the Royal Court, and James Macdonald's *Roots* at the Donmar Warehouse in 2013. By comparison, the French attachment to *Jerusalem* and *Four Seasons*, both widely overlooked in the United Kingdom, suggests sensibilities at variance and directors' motives that deserve to be investigated. In addition, if the relationship Wesker built with John Dexter in England remains unique – Dexter directed six of his plays and they fed off each other's work at the beginning of their careers – Wesker also weaved long-lasting relations with French artists. He developed friendships with French directors (Jean-Michel Ribes in particular, but also internationally recognized director Régy who championed his work in 1968). He also received requests to mount more than one play from directors and other actors: for instance, following *The Friends*, which united revered stage and film actors (and life partners) Laurent Terzieff and Pascale de

Boysson, de Boysson was keen to adapt *Love Letters on Blue Paper* for Laurent Terzieff's company.

Enter: Les metteurs-en-scène

The translator of a number of Wesker's plays, Philippe Léotard also adapted *The Kitchen* for the Théâtre du Soleil, eventually taking on an acting role in the production. The rehearsal process lasted five months.[7] This was partly due to the difficulties raised by the text for a young company – such as the need to learn and embody physical movement, which was practically achieved by the actors taking up restaurant internships, while Mnouchkine herself trained with Jacques Lecoq (Richardson 2016: 307, 313). In addition to this, no firm venue was lined up until they found the inexpensive option of the Cirque Médrano. Wesker attended rehearsals in March 1967 and recounted in his diary:

> The rehearsals were good. The play seemed well set but in a mess. Needed definition. [...] I told her [Mnouchkine] I was really pleased and felt that though the rhythms were wrong they were easily remedied. [...]
>
> I suppose it's at this point that Ariane must have asked me to talk with the actors. [...] I remember explaining to the actors what should happen. 'Count eight in between the first round of orders,' I told them, 'and then seven, and then six, and then five [....]' We rehearsed this method for a short while and it began to work. I left the rest to Ariane.
>
> (Wesker 2001b: n.pag.)

Mnouchkine further shaped the play by excising from the interlude emotional images, a feature of his plays frequently attacked by English critics:

> She had cut out the 'bridge-building' scene and replaced it with a 'horse-building' scene instead. The Horstwesel song had been replaced by the melody from Wagner's *The Flying Dutchman*. She had cut Hans playing the guitar. 'Too sentimental!' And she'd also cut the important 'rose-offering' moment. 'Too sentimental!' I objected but only limply.
>
> (Wesker 2001b: n.pag.)

Wesker concluded from his time in Paris with Mnouchkine, during which she acted as translator with interviewers, that 'we both grew sick of me' but nonetheless suggests that 'perhaps we are just two sides of the same coin' (Wesker 2001b: n.pag., AW4 1970: n.pag.).

Despite their different approaches, Mnouchkine enthused about *The Kitchen* as much as Wesker enthused about her work,[8] explaining that 'the play represents life like no other I have ever read. It does not talk about life, it *is* life. Life is not particularly realistic and the play is not either' (Mnouchkine 1967: n.pag.). To her, Wesker's talent lay in drawing 30 characters, none of which was secondary: 'you get to know them all. You can feel that Wesker loves them, that he understands them, even if he doesn't always agree with them' (Mnouchkine 1967: n.pag.).

This ability to build moving, fully evolved characters 'even if they have only a few lines' also attracted Jean-Louis Martin-Barbaz, who directed the play in 2002 (Martin-Barbaz 2018: n.pag.). Influenced by his work with Roger Planchon in the 1960s and as director of a CDN in the 1980s, he militated for a contemporary, popular theatre. If such issues as abortion and the death penalty would by then be obsolete, *The Kitchen* transcends historical periods because it is 'larger-than-life and socially mimetic' (Martin-Barbaz 2018: n.pag.) – an echo of the early critique of the play as 'at once realistic and representative' (Leeming and Trussler 1971: 26). Brutal and poetic, the text prompts a theatrical, hallucinatory effect – particularly evident in the balletic movement at the end of Act I, where the uniformed bodies expertly waltz past each other and in the tension between allegory and the realistic setting – but also a tragic feeling in the truth of the characters' suffering: just as '*Platonov* sums up Anton Chekhov, *The Kitchen*, through its characters more than the overall plot, reveals entirely the world of Wesker: a broken world' (Martin- Barbaz 2018: n.pag.).

In the case of *Four Portraits – of Mothers* in 1990–91, actress Josiane Stoléru elicited the production, directed by her friend Patrice Kerbrat (a director and actor from the Comédie Française). She had met Wesker in 1987 and was granted rights for both this and the one-act *Yardsale*. She and Kerbrat reworked the 1983 translation (Kerbrat 2019) while trying to secure a venue. Eventually, the opportunity to stage the play at a festival in Sète provided a stage, where it won the Georges Brassens prize, and a successful transfer to the CDN Théâtre de Nice in December 1990. Kerbrat's scenography stood as a counterpoint to Wesker's vision that 'the actress will add or discard one or two garments [and] the four settings are indicated by one or two pieces of furniture [...] all visible on the stage' (Wesker 2001a: 46). Kerbrat explained his conception in the following way:

> A red curtain fell down from the gods and covered the stage, hiding a few pieces of furniture. Front centre were five pairs of shoes, symbolising the five women. That's the only thing that changed. The costume was a lame dress, very music-hall, like the mise-en-scene, but not the acting. Little by little things were revealed from below the curtain: a table etc. [...] Between each sketch I used English nursery songs to evoke the presence of those unseen children.
>
> (Kerbrat 2019: n.pag.)

Kerbrat appreciated the humour and shifts in the play and developed a personal relationship with Wesker, translating *Letter to a Daughter* (*Lettre à ma fille*) and *One More Ride on the Merry-go-Round* (*Un Autre tour de manège*) in 1989. Previously turned down by producer Lars Schmidt as inadequate for a Parisian audience (AW 1980), *One More Ride* appealed to Kerbrat because of its wit (AW 1988). Though it is a comedy which opens with an orgasm in the dark, Kerbrat recognized it as a 'Wesker play' that tackles the same themes as *Yardsale* with different viewpoints but similar characters, and with the same 'interest in the relationship between mothers and children' as in *Four Portraits* (AW 1988: n.pag.). Neither were produced, and one may suggest that the Parisian transfer of *Mères – Portraits* in 1991 at the Espace Cardin, a huge venue ill-suited for the intimate performance of the monodramas and virtually abandoned at the time (Kerbrat 2019), was unlikely to entice other theatres to programme a lesser known play by Wesker. In addition, Kerbrat inferred that the need to secure the involvement of a movie star 'who decide[s] to do some theatre again' was as crucial in the 1980s as that of a suitable venue (AW 1988: n.pag.).

The première of *Betty Lemon* was primarily motivated by friendship. Jean-Michel Ribes met Wesker in the 1980s through their work with the International Theatre Institute where they both represented contemporary authors. He fully engaged with Wesker's 'life as a bellicose woman' (AW 1986b: n.pag.): he not only directed and translated the play but was involved in the English drafts of the play, suggesting that Betty be 'made Handicapped Woman of the Year' (AW 1986a: n.pag.). *Betty Lemon* was part of a show titled 'Révoltes' (Revolts), which included another two short plays: *Malédictions d'une furie* by Jean Tardieu – a contemporary spin on Cassandra – and *Venise zigouillée* by Ribes. Wesker was particularly keen on the play, which fitted Ribes's desire at the time of producing a show with three portraits of women. Much like *Annie Wobbler*, the show revolved around the actress, Judith Magre, who played the three women, moving from the 'metaphysical' atmosphere of Tardieu's poetic text (Debreuille 2010: 224), in a tale of a revengeful woman who destroys Venice, to *Betty Lemon* and her 'daily companion', through the object of a noose (Wesker 2001a: 89), wavering between tragedy and comedy: 'Handicapped Woman of the Year. I can put H.W.O.Y. after my name. I'm a hwoy! Lady Betty Lemon – hwoy!' (Wesker 2001a: 93). The set consisted of just an empty box walled with black velvet, together with changes of costumes and lighting. Wesker's only requirement was that 'the kitchen pieces [be] very very carefully chosen' and that the wheelchair be 'a wonder of electronic science' (AW 1986d: n.pag.).

For Ribes, the more problematic issue hinged on the political climate, at a time when, for the first time in the history of the Fifth Republic, a left-wing president (François Mitterrand) had to collaborate with a right-wing prime minister

(Jacques Chirac) as the result of a swing to the right for the legislative elections in 1986. This situation dominated debates and 'the passages of the play that directly touch socialisme [*sic*] risk perhaps to suffer from this situation, [what] worries me is the possible diversion, the false perception that the public might have' (AW 1986c: n.pag.). Between Betty pondering whether she was 'ever really a socialist' and why she 'never really liked the majority' (Wesker 2001a: 96) to asking her politician husband's colleagues 'why are all your left-wing leaders looking to the right?' (97) and her conclusion that she 'didn't fucking plan it this way' (105), her diatribe could indeed be read as a comment on the conflicting Governmental situation and her crippled figure as the uneasy vision of a 'handicapped society' (Ribes 2019: n.pag.). Both agreed that the solution was to 'center the direction on the moving character of this untamable shrew' (AW 1986c: n.pag.; AW 1986c: n.pag.). Despite attempts to produce *The Four Seasons* and *Love Letters on Blue Paper*, *Betty Lemon* remained their only theatrical collaboration.

Gilles Chavassieux directed two of Wesker's plays – *Roots* (tr. Philipppe Léotard) and *Annie Wobbler* (tr. Chavassieux and Lachaise). He had worked with Planchon until 1972 and founded with Nicole Lachaise the independent theatre Les Ateliers in Lyons in 1975 to 'promote contemporary drama and renew theatre audiences' (Chavassieux 2019: n.pag.). In 1979, 1968 remained a vivid memory, and *Roots* resonated with the spirit of young, working-class rebellion, represented by the revolt of Beatie Bryant.

Though he considered *Annie Wobbler* as a 'pleasant entertainment' with the exception of the character of Annie Wobbler, Chavassieux's 1986 production toured in France and Belgium in 1987 and was further revived in Lyons in 1988. The actress initially chosen for the role, Francine Bergé, disapproved of the translation and was replaced by Christiane Cohendi in October 1986 and Edith Scob in 1987 (Chavassieux 2019). Lachaise confirmed in August 1986 to Wesker that the production was programmed. At this point Wesker shared with Bergé pictures of the London production and notes on sets and costumes, clearly betraying his intention to dictate the design:

> the first 2 [flats] pull aside very simply revealing the set behind. With each new area the indoor light increases so that in the beginning you have a slum attic light, then a little more window light for the student apartment, finally the full slope of window for the chic atelier.
>
> (AW 1986e: n.pag.)

Therefore, Wesker imposed his set designer: he was concerned that Chavassieux found the London set 'too naturalistic' and expressed his disapproval by concluding, 'Well, that's the play it is' (AW 1986e: n.pag.). For the première in Lyons, they nonetheless focused on transforming the naturalistic frame to link the three parts in a more flowing manner (Chavassieux 2019). What remained of Wesker's initial vision was abandoned for the Parisian run on the small stage of the Athénée and the set further evolved for the tour with Edith Scob. For Chavassieux, the three parts had not managed to unify and the link they finally introduced, 'even if it referred to something else, was a mountain of discarded clothes that could evoke [sculptor Christian] Boltanski's focus on memories', a far cry from Wesker's naturalistic approach. Chavassieux realized that the three texts are 'a gift for an actress' – but 'this does not make a play' (Chavassieux 2019: n.pag.).

While similar comments were voiced in the United Kingdom about the one-woman plays, his 1960s plays were read very differently each side of the Channel. *Golden City* – a reflection of and on C42 – is unsurprisingly absent from the French repertoire, but its companion piece *The Four Seasons* clearly appealed to French sensibilities. Following Régy's initial acclaimed production, it was revived in 1976, in the Parisian suburbs, where the leftist town of Villiers-le-Bel was keen on drawing more varied audiences and therefore willing to take chances with experimental texts and radical young directors. Looking for a contemporary play for two actors Serge Lascar was moved by 'its simplicity and its absence of pathos' and the fact that Wesker showed a couple without moral hangs-up (Lascar 2019: n.pag.). Whereas in England, critics condemned the absence of a social environment and the pseudo-poetic language, Lascar embraced this love story across four seasons and the language of the lovers, easy and direct. The publicity materials, 'Will winter ever end?', emphasized an approach that privileged the power of language and further placed the play as a counterpoint to the theatrical and filmic output of the 1970s. When the spirit of the decade could be defined as 'raw rebellion, language games, provocation [...] and widespread female nudity', *The Four Seasons* was devoid of sexual fantasy, simple in its discourse, and as such 'original' (Lascar 2019: n.pag.). Lascar therefore developed two scenic ideas that steered the play towards symbolism – the only pointedly realistic moment being the preparation of the apple strudel: lights were used to evoke the seasons and associated sentiments; in the middle of a high stage rose a staircase which led to nowhere. Possibly 'influenced by Albert Camus's *Myth of Sisyphus*' and therefore observing the situation with an existentialist lens, Lascar directed his actors in an ascending relation to the stairs, so they would 'appear lost in space [or] tall, overlooking the space' (Lascar 2019: n.pag.).[9] These aesthetic choices remedy the ambivalence of the text, where Wesker develops the poetic, stylized language of love in a *huis-clos* composed of a concrete 'mixture of antique[s]' furniture (Wesker 1990: 75). By privileging the power of words to create a world on stage, Lascar also denied any necessity for a social environment.

In contrast, Jean-Claude Bastos, who directed *I'm Talking about Jérusalem* (*Je parle de Jérusalem*) in Toulouse in 1979, was interested by the more overtly socio-political aspects of Wesker's work. His initial project was to present the whole *Trilogy*, but for financial and strategic reasons, the CDN decided to limit its programme to one play. As Bastos explains, '*Chicken Soup* would have resonated in Toulouse, a city very affected by the Spanish Civil War' (2018: n.pag.). However, the choice was motivated by three considerations:

> *Jerusalem* had never been produced in France.[10] Also, it was ten years after the 1968 events and three years – though even as a militant leftist I did not imagine – before the political shift of 1981 with its excitement, and then disillusions. I felt more inclined to look at utopia than political commitment. Finally, in the 1970s, around Toulouse there was a distinct trend to go back to a rural life: even two of the actors cast had come to the region to reinvent their lives in a more autonomous fashion, exactly what *Jerusalem* is about.
>
> (Bastos 2018: n.pag.)

Beyond the political echoes and hippie *zeitgeist*, Wesker's least performed and 'least satisfying' (Hayman 1979: 42) *The Trilogy* play seems an odd choice for a director who shied away from realism, preferring Seneca, Lorca, Calderon and even scientific texts, but *Jerusalem* was a digression that permitted him to explore 'the balance between a representation of reality and a certain abstraction' (Bastos 2018: n.pag.). Yet, compared with the 'Brechtian whiffs' of *Soupe de poulet* and the 'Chekhovian aspects' of *Racines*,[11] he praised the style of *Jerusalem* as more innovative, akin to such upcoming French dramatists as Michel Vinaver, Philippe Minyana or Jean-Luc Lagarce, 'a more open, a more pared down writing'.

Linked to this, and in opposition with Wesker's 'didactic purpose' (Wilcher 1991: 6, 18), Bastos was drawn to Wesker's treatment of utopia, 'positing facts, situations, moments without trying to demonstrate or to resolve anything' (Bastos 2018: n.pag.). The scenography attempted to fuse hyperrealism and stylization:

> There were no walls, so that the room where the action takes place would look like a raft placed on a metaphoric landscape, a space opening onto hills, a countryside with a not entirely naturalistic sky, a space through which you could see kanji as if beneath the surface. The very real behaviour of the characters was seen against this raft on a mythical rurality.
>
> (Bastos 2018: n.pag.)

The inclusion of Japanese kanji on the backdrop (see production picture) remains unclear – perhaps a reference to Wesker's success in Japan or his penchant during the 1970s for sporting kimonos, as hinted at in Pamela Howard's chapter in this volume. Yet, one may suggest that these symbols participate in the stylization of the characters' utopian quest and firmly depart from the aesthetic approach of other productions. For Wesker, the play was 'flawed' because his 'impulse to break out [of a conventional three-act play]' was 'never quite fulfilled' (Leeming 1983: 54–55). His dissatisfaction with the play's structure might have been counterbalanced by the aesthetic approach which broke with naturalistic conventions since he enjoyed the French performance (Bastos 2018).

This overview of French productions since 1967 reveals two tendencies. Whereas the naturalistic aesthetics of the social realist has dominated Wesker's reputation in England, French directors have freely adapted the stage directions to respond to their vision of the text – despite sometimes incurring Wesker's displeasure – yet these productions have successfully released Wesker from the restrictive cliché of the 1950s angry young man. Three productions of *The Kitchen* between 1990 and 2004 also confirm that 'Wesker's early plays were widely performed and enthusiastically received in Continental Europe' (Patterson 1995: 32); however, the 1980s were dominated by an interest in Wesker's one-woman plays, which may be a response, conscious or not, to feminist issues. Abortion in France was legalized in 1975; to elude further protests from the feminist movement in the 1970s, conservative president Giscard d'Estaing also initiated a 'state feminism', which was then furthered by socialist president François Mitterrand when he increased the number of women in ministerial posts, an agenda epitomized by the nomination of Edith Roudy as Minister for Women's Affairs (1981–86), who passed a law against sexism in 1983. Conversely, another explanation could be that the plays simply appealed to actresses because they offered the rare opportunity of multi-faceted women roles by a playwright who could 'marvellously write female characters' (Martin-Barbaz 2018: n.pag.).

Crrritique!

It has been suggested that 'the excitement of going to the circus to see a play certainly accounted for some of the success' of Mnouchkine's *Kitchen* (Bradby 1984: 192). However, the interviewed directors' unanimous testimonials as well as the production's European tour and, later, its transfer to the Elysée-Montmartre theatre indicate that the impact of the show surpassed aspects of location.[12] Yet, the show took on a site-responsive dimension when it toured for a month in French factories on strike during the May events in 1968 (Bradby 2002: 114–15). There the actors would bring in the props in front of a first-time and non-paying audience seated on benches, boxes or scaffolds, transforming the workplace into a theatre which showed a workplace: 'Nowhere but within the factory setting, as sordid as the play's décor itself, could *The Kitchen* be more meaningful' (Zand 1968: n.pag.). Beyond the encores, the show elicited a new demand for 'theatre in the factory', one that reverberates through Wesker's C42 project. While some reviews spinned the existential crisis at the core of the play (Leonardini 1967; Kourilsky 1967), others focused on the documentary qualities of Wesker's writing (Poirot-Delpech 1967); but they concurred that the play is both political and a tragedy that reveals the human condition. As such, Wesker's microcosm of an alienating universe raised advantageous comparisons with Eugene O'Neill's *Hairy Ape* (1922) (Poirot-Delpech 1967) or Zola and Dickens (Baignères 1967). No subsequent production earned similar praise for Wesker, and, according to Martin-Barbaz, 'it's the kind of shows that has marked a generation with such force that it becomes a sacred taboo' (cited in Thébaud 2003: n.pag.).

Like in the United Kingdom, *The Kitchen* was not his first play performed. At one of the first Maisons de la Culture launched by André Malraux, Tamiz created *Roots* with the troupe of La Comédie de Bourges. Despite its regional opening, the production was covered by national magazines. The *Figaro Littéraire* and *L'Entracte* praised the 'rigorous mise-en-scène, devoid of excessive realism or mannered populism' (AW 1967a: n.pag.); the *Nouvel Observateur* applauded Wesker's play but lamented a certain 'lack of poetry', which heightened the characters' trivial reality (AW 1967b: n.pag.). Interestingly, critics chose to focus on the political agenda not only of Wesker – 'socialism is possible only when one reconnects with one's roots' (AW 1967b: n.pag.) – but also of the cultural context of the Bourges production: 'despite the animosity of stubborn, conservative parties' (Wolff 1967: n.pag.) the theatre was packed, in great part with young theatre goers, which showed that the mission of the Maison de la Culture to develop a popular programme had been successfully achieved (AW 1967b). It is unlikely that Wesker was aware of this context as he was reported to have declared after the show that the play's aim was to 'demonstrate that intellectuals were revolutionary in their statements but disappeared when it was time to take action', but *Roots*' discourse and venue proved relevant in pursuing the popular and decentralizing agenda initiated by Planchon, one that was similar to C42 (Wolff 1967: n.pag.). Like *Roots* in England, with its provincial premiere in Coventry and subsequent transfer to the Royal Court in London, its French counterpart moved to the Théâtre de l'Ouest Parisien (Boulogne-Billancourt) between 27 November 1968 and 11 January 1969, with a revised mise en scène that aimed to distance itself from naturalism by stripping the set to 'a clinical whiteness' (*L'Humanité, La Croix*) (AW1968: n.pag.). The play divided critics, from the condemnation that Parisian audiences were too removed from such English, rural and trite issues (*Le Nouvel Observateur, Le Figaro*) to the encouragement to see 'one of the best plays I have seen in a long time' (*Combat, L'Humanité-Dimanche*: n.pag.). This, following the much praised production of Régy's *The Four Seasons*, might explain why *Roots* was not produced again before 1979.

If the dramaturgy was deemed monotonous (Gautier 1968a) due to the repetition of 'psychological monologues interspersed with poetic effusions', what critics applauded in *The Four Seasons* was its innovative writing, 'violent, tender and disillusioned' (Galey 1968a: n.pag.), and its rhythm, for which the play was likened to a song or a poem (Kanters 1968). Hence, the absence of plot and social background did not irritate – understandably in a country that saw the premiere of plays by Beckett or Ionesco. Away from Britain, where the autobiographical elements could be easily read – in French Alain and Catherine have replaced Adam and Beatrice, whose initials recalled those of Arnold and his C42 assistant and paramour Beba Lavrin – the play appeared 'unsentimental, cruel and sharp' (Cartier 1968: n.pag.). The couple's inevitable fate endeared all critics towards the unanimously praised actors, and Régy's delicate direction proved ideal for a play which exists 'not in dialogues but in the background which prevents the words spoken to become true or even believable' (Madral 1968a: n.pag.). Once again, parallels were made with O'Casey and Brecht, but also Gorki, Gatti and Adamov (Galey 1968a; Schifres 1968: 98), and for the first time, the notion that Wesker is 'English only by chance, through nationality' suggests that his work's texture and inspiration was coloured by his European Jewish roots (Galey 1968a: n.pag.). Served by star actors Claude Rich and Nicole Courcel, the production's impact can be assessed by the fact that it was even covered by the popular magazine *Paris Match*, where it was acclaimed somewhat sensationally as an 'avant-garde' event that would enable 'the survival of theatre' in the wake of May 1968 (Hanoteau 1968: n.pag.).

In 1972, on the main stage of the TNP, *Chips with Everything* proved a poor choice due to context: established in France in 1798, National Service remained mandatory until 1997. The actors and Vergez's scenography were applauded – minus rumblings about the inappropriate 'plastic' props (Marcabru 1972a; Leonardini 1972). However, beyond an honourable mention for the 'first part [...] intelligent, humorous, psychologically well-observed' (Gautier 1972: n.pag.), reviews condemned the play as dated in a country where the standards of army camps had prompted many stage and filmic versions (Galey 1972; Poirot-Delpech 1972; Marcabru 1972b; Poirot-Delpech 1972; Gautier 1972). Whereas the play's study of the mechanics of rebellion was controversial in England, famously defined as 'the first play of which the Establishment need be afraid' (Hobson 1962: n.pag.), in France the brutal treatment of the men appeared so conventional that it became cliché blending satire and antimilitarist melodrama (Gautier 1972). Moreover, in France, Pip's and Chas's fascination for each other's social class failed to find a convincing echo, and Pip's journey between decadence and treason lacked a cultural explanation and seemed to hesitate between political documentary and Pip's story (Galey 1972). This failed gallic adaptation may easily explain why *Chips* has never to date graced the French stage again.

By contrast, *Jerusalem* took on contemporaneous accents in 1970s France, as Bastos explained. In 1974, though Pierre della Torre framed his direction to reflect international events – 'a questioning youth, a world running on petrol, the Watergate and other scandals' (AW2 1974: n.pag.) – yet the production suffered from the context of the French presidential election, where the high hopes of the Left crashed when Gaullist candidate Valery Giscard d'Estaing won with a 1.6% gap to François Mitterrand, rendering the characters' debates on the socialist experience and the relationship between workers and employers tiring and naïve (Gautier 1974; Kanters 1974). Gautier further condemned the excessively natural-istic design – also present in Loriol's production of the *Trilogy* in 1994–96 – which marred Beatie's sentimental woes by turning it into a television soap episode. In his stylized realist scenography, Bastos avoided such reproach.

Like *Chips with Everything*, *The Friends* was produced only once in France; unlike *Chips*, it was very well received, engendering none of the 'violent reactions' it suffered from in England (AW 1970: n.pag.).[13] The setting remains English in translation, but the location is that of an 'eternally conformist England barely offset by rebellion', therefore suggesting a timeless story rather a specific context (Jamet 1981: n.pag.). Two aspects differentiate the English and the French produc-tions: where the characters appeared on the enormous stage of the Roundhouse, the intimacy of the Parisian venue fitted the intimacy of the huis clos; the conclu-sions Wesker draws from C42 and his generation of working-class, utopian and now disillusioned friends were lost on the French audience, the only similarity raised being that the characters' drama is that of Wesker's generation (Jamet 1981). Most critics focused on the characters' class consciousness and 'subverted political aspirations, which reflect a disappointed society where sadomasochism competes with humour' (Dumur 1981: n.pag.), alluding either to the decline of the com-munist party in France or to the spirit of May '68 (Gautier 1981; Broussouloux 1981). The leftist *Canard enchaîné* lamented the selfishness of these socialists and doubted their revolutionary instincts but ended up seduced by the beautiful mono-logues on revolution (Tesson 1981).

Wesker had wanted 'to write it like a symphony' (AW 1966: n.pag.), a desire which director Yves Gasc had felt through 'this collation of overlapping situations [which] cannot be told by words' (AW 1981b: n.pag.). Symphony or concerto (Gautier 1981), the complexity of the characters, 'both heroes and victims' (Frazier 1981: n.pag.), and the physical presence of death as a pretext to tell about life, prompted lyrical reviews (Broussouloux 1981). In its treatment of Esther's death the play 'could have been a sombre drama but Wesker turns it into something ethereal, where the atmosphere and the ideas prevail over the circumstances' (Galey 1981:

n.pag.). This central event will not prompt a sudden realization because the friends are dreamers who cannot face reality. For Galey, the quality of Wesker's writing is defined by his instinct to use an 'impressionistic brush: he is the Vuillard of the Angry Young Men', an aesthetic description which Wesker has applied to many of his plays, as noted in Chris Megson's chapter (Galey 1981: n.pag.).

The critical reflections studied here outline two ideas. Firstly, the later plays either received moderate success (the one-woman plays) or were disregarded (even when a translation was effected, no production ensued). Secondly, Wesker's stylistic experiments did not bemuse nor alienate French audiences and critics. Based on his work up to the mid-1960s, literary critic and author Matthieu Galey describes Wesker as:

> an author fluctuating between the naturalist intimacy of his autobiographical plays (*Trilogy*) and a more poetic lyricism (*Four Seasons*). Inbetween are documents, lived experiences (*The Kitchen* and *Chips With Everything*) that lack the presence of the former (the family is missing) and the ethereal soaring of the latter.
>
> (Galey 1972: n.pag.)

Possibly because his plays were not produced chronologically in France, the perception differed from British reviewers who categorized Wesker as a social realist writer and were at best unconvinced by his stylistic shifts. In France, where *The Kitchen*, *The Four Seasons* and *Roots* were performed a few months apart, he evaded such labelling and was not expected to write continuously in the same vein, giving him the freedom to cultivate 'the lyrical, the paradoxical, the absurd, the ironic, the musical, the farcical and so on' (Wesker 2000).

Conclusion

Reflecting on his popularity abroad, Wesker mused that 'the plays are demanding in a way that the English temperament is not prepared to meet: emotionally and intellectually demanding and, what's worse, financially demanding as well' (Billington 1977: n.pag.). Indeed, though his general take on 'the Continent' fails to observe national variations, Michael Patterson has argued that the economic structure of British theatre and 'continental' theatre translates into values of 'show business' versus 'culture' (Patterson 1995: 32). Yet, Wesker's unequalled success in France with *The Kitchen* took place on a minute budget and outside the state-subsidized venues.

The hint of an 'un-English' quality in his writing (Wesker cited in Cleave: 38) was acknowledged in France and expressed by directors and critics alike in terms of his Jewish heritage: 'His realism is always tempered with lightly Chekhovian poetry and derisive humour, a typically Jewish self-mockery' (Galey 1981: n.pag.). Beyond the Jewish influence, his European roots may inform the musical and poetic rhythm of his plays, a pivotal quality that he insists emerges in performance and which was noted by French critics who likened the characters to instruments. Although the French enjoyed his political plays, sympathetic to Ronnie Kahn's utopian visions and then lamenting the death of an era, they were also able to appreciate spectacles like *The Kitchen* that raised philosophical questions, as well as delighting in the ascetic poetry of *The Four Seasons*. Wesker once suggested that he 'would like to write a play that begins with Once upon a time…', and if his plays cannot be described as fairy tales – as the absence of happy endings betrays – the French viewpoints garnered prove that 'a socially-committed dramatist may also reveal himself to be a poet' without contradiction nor controversy (AW 1965: n.pag.). When his alienation in England led him from irritation to despair, his optimism and faith in his plays prompted him to look beyond national characteristics, and always towards Europe: 'Any day can bring anything. Letters from abroad about productions in France, Portugal, Italy, maybe Germany […] reminding me I'm European, I'm European, I'm European' (AW 1993: n.pag.).

NOTES

1. *The Journalists*' UK premiere (27 March 1977) was an amateur production directed by Geoff Bennett at the Criterion Theatre in Coventry. The play was originally commissioned by the Royal Shakespeare Company for their 1971–72 season.
2. The TNP was founded by Firmin Gémier in 1920 to create a people's theatre. When Jean Vilar was given financial support to direct it from 1951, the TNP was able to have a permanent company and to produce and tour extensively. As part of the decentralizing impulse of the government towards the arts, the name TNP was transferred in 1972 to Planchon's theatre in Villeurbanne.
3. The 38 CDNs in France are subsidized producing structures developed since the 1940s in response to the decentralizing impulse of the government.
4. See Greenstein 2000 for details. To explain its limited impact, Wesker suggested that the six theatres where the plays were presented in rep could not raise the interest of Parisian audiences and prominent venues because they were located in the suburbs. The timeline of the project – *Chicken Soup* premiered in May, *Roots* in October, and *Jerusalem* in November – made for fragmented and sparse press coverage. Added to that, Loriol himself admitted that his direction raised criticism and that he was still working through difficult passages during the run. Finally, Loriol constantly struggled to secure enough funding (and new venues) to put on each successive play (AW1994d).

5. This includes *Circles of Perception*, a play so personal that it was never intended for performance. Originally titled *The New Play* in 1969, Wesker revised it in 1996.
6. It is worth noting that Wesker also wrote *Barabbas* (2000), a monologue for one man, for a BBC television series in Easter 2000.
7. Incidentally, this lengthy process is also favoured by Mnouchkine, who declared she could not rehearse a play in a month (Mnouchkine 1967).
8. He was not entirely enthusiastic about her production of *1789*, which he detailed to her in a long letter, but ends with congratulations and the assurance that he will ring Oscar Lewenstein to bring the production to the Roundhouse (AW4 1970).
9. The initially planned tour could not take place due to the size of the set and the availability of the actors.
10. Though the production had a limited impact, Bastos has overlooked Pierre della Torre's 1974 production of *Jerusalem*.
11. Glenda Leeming (1983: 54) also points to the Chekhovian qualities of *Jerusalem*.
12. For production details, see Williams (1999: 239).
13. The only adverse notices came from Pierre Marcabru (*Figaro Magazine*), who had previously condemned Wesker for *Chips* and whose scathing views were not representative of *The Friends'* reception.

REFERENCES

Baignères, Claude (1967), 'La Cuisine d'Arnold Wesker', *Le Figaro*, 10 April.
Bastos, Jean-Louis, and Etienne, Anne (2018), Telephone interview, 20 December.
Billington, Michael (1977), 'Wesker bounces back', *The Guardian*, 19 January.
Bradby, David (1984), *Modern French Drama 1940–1980*, Cambridge: CUP.
—— (2002), 'Cultural politics and theatrical practice in the history of the Théâtre du Soleil', in D. Bradby and M. Delgado (eds), *The Paris Jigsaw: Internationalism and the City's Stages*, Manchester: Manchester University Press, pp. 113–30.
Broussouloux, Claude (1981), 'Une mort amicale', *Combat*, May.
Cartier, Jacqueline (1968), 'Les quatre saisons', *FranceSoir*, 7 October.
Chavassieux, Gilles (2019), E-mail to author, 14 April.
Cleave, Maureen (1981), 'If it weren't for the foreigners, I should be in despair', *The Observer*, 4 October.
Debreuille, Jean-Yves (2010), 'Le clavecin bien tempéré de la dramaturgie', in J-Y. Debreuille (ed.), *Jean Tardieu: Des Livres et des voix*, Lyon: ENS éditions, pp. 219–32.
Dumur, Guy (1981), 'Les amis', *Le Nouvel Observateur*, 22–28 May.
Frazier, Arlette (1981), *Pariscope*, n.d.
Galey, Matthieu (1968a), 'Un poème à deux voix', *Combat*, 9 October.
—— (1972), 'Frites, frites, frites: Une démonstration consciencieuse', *Combat*, 17 January.
—— (1981), 'Agonie', *Les Nouvelles littératures*, May.

Gautier, Jean-Jacques (1968a), 'Les Quatre saisons', Le Figaro, 7 October.

——— (1972), 'Des Frites, des frites, des frites', Le Figaro, 17 January.

——— (1974), 'Je parle de Jérusalem', Le Figaro, 18 May.

——— (1981), 'Symbiose en chambre', Figaro Magazine, 13 June.

Greenstein, Rosalind (2000), 'La Trilogie d'Arnold Wesker: Récit d'une transposition', Coup de théâtre, 16, December, pp. 63–83.

Hanoteau, Guillaume (1968), 'Pour survivre le théâtre mobilise toutes ses gloires', Paris Match, 21 Sept.

Hayman, Ronald (1979), Arnold Wesker, 3rd ed., London: Heinemann.

Hobson, Harold (1962), 'Chips with Everything', The Sunday Times, 29 April.

Jamet, Dominique (1981), 'L'avenir n'est plus ce qu'il était', Le Quotidien de Paris, May.

Kanters, Robert (1968), 'Quatre saisons aux couleurs de l'automne', L'Express, 14 October.

——— (1974), Review of Je parle de Jérusalem, L'Express, n.d.

Kerbrat, Patrice, and Etienne, Anne (2019), Telephone interview, 15 January.

Kourilsky, Françoise (1967), 'Un "trois étoiles"', Le Nouvel Observateur, 19–26 April.

Lascar, Serge (2019), E-mail to author, 27 May.

Leeming, Glenda (1983), Wesker the Playwright, London: Methuen.

Leeming, Glenda, and Trussler, Simon (1971), The Plays of Arnold Wesker, London: Gollancz.

Le Masque et la plume (1967), France Inter, France, 23 April, https://www.ina.fr/audio/ PHD99205692. Accessed 28 May 2019.

Leonardini, Jean-Pierre (1967), 'L'enfer c'est les fourneaux', L'Humanité, n.d.

——— (1972), 'La petite illusion', L'Humanité, 18 January.

Madral, Philippe (1968a), 'Une distance jamais comblée', L'Humanité, 8 October.

Marcabru, Pierre (1972a), 'Des frites, des frites, des frites… Indigeste', FranceSoir, 15 January.

——— (1972b), 'Des frites à la sauce anglaise', Journal du Dimanche, 16 January.

Martin-Barbaz, Jean-Louis, and Etienne, Anne (2018), Telephone interview, 11 December.

Mnouchkine, Ariane (1967), Interviewed by Paul Louis Mignon, Le théâtre, Office national de radiodiffusion télévision française, 23 April, https://www.ina.fr/video/I18149785. Accessed 7 January 2017.

Patterson, Michael (1995), 'The reception of Arnold Wesker's plays in Europe', History of European Ideas, 1:3, pp. 31–34.

Pierre, Henri (1972), 'Le naturalisme selon Bond et Wesker', Le Monde, 6 January.

Poirot-Delpech, Bertrand (1967), 'La Cuisine d'Arnold Wesker', Le Monde, 9–10 April.

——— (1972), 'Des frites, des frites, des frites', Le Monde, 18 January.

Ribes, Jean-Michel, and Etienne, Anne (2019), Telephone interview, 16 January.

Richardson, Helen (2016), 'Jacques Lecoq, Ariane Mnouchkine and the Théâtre du Soleil', in M. Evans and R. Kemp (eds), The Routledge Companion to Jacques Lecoq, Oxon and NY: Routledge, pp. 307–15.

Schifres, Alain (1968), 'Racines triomphera-t-il à Paris', Réalités, 275, December, pp. 98–100.

Tesson, Philippe (1981), 'Les amis (Tchékhov à Chelsea)', Le Canard enchaîné, n.d.

Thébaud, Marion (2003), 'Le défi de Jean-Louis Martin-Barbaz', *Le Figaro*, 11 April.

Vigouroux-Frey, Nicole (2000), 'Caryl Churchill et la France', *Coup de Théâtre*, 16 December, pp. 135–48.

Wesker, Arnold (1977–78), 'A sense of what should follow', *Theatre Quarterly*, 7:28, pp. 5–24.

—— (1990), *The Kitchen and Other Plays*, London: Penguin.

—— (2000), 'What makes a work of literature last through time and able to cross frontiers?', *Coup de Théâtre*, 16, December, pp. 135–48.

—— (2001a), *One-Woman Plays*, London: Methuen.

—— (2001b), 'Ariane', unpublished memoir, 15 April. Personal copy.

Wesker, Arnold Papers (AW) (1965), Review of *Four Seasons* by Daniel Salem, n.d., Austin, Texas: Harry Ransom Center, Box 109.1.

—— (1966), Notes on initial manuscript of *The Friends*, 5 July, Austin, Texas: Harry Ransom Center, Box 35.6.

—— (1967a), *Figaro Littéraire*, 2 March, Austin, Texas: Harry Ransom Center.

—— (1967b), *Nouvel Obs*, 1–8 March, Austin, Texas: Harry Ransom Center.

—— (1968), Foreign press, Reviews of *Roots*, 1–15 December, Austin, Texas: Harry Ransom Center, Box 111.5.

—— (1970), Letter from Frank Marcus, 4 June, Austin, Texas: Harry Ransom Center, Box 36.11.

—— (1980), Letter from Lars Schmidt, 8 October, Austin, Texas: Harry Ransom Center, Box 68.4.

—— (1981a), Letter from Jacques Huisman to Wesker, 27 February, Austin, Texas: Harry Ransom Center, Box 96.3.

—— (1981b), Director's note in programme of *The Friends*, May, Austin, Texas: Harry Ransom Center, Box 38.3.

—— (1986a), Second draft of *Betty Lemon*, 18 January, Austin, Texas: Harry Ransom Center, Box 102.9.

—— (1986b), Letter to Jean-Michel Ribes, 13 May, Austin, Texas: Harry Ransom Center, Box 102.9.

—— (1986c), Letter from Ribes, 16 May, Austin, Texas: Harry Ransom Center, Box 102.9.

—— (1986d), Letter to Ribes, 20 May, Austin, Texas: Harry Ransom Center, Box 102.9.

—— (1986e), Letter to Francine Bergé, 31 August, Austin, Texas: Harry Ransom Center, Box 2.3.

—— (1988), Letter from Patrice Kerbrat, 26 May, Austin, Texas: Harry Ransom Center, Box 68.3.

—— (1993), Diary entry, 16 January, Austin, Texas: Harry Ransom Center, Box 292.2.

—— (1994a), Draft letter to Stephen Daldry, 31 August, Austin, Texas: Harry Ransom Center, Box 48.5.

—— (1994b), Correspondence with Anne Mayer, 9–10 February, Austin, Texas: Harry Ransom Center, Box 48.7.

——— (1994c), Diary entry, 2 December, Austin, Texas: Harry Ransom Center, Box 294.9.

——— (1994d), Correspondence between Wesker, Loriol and Greenstein, 13 May–15 December, Austin, Texas: Harry Ransom Center, Box 100.2.

AW2 (1974), Director's note in programme of *Jerusalem*, 7–30 May, Austin, Texas: Harry Ransom Center, Box 39.9.

AW4 (1970), Draft letter to Ariane Mnouchkine, 18 November, Austin, Texas: Harry Ransom Center, Box 12.

Wilcher, Robert (1991), *Understanding Arnold Wesker*, Columbia: University of North Carolina Press.

Williams, David (ed.) (1999), *Collaborative Theatre: Le Théatre du Soleil*, London: Routledge.

Wolff, Stéphane (1967), '*Racines* d'Arnold Wesker', *L'Entracte*, 1–15 March.

Zand, Nicole (1968), '*La Cuisine* à l'usine', *Le Monde*, 17 June.

Drawings by Felix Topolski of Nichola McAuliffe and Arnold Wesker
in rehearsal for *Annie Wobbler*

FIGURE 10: Drawings by Felix Topolski of Nichola McAuliffe and Arnold Wesker in rehearsal for *Annie Wobbler*, 1983.

9

Wesker the Visual Artist – 'Ah! Sweet Mystery of Life!'

Pamela Howard

How I met Arnold Wesker

Birmingham Repertory Theatre, March 1959. I am in the paint shop cleaning buckets. I am 19 and imagining this is how one begins a career as a theatre designer. The air is heavy with the smell of size and rabbit glue and poisonous pigments. In between cleaning the buckets, I am cutting out canvas ivy leaves, dipping them into size and, when dry, wiring them on to lengths of rope to be draped over the gaps in the scenery, where the flats depicting drawing rooms and grand houses never quite met. Into this mouse-ridden temple of the arts, suddenly came a young man... an actor... and he actually spoke to us. This was extraordinary as actors never came up those black iron spiral stairs. He had momentous news. He told us that just 'down the road' in Coventry, in the new Belgrade Theatre, some writers were putting on plays about 'people like us', and furthermore, if the M1 motorway was to be finished in time, he was going to hire a car and drive 45 miles to Coventry to see these plays, and stay overnight, or possibly even two nights. He urged us to join him saying it was the most important event ever. We were shocked and filled with disbelief. 'Don't be silly', we said to the young Albert Finney, for it was he. 'No-one is going to write plays about people like us!' Rather primly we said we would have to ask our parents first. That night, I related this to them, and my parents firmly warned that if I went, I would die of 'motorway madness' ... and since this was the first motorway to be built, I believed them.

However, we three bucket cleaners and ivy leaf makers decided to defy fate, and I was deputed to leave a polite note in the young man's pigeon hole at the stage door saying we would go. The motorway opened, and tragically just before these plays opened, the Director of the Belgrade Theatre Bryan Bailey was indeed killed in a crash on the motorway. The other two girls dropped out, but I was determined to defy fate and go, and so we drove those 45 miles and went to the theatre and saw the last part of the Wesker *Trilogy*, and I couldn't believe it. Not only were the plays totally different from anything I had ever seen, but they were beautiful and poetic to look at. There were no dead ivy leaves. Just a line of washing… a well-chosen chair… a perfect table, and the words! Who has written this, I wondered, and who has made this beautiful staging? There was a small café, and we went to have a cup of tea. And then a tall elegant lady came up to us, and said she knew we came from the Birmingham Rep, and thanked us, and introduced herself as Jocelyn Herbert, the designer. She said she had been in Germany and met Bertolt Brecht, and that was where she had learned to 'place things beautifully in the space'. Thus started a lifetime's friendship. I asked her timidly who had written these plays, and suddenly a little jovial man behind us said, 'well actually I have – I am Arnold Wesker'. He sat down with us and asked us if we liked what we had seen. 'Oh yes,' we said, and we are staying in Coventry to see them all, and something called *Look Back in Anger* – 'well, that's not mine', he said dismissively. Then he looked at me quizzically and said those familiar words… 'are you…?' and I said 'yes' and I knew we would go on knowing each other.

Artistic collaborations

It was several years later, when my career was well on its way, that we met again. I was working in France during the 1970s, and while in Paris, I saw Ariane Mnouchkine's marvellous spare production of *The Kitchen*. This was the theatre I wanted to make. Then, in Lyon, at the Théâtre National Populaire, I re-united with my old Jewish Study Group friend, the late and much missed Michael Kustow, who was also working there. We talked about the impact of the Wesker plays, and Michael told me he knew the Weskers well and would introduce me. And so it was that Arnold and Dusty (CEO of the Arnold Wesker Industry) invited me to Bishops Road dinners – famous for food and talk and arguments. On the walls were paintings of artists they admired, Philip Sutton's Japanese prints, Lisa Dalton's paintings and John Allit's wonderful detailed paintings of Whitechapel life, especially the one of Gardiners Corner and the Cable Street uprising. Apart from words, Arnold loved and appreciated art and was himself a good artist. This consolidated our connection.

In 1982, Arnold began to think about another of his mini-cycle of One Woman Plays – in this case *Annie Wobbler*. He conceived it as a vehicle for the actress Nichola McAuliffe, and it was, as the initials of Annie Wobbler suggest, a version of himself. In the very early stages, he talked to me about his admiration for the Polish-born artist Feliks Topolski, and he was amazed to discover that I too admired this prolific illustrator, war artist, chronicler of world history, painter and mural artist, to mention just a few of his skills. Topolski worked in a large studio under the arches in Waterloo, and Arnold invited me to accompany him on a memorable visit. We entered a huge dark subterranean world which was both a work space and a haphazard exhibition. My passion, then as now, is drawing, a habit drummed into me from daily compulsory life classes at art school. There, in this spidery railway arch, I saw hundreds of lyrical black pen line drawings, fluidly racing over the paper as if singing and flying at the same time. The result of this visit was that Arnold was able to get Topolski to agree to come to some early rehearsals of *Annie Wobbler* that took place in the lounge of the Wesker house and to draw Nichola. Topolski allowed Annie Productions to use one of the drawings for the poster and in the programme. In this drawing (Figure 10), Topolski has captured four wonderfully mobile faces of Nichola McAuliffe and then a small Arnold Wesker sitting on the floor against a wall, deep in thought, possibly contemplating the 'sweet mystery of life', the musical theme in *Annie Wobbler*.

A visual artist

Arnold was a collector of art but was not known as a visual artist. In his cottage above Hay-on-Wye, over the space of three years in the mid-1980s, Arnold started drawing his immediate surroundings, using a direct technique of ink on paper. Later he said he surprised himself and that he had found it the most intense and absorbing process.

When I first saw these drawings on the walls of the house in Hove, I too was immensely surprised, for I recognized immediately how unusual it is to have the confidence and courage to draw directly with ink on paper where it is not possible to make mistakes. As far as can be seen, there is no pencil drawing that could be erased, and unlike writing no crossing out, second thoughts, additions, subtractions: these drawings are just what they are. To be able to compose these images, he had to start with the foreground, much as Michelangelo did with a block of marble, and work through to the background, composing the picture as he 'walked through the paper'. It is immensely brave. This is not photography, or documentary – it is a poetic realization of a private space. But look carefully at the composition (Figure 11). The central focus of the image is an empty space, and all the objects ranged on three sides, almost like a conventional stage setting. There is an air of expectancy, as if something is going to happen. In the foreground is a view of 'the chair' so carefully drawn, an object that re-appears

FIGURE 11: Drawing by Arnold Wesker of his study in Blaendiggedi, his home in the Black Mountains above Hay-on-Wye, 1986.

again and again in these images. This drawing must have started with this chair, so surely rendered in pen and ink, facing the apparatus of a writer – blank pages and an empty typewriter.

All of Arnold's drawings have a very particular 'point of view' as if he has been choosing the shot through a camera lens to best tell the story. Here is the second most important icon: the kitchen table (Figure 12). So much happens around tables in his dramatic works, and in Jewish families everything happens around a table. Here the great issues of life, personal and political, are argued and battled with, and however opposing, the views always contain a degree of hope. One chair is pulled out as though someone has just left the room maybe as a result of a telephone call, that the caller had to look up the number in an old paper telephone directory, which is on the table. This small gesture creates an air of expectancy and uncertainty, and the viewer may speculate on what happened in that moment before. Further analysis of this drawing reveals that Arnold instinctively understood that in order to emphasize the importance of the table, there would have to be a contrast in the background, and so with a fine pen he has carefully textured the cushions, the carved sideboard, the textile

FIGURE 12: Drawing by Arnold Wesker of the kitchen in Blaendiggedi, 1984.

FIGURE 13: Colour drawing by Arnold Wesker of the kitchen in Blaendiggedi, 1988.

on the armchair and the lampshade above. As in the previous drawing, this must have started with the centre downstage leg of the table and then worked backwards through the paper. It is astonishingly competent because it is incredibly hard to start with the first thing nearest to you and then work back into the paper.

The next drawing (Figure 13), which appears to be the other side of the previous image, is a curiosity. By placing the table almost out of the picture, he has allowed his pen to flow more freely. The lines are less rigid; the plates are leaning forward eagerly, almost like spectators. He has acquired a watercolour box and used a small brush delicately and playfully to colour in the surfaces. Here, however, he draws attention to the outside world. The collection of china plates and bottles lead the eye to a vase of Chinese Lanterns and, in the outside world, a tree whose leaves have fallen. Did he re-arrange the chairs for this image? In the far right corner, the hint of a chair at the head of a table where Arnold so often presided.

Figure 14 shows an extraordinary drawing of Arnold's workplace high up in the hills. Its empty central space is full of mystery and tension and question, so many questions, so characteristic of our Jewish culture. Where was he sitting to draw this perspective overlooking the valley below, the curtains fluttering in the breeze from the open door? Once more, this recalls a stage setting for a play when

FIGURE 14: Drawing by Arnold Wesker of his study in Blaendiggedi, from another perspective, 1984.

the central character will shortly arrive, and is a good example how Wesker often used the 'quotidienne' assembly of objects to reflect visually the story he had in mind. However, there is no evidence of the familiar typewriter, but on the work table and in exactly the central focus of the drawing an old fashioned tape recorder/radio; to the right a large box of what looks like scripts or papers, and below a small open notebook. The chair is firmly pushed into the table as if the author has finished the work in hand. Above over the door and on the walls are what could be Japanese fans and a Japanese straw hat and on the side workbench a Japanese water bottle. Japan had a special place in Wesker's heart because he developed a rich production history since his first invitation there in 1968. (I possess his collection of kimonos!) We glimpse by the open door an arm of a Victorian button back sofa. It might be concluded that this is where Wesker was recording his biography as he did throughout his working life. Like any recording it has his life but not his body, but we feel his presence precisely through his absence.

A sitting room drawn from an extraordinary perspective, in a masterly fashion, where Wesker must have been standing or sitting at the bottom right of the picture (Figure 15). The contrasting textures of materials, eclectic collection of furniture (where did he get it all from?) speak of security, comfort, home – the door

FIGURE 15: Drawing by Arnold Wesker, a sitting room, 1985.

firmly closed to the outside world. The back of a chair waiting for its sitter in front of the open fireplace adds to the dynamic of the perspective, and this chair is engaged in a conversation with the wing back armchair. It is the most homely of all the drawings, and the amount of observation and detail is more elaborate than a quick sketch. The astonishing accomplishment is the direct drawing on the paper. Working from the two floor cushions and the coffee table down front to the fireplace at the back, the perspective is both accurate and lyrical. Since the viewer sees the full surface of the coffee table, Wesker must have been standing well above or maybe sitting on a high stool. They say every picture tells a story, and these drawings, relatively unknown, made before Parkinson's disease struck, demonstrate the synchronicity of word and vision that is central to the understanding of Wesker's dramatic visions.

Finally, a surprise. A portrait of his chair (Figure 16), created freely in impasto paint, seemingly with a palette knife, or more likely with a kitchen knife. This wonderful painting set against a plain background has nothing to deflect its impact. Only an imagined, almost oriental beautifully placed green twig, its leaves pointing in the opposite direction to the chair. It is a sophisticated image that reads as a self-portrait without the human figure… and in all these works of self-imposed isolation, Arnold never drew people.

FIGURE 16: Painting by Arnold Wesker of his chair, 1966.

In *Annie Wobbler*, the musical theme is an old 78 record of 'Ah Sweet Mystery of Life', sung by Richard Crooks. At the end of Act III, in the final moment, the famous Annabella Wharton recalls how the record that belonged to her father always stuck at 'myst' and would repeat itself over and over again. These drawings are also a mystery in Arnold's life. How did he know how to do this highly sophisticated work with such eloquence and confidence? If he had not become a writer, might he have become an artist like Topolski? Ah! Sweet Mystery of Life...

FIGURE 17: A painting of Arnold Wesker as Annie Wobbler, by Pamela Howard.

10

A Charming Rogue: Wesker's Relationship with Women – and with Himself

Michael Fry

He tells me that he keeps everything – letters, programmes, memorabilia, trivia, and, I suspect, injustices.

(AW 1997: n.pag.)

Letters and liaisons

The Wesker collection of works and papers, which was acquired by the Harry Ransom Center at the University of Texas in 1999, is among the largest in the Center's extensive library. The archive, at 286 catalogued boxes, is far larger than, for example, Tom Stoppard's (149 boxes), John Osborne's (50 boxes), Tennessee Williams's (76 boxes) or David Hare's (37 boxes), and Wesker was peeved that these other files were deemed more valuable, in pecuniary terms, than his own – references to income and wherewithal are a recurrent motif throughout his correspondence. The archive is voluminous because Wesker appears to have retained every letter, contract and article (and draft articles) connected to his work and daily life, as well as the various manuscripts (and drafts) of the plays themselves. He was an inveterate diarist, as indicated in his autobiography, *As Much as I Dare* (1994), and in his lengthy reflection on the American production of *The Merchant*, which became *The Birth of Shylock and the Death of Zero Mostel* (1997).[1] He had protracted communication with many friends and colleagues – mainly women – and kept not only their letters to him but usually a (typed) copy of his own to them as well. Whether this suggests sentimentality or a sense of his own posterity is equivocal.

187

This chapter assesses, through some of the key correspondence, the importance of Wesker's relationship with women both in his life and in his plays (though the two are intricately connected as he frequently asserted), with particular reference to the one-woman plays that he wrote during the 1980s and which seem to reflect his own concomitant frustrations quite as much as those of the wives, mothers and mistresses he depicts. One of his favoured vocations during the 1990s was to give his own epic (up to five-hour) readings of the one-woman plays, which he performed variously, and with surprising success, over three continents.

The 'charming rogue' allusion is by his close friend, the actor Frank Barrie, suggesting both Wesker's geniality and his obduracy (as well as his philandering) (2018: n.pag.). It also reflects on the curious dichotomy between his public persona as a belligerent confrontationist and the convivial, compassionate man described by his many acquaintances and expressed through his letters. His widow, Dusty Wesker, from whom he was estranged for a number of years, confirms both his 'thick skin' and his 'vulnerability', a paradox that may account for the anguish at the hostility towards his later plays, manifesting itself in countless abusive broadsides (some private, many public) at the critics and artistic directors who rejected his work (Wesker 2018: n.pag.). The characters in the one-woman plays also seem to exemplify a disenchantment with the world and their perception of how it has treated them. They too possess a resilience, a stubbornness and an engaging liveliness, if not always the palpable wit and hilarity that Wesker claimed for them in the correspondence.

While there is some bitterness, there is no sense of envy in the correspondence (he was bemused by Pinter's and Osborne's success, according to Dusty Wesker, but not jealous of it) nor anything malevolent or vengeful. What comes across is mostly disappointment and exasperation, or a sense of what he described in the autobiography as 'a need, a wish, to see all humanity as equally good and sensible, and the experience of much of humanity as stupid and irrational, often cruel' (Wesker 1994: 326). There is certainly ego, a brazen lack of humility and a predetermination to have the last word, but there is also ebullience, loyalty and transparent family obsession. His humanitarian causes have been frequently chronicled, and the Weskers' hospitality was legendary, but the correspondence also records his generosity to many aspiring writers and artists – requests were answered, professional advice offered (not always positive) and accommodation provided where necessary.

His parents brawled throughout his childhood. Wesker maintained that as a result he always steered clear of confrontation, and while this may have been largely true in his personal and working relationships – Garry O'Connor, who documented the rehearsal process of his production of *The Friends* (1970), was astonished by his 'extraordinary tenacity' in the face of a barrage of abuse from the cast – his correspondence shows an astonishing unreserve and provocation, whether the recipient was a critic or an ingenuous member of the public (O'Connor 1971: 85). An audience member for one of his readings of the one-woman plays at the Young Vic (Carole Denton) wrote to explain why she walked out at one of the intervals, suggesting that she was bored and the characterizations were trite:

> As a mother of two, and Jewish, I could neither recognise anyone I knew in them, nor in any way identify with them [...] I suggest you see 'Shirley Valentine' or Jackie Mason who, in their different ways, are hitting truths that ring the bell of interest and depth of understanding.
>
> (AW 1990b: n.pag.)

Wesker replied:

> If you register Shirley Valentine then I don't think my work is for you [...] I do think you ought to reflect on the notion that all that matters to you is that you must be able to 'identify' with characters. That would pre-suppose that every woman in literature must exist within the intellectual and emotional confines which are Carole Denton.
>
> (AW 1990c: n.pag.)

Wesker was not the only prominent post-war dramatist to suffer from early acclaim and future indifference. John Arden, Peter Barnes, Edward Bond and Ann Jellicoe experienced a similar lack of regular revival or interest in later works, but (and while Bond is hardly docile) they did not pen recurrent articles haranguing the critics and berating artistic directors for their lack of taste and foresight.

While the majority of his correspondents are women, Wesker appears to have replied volubly to anyone who wrote to him. 'My character is tattered with many flaws but the courtesy of acknowledging the effort someone has made to contact me is inviolate' (Wesker 1994: 397). It seems not to have mattered whether the writer was mentally ill, such as the prisoner in Broadmoor ('Daryl, Block 4') sentenced for smashing the cross in Westminster Abbey – or as Daryl put it, 'this ghastly, gilded, grave image, the Golden Calf of the Establishment and a false symbol of Christianity' – a virulent racist such as 'Butch' of Southwick, Sussex, 'c/o the Canadian Anti-Semitic Association – H.Q. Berlin' or a volatile, aspiring playwright:

> Dear Arnold Wesker,
> Yes it is a bastard when some fuck pig of a Critic who can't write a sausage has the gall to say anything about an artist; any fucking thing [...] Why don't the IRA blow up all fucking theatres and the bastards who run them.
>
> (AW 1954: n.pag.)

Wesker entered into a long and implausible correspondence with a 'Flossie B Avon', who may have been a pseudonymous satirist (although Dusty Wesker thinks they met on at least a couple of occasions) and who wrote a series of increasingly besotted letters during the 1990s. The correspondence includes a poem – 'I like your NOSE, It's not too long, I even like your EYES, your hairy arms look oh so STRONG, and Flossie never LIES' – a Valentine's card and passionate commiserations during his estrangement from Dusty, about which he presumably confided in Flossie (AW 1991b: n.pag.).

His principal correspondents in the archives are three women with whom he seemed to have had deeply intimate yet platonic relationships: the actor Brenda Bruce (three crammed boxes of hundreds of mail and faxes – Bruce regularly wrote ten-page rambles through the night to 'Boss A'), the screenwriter Linda Aronson (written mostly from and to Melbourne and of a similar length and passion to Bruce's) and the Spanish actor and director Nuria Espert (slightly more pithy, and with English as a second language). Wesker confided in all three of them about his infidelities. He told the psychiatrist Anthony Clare (during a recording of the BBC's *In the Psychiatrist's Chair*) about his uncontrollable 'need to tell all', but the intimacy of these letters – to other women, about his relationships – is unusual (Clare 1982: n.pag.). 'I've stayed in Ashley Road the last two times I've been in London', he wrote to Espert during the breakup of his marriage:

> which was both good and bad, and confusing for everybody – friends, family, Dusty and me. But it seemed so natural being there. That's the problem of my life – everything I do seems natural. I'm not sure how to describe it, what to call it, but just as some people are colour-blind, tone-deaf, dyslexic so there is something wrong with my – what? Head? Heart? Emotions? Intelligence? Sensitivity?
>
> (AW 1992a: n.pag.)

There are also a good number of discrete boxes for various female agents, producers and translators, which similarly transcend a business relationship. Those to Berit Gullberg, his Scandinavian agent, Connie Ricono, his Italian translator and Nina Adler, his German translator, are particularly striking in their combination of the commercial and the personal. After Adler's early death, Wesker wrote to their mutual friend Ursula Pegler to say that he was disappointed (and 'astounded') that his letters to Adler had gone missing and 'should have amounted to at least a box file full. Her letters to me occupy at least three files. There was vast correspondence between us over her translation of *Shylock*' (AW 1993a: n.pag.).

Women and one-woman plays

'Women! Ah, women! I love them! Their touch, their looks, their smells [...] I can't bear to be without them', declares Dominic in *The Journalists*, and Wesker expresses similar feelings throughout his letters and journals (Wesker 1979: 119). In *As Much As I Dare*, he references Charlie Chaplin's claim that he'd 'never looked at a woman without measuring the possibility of what could be between us', rationalizing that for himself he 'simply measure[s]; but there were times, too many perhaps, when I argued with myself: how can you deny this woman's uniqueness, her spirit, her smell, her intelligence, [...] the explosion of passion, how?' (Wesker 1994: 69). In the revealing radio interview with Anthony Clare, Wesker speaks more equivocally about his relationship with women, acknowledging that while he happily flirted with nearly every woman he met, any liaison had always been prompted by the other party. He ponders on how he simply preferred the company of women over men. 'Even now, with few exceptions, I don't enjoy male company' (Clare 1982: n.pag.). According to his friend and collaborator Nichola McAuliffe, he always looked completely at ease when surrounded by women, while there was evident antipathy, on both sides, between Wesker and what she terms 'certain types of men' (such as her own husband, the Scottish journalist Don Mackay). McAuliffe also suggests that his reputation for flirting may have been overstated. 'I never saw any sight of it – although perhaps it was just me. He was always completely professional and very respectful of my ideas' (McAuliffe 2018: n.pag.).

His preference for women over men is reflected in his work. Even before the one-woman plays, Wesker had been unusual among his male contemporaries in writing leading roles for particularly spirited female characters, a feature he attributed to his upbringing. 'My mother runs through all my work; seventy-five per cent of my characters are women', he claimed (cited in Cleave 1981: n.pag.), noting that in all his male/female relationships, 'it's the woman who emerges as the strongest and often most sympathetic of the two' (Wesker 1971: 162). He often cited the *Book of Genesis* in his letters and interviews, pointing out that 'boring old Adam wanted to hang around paradise bathing in the bliss of ignorance; Eve, bolder and more adventurous, was prepared to take the risk and explore knowledge' (Staff 2001: n.pag.).

His writing for women became a badge of honour. In the programme note for the first production of *Annie Wobbler* (1983), he wrote:

> Wesker, whose Beatie Bryant in *Roots* gave Joan Plowright her first leading role and whose Sonia in *Love Letters on Blue Paper* won Elizabeth Spriggs a SWET award has again given a relatively unknown actress the enormous challenge, and gift, of three dramatic studies of women ranging from 25 to 60 years of age.
>
> (AW 1983: n.pag.)

While writing *Roots* (1959), he wrote to Dusty in Norfolk outlining the plot and acknowledging the clear autobiography:

> In the play I fail to turn up – ever, and after some terrible misery and 'there I told you so' from the family you turn round and say 'So what! I do not need him now!' [...] And the triumph of the play is not my triumph but yours. The intellectual has betrayed but the ordinary man – girl – had found her own voice, her own language. Funny that, the triumph of Chicken Soup is also not my triumph but my mother's. I wonder why.
>
> (AW 1958b: n.pag.)

His identification with women was also shaped by his belief, continually noted in the autobiography, that male writers have a 'stronger feminine nature' than other men, although his empathy was sometimes excessive. 'All mothers fight for their children, and I'm a very Jewish mother!' he wrote to Max Stafford-Clark suggesting he produce *Caritas* as the Royal Court (AW 1982: n.pag.). He also told Clare that he regretted not being able to physically give birth to his three children, a sentiment that perhaps finds its fictional outlet through Deborah, the earth mother in *Four Portraits – of Mothers*, rhapsodizing about new motherhood, 'I loved carrying them, giving birth to them, suckling them' (Wesker 2001: 64).

The combination of hope and dejection that runs through all the one-woman plays perhaps reflects Wesker's quaint notion of himself as a 'happy pessimist' (Drabble 1998: 82). In the press release used to advertise his European readings, Wesker referred to the linking theme of 'time, the thief' in the plays (literally in the case of *Yardsale*, where the ticking of a clock divides the eight parts), but at the same time each one leaves the audience with an abstruse sense of affirmation at their conclusions. They have, as Robert Wilcher puts it when summarizing Wesker's writing, 'celebrated the resilience of those who persist in the face of discouragement and defeat and [...] devised ways of communicating the occasional victories that can sustain and console the human spirit' (Wilcher 1991: 154).

Where his earlier works offer an ostensible objectivity in the narrative pockets of East End (or East Anglian) society, the one-woman plays are brazenly subjective. A monologue gives no opportunity of comeback or contradiction, which perhaps suited Wesker's later years of dissent. The dialogue in the plays also advances from the routine realism of the earlier works to something more heightened and structured. The streams of consciousness, frequent repetitions and interminable lists offer a sort of meta-naturalism that is a strange and paradoxical mixture of both empathy and disengagement.

Wesker's correspondence during the 1980s and 1990s increasingly champions the one-person play and he points out, defensively, on more than one occasion that no one dismisses Beethoven's sonatas (for one instrument) as being lesser works than his symphonies and concertos – 'not that I would compare myself to Beethoven...' (AW 1992c: n.pag.). He also contends that he has not written monologues. 'A monologue is one person being reflective in various stages of emotion,' he wrote to Connie Ricono (AW 1990d: n.pag.). 'In my plays for one person there is always action – scrubbing a floor, cutting a pattern for a dress, making up etc. and there is always somebody else off-stage being addressed' (AW 1990d: n.pag.). Yet, being reflective in various stages of emotion is precisely what most of the characters are doing in the plays. They are monologues in that there is no one else physically on stage with whom to interact or verbally spar, and the action is limited: dressing or cooking or watching television are not especially animated exploits, and internal or imagined quarrels are not the same as those between two (or more) individuals, that Wesker himself conveyed so effectively in the early plays.

Annie Wobbler *(1983)*

The short monologues that comprise *Annie Wobbler* were the first of Wesker's one-woman plays. Like most of the later works, these were written for a particular actor, Nichola McAuliffe, whom Wesker had originally wanted for the central role in *Caritas* at the National Theatre, but who had been vetoed by director John Madden. The three women in *Annie Wobbler* share the same initials as their author, a blatant acknowledgement of some shared sentiments, although the title character was based on a cleaner from Wesker's childhood, with a genuine (if improbable) name. In many ways hers is the most vivid portrayal, perhaps because as in his early realizations Wesker was able to recall and keenly animate someone he knew well. Annie's dialogue and accent are well rendered, and her rhetoric rarely offers a false note. She is the only one of his solo characters whose preoccupations are not to do with sex or success, and Wesker offers a persuasive account of her deprivation and resilience. The directing of her thoughts to the off-stage 'Madam' (Wesker's mother), and occasionally to God, is convincing and less tenuous than the supposed addressees in some of the later plays. What she does have in common with all of the one-woman protagonists is an ability to reflect on her life's choices (and lack of choices), a need to make some sense of her existence and identity and an unexpected lucidity of expression.

The second monologue concerns an attractive student, Anna, dressed in black underwear and preparing for a date with her new boyfriend. The complete contrast with Annie Wobbler was designed partly as a brilliant acting coup (and costume change) for Nichola McAuliffe, and Wesker confirmed in the programme that the character of Anna ('over-brimming with energy') was inspired by

McAuliffe – though his description of her as 'an unknown actress with protruding teeth and a nose that seemed to have grown straight out of her forehead' is hardly gallant (Wesker 2001: xii).

Although Anna appears to have many positives in her life (a recent first-class degree, relative affluence, a good-looking boyfriend), the stage directions suggest that '*disturbing her sense of the future is a fear of what she might be leaving behind, that she may not be what she feels she* can *be*', a sentiment that Wesker often expressed in his journals (Wesker 2001: 16). Throughout the monologue she talks to herself in a tall mirror, delighting in what she sees, but concerned that the new boyfriend is attracted to her breasts more than her brains and the newly acquired Cambridge degree. 'Why *don't* men like their women to be clever? They like them to be clever, but not cleverer than them' (Wesker 2001: 20, original emphasis). While this seems a generically implicit criticism of his gender by Wesker (and one that he often substantiated in other writing), his own relationship with Dusty Wesker, as the principal theme in *Roots* infers, was not, from his perspective, one of intellectual equals. Dusty recounts:

> He never showed me the drafts of any of his plays, preferring to send them to Mike Kustow[2] and other friends for comments [...] He changed my name [from Doreen], insisted on planning every detail of our wedding himself and even designed my wedding dress, with an empire line that made me look pregnant.
> (Wesker 2018: n.pag.).

There is a patronizing, if affectionate, tone from the start, in his early courtship letters: 'Your flowers are carefully putaway [*sic*] in the covers of a book – though I somehow feel that flowers are meant to be alive and not dead and lost in a book but I like the thought' (AW 1958a: n.pag.). Despite being a bright, independent woman, until the end of the monologue Anna still needs the approval of a man to feel truly assured, and perhaps, despite his declared regard for women as the superior sex, Wesker also needed to play a more assertive role in his marriage and relationships.

The third character, Annabella Wharton, was loosely inspired by the American novelist Judy Rossner, whom Wesker got to know in New York during the rehearsals of *The Merchant* and whose recently acclaimed fourth novel, *Looking for Mr. Goodbar* (1975), had just been filmed. When he asked what it felt to be unexpectedly rich and famous, her retort – like the 'fucking Empress of China' – impressed him (Wesker 2001: xii). Annabella is a newly celebrated writer practising a series of press interviews in which she rehearses three entirely different persona – the diffident writer, the self-important writer and the more candid writer hindered by distrust and belittlement. A writer 'like myself', wrote Wesker, 'stumbled between arrogance, modesty and searing self-doubt' (Wesker 2001: xiii). He tended to be disarmingly honest in all his interviews and unlike Annabella relished the opportunity to talk about his work and his values. Here he supposes a vengeful deriding of the media, as Annabella offers contradictory, fabricated details to each journalist – for one she has a husband and four devoted children, for the next she is single and childless.

All three Annabellas make observations about the art of writing that are reminiscent of published remarks by Wesker himself, and while he sends them up for pretentiously quoting Dr Johnson, he himself cites Johnson twice in his radio interview with Clare. In the final moments of the play, Annabella is asked by the voice-over interviewer whether she has any fears. The reply seems much more Wesker than Annabella (who has by now assured us she has no children): 'Of being afflicted with a sense of futility. Of violence and certitudes. Of failing my son. Of being disliked [...] mediocre' (Wesker 2001: 44). Michael Billington shared this view, writing that 'the final unburdened self struck me as more Arnold than Annabella, more a personal projection than a real character' (Billington 1983: n.pag.). However, Michael Coveney, not a pervasive admirer of Wesker, concluded that 'a marvellous technical feat of writing sees Wesker both penetrate the skin of each woman and, at the same time, conduct an organised debate of issues close to his heart' (Coveney 1983: n.pag.). Nichola McAuliffe, in retrospect, maintains that only the first monologue offers a properly authentic character:

> The other two were much harder to play. They were too polemical, like a lot of his later works. If a character knows herself too well, as Annabella does, then there is nowhere for the actor to go with her, and nowhere to take an audience on a journey. Whereas Annie herself helps you discover the woman through her ignorance and imprecision.
>
> (McAuliffe 2018: n.pag.)

Whatever Happened to Betty Lemon? *(1986)*

Set in an Edwardian mansion flat, *Whatever Happened to Betty Lemon*, with its unmistakable reference to the film *Whatever Happened to Baby Jane* (1962), opens on an empty set, at the centre of which is an electric wheelchair and '*off centre [...] a rope looking like a noose, but without the hangman's knot*' (Wesker 2001: 89). That the first sound is a lavatory flush suggests the raw detail in which the protagonist's life will be conveyed, and the opening stage directions in many ways sum up the entire narrative. '*Betty Lemon appears, an old woman crippled by everything old age brings. Eccentric. She hobbles in with the aid of her walking frame. Surveys her flat. Another day is beginning. Gloom*' (Wesker 2001: 89).

Like most of the women in the plays, Betty's life has been sustained but mostly spoiled by men, principally her late husband, a Labour MP whose knighthood has left her with a title but little capital, and who was a 'philandering bastard [who] spent his seed more than his pennies' (Wesker 2001: 90). The plot, such as it is, revolves around a letter that Betty has just received inviting her to attend an event as 'Handicapped Woman of the Year', which makes her reflect on her life, her marriage and her disability. She is as contemptuous of the accolade as she is with its lack of tact, 'They telling me there's no one more handicapped in the entire fucking universe than me?' and derives amusement from fantasizing about the sort of inflammatory speech she will give should she decide to attend the ceremony (Wesker 2001: 91).

Her ruminations are principally directed at the noose (*'her daily companion with whom she converses'* (Wesker 2001: 89) and sometimes at her daughter's telephone answering machine, with its curt message 'I'm not here', suggesting that there is no love lost on either side of that relationship either (Wesker 2001: 103). In a rare acknowledgement of dramaturgical assistance, Wesker wrote to Krista Jussenhoven that

> the most helpful observation Nina [Adler] made about BETTY LEMON was that the daughter should appear sooner. I absolutely agree and have some additions (which I send). I'm very grateful because it has given the play another thread in the weave and also the opportunity for further comic invention and funny/charming moments.
>
> (AW 1986: n.pag.)

Betty is both crude and crabby, but Wesker evidently identifies with a character who rails at the injustices in society, reflects on her own disappointments and how the world has treated her and reassesses the meaning of incapacity: 'What about those handicapped by the wrong relationship until death do them part? [...] What about those handicapped by talent, taste, a touch of colour, style? [...] And what about those handicapped by despair'? What about *them*?' (Wesker 2001: 101–4). During the early previews of the play, Wesker sent Brenda Bruce a late-night fax reminding her not to make the character too likable:

> Perhaps you've hit the old problem actors have of wanting to be received sympathetically [...] I don't mean you should comment on your character in the way you perform her but if you're truthfully her, and you don't like *her*, then the hope is the audience won't like her and *that* will be your victory.
>
> (AW 1993b: n.pag.)

To Claretta Carotenuto, an Italian actor about to play the role, he suggested that

> She is a fierce personality who attracted irritation by her irreverent and uncon-
> ventional attitudes; and she probably irritates some people in the audience too!
> But she should finally be loved and respected by the audience for her honesty
> and the originality of her attitudes and her courage and her humour.
>
> (AW 1989: n.pag.)

He used similar expressions when defending his own behaviour to friends, although there is some irony here in the fact that he was empathizing with a seri-ally betrayed spouse.

There is a tendency to overwrite, as in all of these plays – 'what glorious son of man conceived such blushing laurels, such awesome accolades, such canon-isation?' – but a curious surreal element is also introduced (Wesker 2001: 91). The wheelchair moves of its own accord around the room and away from Betty, who is attempting to sit in it. It was a crucial part of the premise for Wesker, who reminded potential European producers that an autonomously moving chair was a dramatic (and licensing) stipulation. Aside from the metaphorical implication of an errant wheelchair, this ruse results in neat *coup de théâtre* when Betty uses the rope (which the audience assumes will be employed in a probable suicide attempt) to lasso the wheelchair and finally gets to sit in it at the end of the play, with the rope discarded. She, like Wesker and most of the other women, is too indomitable to submit to life's adversities, and the concluding lines are defiant and stoical: 'I didn't fucking plan it this way' (Wesker 2001: 105).

Yardsale *(1987)*

Written as a radio play for the actor Sheila Steafel and first broadcast by BBC Radio 3 in 1984, *Yardsale* (the American term for a car boot sale) was developed into a companion piece to *Whatever Happened to Betty Lemon?* and performed by Brenda Bruce at the Lyric, Hammersmith, in 1987. Set in Brooklyn (and later Manhattan), Stephanie, a middle-aged primary school teacher, returns home from work to prepare a meal for herself and Sheldon, her husband of 25 years. While cooking, she reflects on her marriage and how agreeable their companionship has proved now that the children have left home. In the second scene, she learns (from a letter placed in the bedroom) that Sheldon has left her to move in with a friend of theirs.

During the remainder of the short, eight-scene play, Stephanie attempts, on the advice of various girlfriends, to venture out and visit some of New York's iconic sites, while all the time bemoaning the 'husband-thief' and decrying her husband's lack of personality and other faults (including sexual inadequacy) (Wesker 2001: 75). Her animosity towards Sheldon, while logical, seems to indicate that perhaps they were not as well-matched as the first scene suggested, and a separation was inevitable. After visiting the Whitney Museum, the Serendipity restaurant and a Barnes and Noble bookshop, the final scene sees Stephanie arrive at a yardsale – not to dispose of her home contents but to buy new (second-hand) goods in an attempt to refresh her life. As she reflects that it was her husband's new partner who in fact introduced them to yardsales, and that 'from yardsales like this she furnished *his* new home', she ends the play suddenly weeping (Wesker 2001: 83, original emphasis).

A play about downsizing and children leaving home had obvious parallels with Wesker's life (financial imperatives had obliged him to sell his large house in Highgate, bought on the proceeds of *The Trilogy*, in 1986). Moreover, Arnold and Dusty Wesker had also been married for just over 25 years and their own separation was impending. In a series of letters to Brenda Bruce and Nuria Espert, he reveals the extent of the acrimony: 'I'd like to love Dusty again as I once did but she has destroyed too much in her anger – justified maybe, but destroyed even so' (AW 1992b: n.pag.). In *Yardsale*, in an inverse shift, Wesker writes himself into the character of the aggrieved wife of a fickle and insensitive spouse. There is a disassociation in making her American (the rhetoric is largely convincing although there are some anachronisms), but the characterization is striking, and Stephanie possesses a good deal of Dusty Wesker's warmth, sincerity and domesticity (during the entire first scene she is 'slicing, slapping and frying' (Wesker 2001: 72).

Stephanie is the most verbose of the women in the monologues and speaks in long sentences with extensive lists. Her speeches offer a rapid, New York-style pace, perhaps an indication of her latent hysteria: '*Not* because the bus was held up by all this snow which made my boots wet and reminds me I've got to buy a new pair which it so happens I saw on sale in that store which seems to have a non-stop-all-year-round sale so you wonder where they got their stock from' (Wesker 2001: 71, original emphasis). Perhaps because of its derivation as a radio play, Stephanie does not talk to an object or offstage person as the other plays do. Her monologue is a bewildered self-examination of her past and present life.

There is a letter in the archives from an unidentified 'Fran' thanking Wesker for basing the character of Stephanie on herself but regretting that the character is so fixated on disaffected reminiscences: 'I feel good about having inspired it, but I wish the woman had not remained self-pitying and bitter' (AW 1984: n.pag.). In fact, the dialogue in *Yardsale* is more compelling than in some of the other plays, because

Stephanie is witty and wry. Even on reading Sheldon's parting letter she is able to note its inconsistencies: ' "My dear Stephie." *My* dear Stephie? His? He's leaving me and claiming me at the same time' (Wesker 2001: 74, original emphasis). Later on, she reflects on his opinion of their relationship: ' "We are boring. I need to be able to surprise someone." I'm surprised Sheldon, am I surprised! [...] I laid on my back more times than I cared to for you. Surprises? You want surprises?' (Wesker 2001: 76). Some of Stephanie's self-probing questions at what she might have done to elicit her misfortune bear an uncanny resemblance to Wesker's own self-interrogation: 'Was my skin clammy? Was my voice droning? Were my thoughts boring?' she asks (Wesker 2001: 75). Reflecting on what he sees as his professional disregard in *As Much as I Dare*, Wesker writes, 'Does my breath smell? Are my armpits unwashed? I don't remember murdering anyone' (Wesker 1994: 8).

Yardsale is an urbane play that references the failure of a marriage, disappointment, loneliness and bitterness, all of which preoccupied Wesker (living on his own in Wales at the time) in varying degrees during the 1980s. There is both compassion and nostalgia in the play's concluding metaphor: Stephanie, the discarded wife, arriving at a sale for discarded objects and marvelling that people can just throw parts of their life away: 'A box full of postcards? [...] People write to you – it means something [...] I hang on to hellos – you need all the hellos you can get' (Wesker 2001: 83). Wesker, the inveterate letter hoarder, would undoubtedly have concurred with that sentiment.

Letter to a Daughter *(1998)*

In *Letter to a Daughter* ('a play in six parts with songs for an actress who can sing'), written in 1991 and first performed, in English, in 1998 at the Edinburgh Fringe Festival, a 35-year-old professional singer, Melanie, is preparing to write a letter to her 11-year-old daughter, Marike.[3] Melanie wants to apologize for failing as a single parent and to encourage the pre-pubescent Marike to make more positive choices as a woman than she did herself. Her protracted deliberations during each scene as she works out what she wants to say are in prose, but the finished letters that conclude it are sung. A series of mooted productions saw the role offered to an eclectic range of prominent performers, including Maria Friedman, Ute Lempe, Juliet Stevenson and even the Iranian ballad singer (but non-actor) Shusha Guppy, who all showed interest but ultimately declined.

The monologue is set in Melanie's workroom/studio – evidence of a successful career – and Wesker gives her four principal actions during its progression: watering her plants, fixing a fuse (when the lights go out), completing a photomontage of her daughter and preparing for 'an event'. She principally addresses her answering machine (*pace* Betty Lemon) – by responding to the messages left by Marike's father, who disappeared when Melanie was pregnant but now wants to re-enter her life – and the pictures in the photomontage.

At about the same time as the play's gestation, Wesker was writing a series of letters to his older son, Lindsay, who had ceased contact following his parents' separation.[4] Wesker's granddaughter – with whom he was also denied contact – was herself approaching teenage years, while Wesker, like the unnamed father at the end of the answering machine, had been a ruefully absent parent to Elsa, his daughter with the Swedish journalist Disa Håstad (Marike's name has Scandinavian overtones, for no discernible reason[5]).

While the play ostensibly depicts a mother's counsel to her child, as Melanie herself acknowledges, it increasingly reflects on the artist's – whether singer's or playwright's – career and familial challenges. From the first, sung lines of the play (reprised at its conclusion), Melanie's nostalgia seems to chime with Wesker's:

> No one can take
> From our time
> No one can shake
> The halcyon memories
> When nothing was beyond
> Our hopeful energies
> And every day
> In every way
> Was our time.
> (Wesker 2001: 144)

Yet, Melanie, like Wesker, has become cynical. She has few positive things to tell her daughter about humanity, and her preparative comments serve mostly as a warning against the individuals she will encounter: 'And here's the fourth and most important thing I have to tell you: select your peers. [...] *I* know sensitive people who got it wrong [in not recognizing her work]. Sensitive, intelligent, knowledgeable – wrong! Should have known better – wrong!' (Wesker 2001: 163, 144, original emphasis).

Like many of the women in the one-woman plays, Melanie is trying to work out what it is she wants to say and how she wants to say it. 'One of the reasons why the character keeps changing her mind is because she's full of doubts and uncertainties. We should see her in pain with those doubts and uncertainties', Wesker wrote to Giorgio Albertazzi, director of an Italian production of *Letter to a Daughter* (AW 1994: n.pag.). This generates an honesty in the writing – the streams of consciousness have a logical rapidity and a lack of rhetorical sophistication, but it doesn't always make for riveting drama. Melanie also speaks in cascades of lists

('Not a really kind, gentle, tender, intelligent, imaginative, interesting, supportive, thoughtful, respectful, educated, courageous, chivalrous, witty, thrilling, thrilling, thrilling man', which might suggest passion, or obsession, but is also so distractedly hyperbolic that it can disengage (Wesker 2001: 181). 'You do tend fearfully to over-write', wrote Lindsay Anderson on being sent a copy of *The Wedding Feast*, 'I know you dislike being told this, dear Arnold, and always resist the criticism fiercely, but it's true' (AW 1983b: n.pag.).

There is also a slightly awkward focus on Marike's developing bosom. It seems questionable whether a mother would be as continually fixated on her daughter's breasts as Melanie appears to be (there are over seven references) or whether she would refer to them as 'tender tits' (Wesker 2001: 152). Melanie herself also alludes more than once to her own youthful 'firm bum and erect nipples' (Wesker 2001: 155). The relative success of the one-woman plays owes much to Wesker's effective empathy with the status of women in society and relationships, but the plays take on a more doubtful aspect when he starts to personify female sexuality – especially since some of the imagery is analogous to passages from his avowedly erotic novel *The King's Daughters* (1998) (where twelve princesses have rather eye-opening encounters with princes and mythical creatures) and to intimate biographical experiences from *As Much As I Dare*. His own performances as the more voluptuous women in *The Mistress,* Anna in *Annie Wobbler* and *Letter to a Daughter*, in particular, must have been disorienting.

In the end, as Melanie acknowledges, 'this letter is going to be of no use to you at all' (Wesker 2001: 184), which rather substantiates her earlier comment that 'perhaps it's not a letter to Marike aged fourteen, but to Melanie aged thirty-five' or, it could be surmised, to Wesker himself, aged 60 (Wesker 2001: 152).

Director/playwright/player

When David Edgar, in a Conversation at the ICA, asked why if Wesker was so frustrated by the theatre he didn't turn to the novel, where he would have total autonomy, Wesker replied that he did not want to leave the theatre, but 'to get out of the clutches of people on whom one depends in the theatre' (Edgar 1985: n.pag.). One of the significant aspects of the one-woman plays was that they coincided with Wesker's immutable decision to direct all his new plays himself. He had already directed *The Friends* (rather disastrously) and *Love Letters on Blue Paper* (more fruitfully), as well as occasional European productions, but during the late 1970s, and in response to the failure of John Dexter's production of *The Merchant* in particular, he became increasingly proselytizing about the role of the writer/director. 'Directing is the continuation of the act of writing: you're really getting your last draft when you're directing' (TQ Symposium 1976: 70). The one-woman plays not only provided him with a vehicle to express his feelings, thoughts and prejudices through the mouths of these resolute women, they also afforded him the opportunity to serve as complete *auteur*.

Wesker's 400-page treatise on the rehearsals for *The Merchant* in *The Birth of Shylock and the Death of Zero Mostel* comprehensively documents his and Dexter's conflicting perspectives on the play and their deteriorating relationship. The archive contains the increasingly rancorous exchanges between them, and Wesker includes much, though not all, of their correspondence in a postscript to the book. In particular, Dexter posits that Wesker should not be so constantly interfering in the rehearsal process as he does not have a director's sensibility and cannot appreciate an actor's need to grow and develop:

> Your manner of delivering notes to me is, God knows, patronising enough. To the actors it is more dangerous in the depression and confusion it produces. From *The Old Ones* to *Shylock*, I have been begged by actors not to let you give them notes.
>
> (Wesker 1997: 346)

In an interesting presentiment of some of the problems of the one-woman plays, as well as Wesker's increasing compulsion for artistic control, he adds:

> You believe yourself to be a poetic writer. I believe you to be a superb writer of theatrical prose who can invent or provoke poetic theatrical moments, but whose glutonous [*sic*] poetics display neither your true voice nor a feeling for poetry itself. You must go on to find a director who shares your views, or direct your plays yourself.
>
> (Wesker 1997: 346)

The commentary in *The Birth of Shylock* has Wesker's characteristic candour, though Dexter is often portrayed as monstrous and Wesker himself as a reasonable, placatory force. Dusty Wesker has a different take on the culmination of their professional and personal relationship.[6] She suggested that in fact Wesker 'was impossible during the rehearsals, refused to cut the section about the gas chambers that ultimately inflamed the critics and was partly responsible for its failure – and he was having an affair with one of the actresses' – presumably Gloria Gifford, the actor playing Nerissa to whom he frequently refers in the book and who would seem to be the prototype for the eponymous *Lady Othello*, the black, New York single parent who has a relationship with an older, English, Jewish professor in a 1980 film script that remains unproduced (Wesker 2018: n.pag.).[7]

Thereafter, Wesker almost always directed the first productions of his plays, while grudgingly permitting an impressive array of British theatre directors (including Stephen Daldry, James Macdonald and Dominic Cooke) to mount the revivals.

Wesker in fact proved himself to be a more than competent, and sensitive, director of his own plays. His writing had always shown an alertness to theatrical craft, with a developed sense of action and stage pictures, perhaps related to his brief film school training. During their earlier, more congenial relationship, John Dexter averred that in Wesker's plays, more than most other playwrights, 'all the physical movements are all firmly indicated. *Tempi* are indicated. Development of characters during those passages are indicated. *Always*' (Hayman 1974: 66, original emphasis). Wesker's letters show an empathetic understanding of character and are written as much from a director's perspective as a playwright's. Two letters to actresses emphasize this – one to the Italian actor Claretta Carotenuto, who was performing *The Mistress* in Florence, comments: 'Great actors make an audience *listen* to them. Superficial actors make an audience merely *look* at them. I want you to belong to the first group' (AW 1991a: n.pag., original emphasis). Giving notes in a letter to Elizabeth Spriggs during the production of *Love Letters on Blue Paper*, he suggested:

> Each letter should have a different mood. I'm interested in the moods *you* find but I have a definite idea about the last two. The letter before the last is of course the *one* emotional letter. It's a breakdown. She loses control [...] And the last one must be simple, straight-forward. The emotion will be in the scene we are watching [...] There will be 'speakers' all around the audience so it will seem as though Sonia's voice is speaking in each person's ear, for them alone.
>
> (AW 1979: n.pag., original emphasis)

Most of the actors he worked with on the one-woman plays seemed to have found him helpful and accommodating. Nichola McAuliffe confirms that he was flexible and responsive in the rehearsal room and that an actor always felt comfortable making suggestions.[8] 'Like Peter Hall and unlike a lot of directors, he never said no' (McAuliffe 2018: n.pag.). Brenda Bruce's letters contain numerous and effusive thanks for his rehearsal guidance, while Frank Barrie, who played Archie Rice in Wesker's production of Osborne's *The Entertainer* (Theatr Clwyd 1987), the sole production he directed of another writer's work in England, described him as 'always encouraging and appreciative' (Barrie 2018: n.pag.).

His international collaborators sometimes found him less compliant. His friend, Anne Cuneo, replying to his criticism of her Italian productions of *Annie Wobbler* and *Four Portraits – of Mothers*, wrote that

You want too much your play to go just as you want it and no allowances made for other people, for life [...] No, actors are not the 'tools' of your idea. Actors are people. The director is a person. And the finished play is not YOUR PLAY ALONE [...] In real life, if I may say so, you are one of the most open and fairest people I know. Why not write a play where you leave total liberty to the director, where you 'dictate' nothing? Would that be so terrible?

(AW 1987a: n.pag.)

Wesker's reply is faintly disturbing, both in its certitude and metaphor: 'We must disagree. My work is my body. And like your body I don't want it raped' (AW 1987b: n.pag.). He describes actors' choices as 'generally masturbatory when they ignore the text, play their own emotions and can't face or produce the real thing themselves'. Although this seems counter to his more benevolent reputation among British actors, Wesker, like many of his contemporaries, was often frustrated by the wayward and ornery approach to his works taken by European directors and actors.

Perhaps Wesker's working ideal were the heroic readings that he undertook for over twenty years. Not only could he write and direct, he could also perform the plays in exactly the way he wanted them to be heard and present their meaning and creativity unencumbered by misconceived contributions from other artists. Writing his own copy for the Young Vic press release, he proclaimed, 'Wesker, whose first ambition was to be an actor, is a superlatively dramatic reader of these works [...] Against reason, though male, Wesker becomes the woman he has created. Tension and excitement mount after each interval' (AW 1990a: n.pag.). In *As Much as I Dare*, he reminds the reader that he was offered a place at RADA but had to turn it down when the London County Council twice refused him a grant. 'Give me a bar stool, a table, a glass of water and an audience and I glow with that power I first experienced playing King Cophetua.' Not a talent, more a facility to capture, hold, control an audience' (Wesker 1994: 231). This *braggadocio* is mostly corroborated by those who saw the readings. 'Wesker gave a mesmerizing, 90-minute performance of *Annie Wobbler*,' wrote the Chicago critic, Hedy Weiss (1988: n.pag.). 'Wesker brought them all to life, quietly but brilliantly, without ever lapsing into female impersonation. It was the most exhilarating theater I'd seen in days' (Weiss 1988: n.pag.). Anne Mayer, who became Wesker's publicist and friend, confirms that he was a compelling and surprisingly effective performer whose vitality never flagged (Mayer 2018). Nichola McAuliffe, who attended a couple of the readings, found them 'reasonably well played, but Arnold never really got the light and shade of the characters. He was a bit grand and enjoying the reading too much to give the women some of the deeper, more distressing areas he goes into' (McAuliffe 2018: n.pag.). The readings provided the most positive professional experiences of his later years, and Wesker continued to perform them until he was no longer physically able to travel.

Forerunner

The Wesker archives are a reminder that for all his bluntness and conceit, Wesker can be seen as a forerunner in many ways. His dedication to working-class audiences (through years of commitment to Centre 42 (C42)), his humanitarian activism and his essays on craft are now routine notions for contemporary playwrights but were less habitual at the time he was confronting the traditionalists. His focus on older (and younger) women and sexual equality, both in his life and in his writing, has also emerged as a twenty-first century dramatic inevitability. The tone of some of the one-woman plays may be outmoded, and his focus on female sexuality is sometimes disconcerting. But both his correspondence and his dramatic works ultimately show Wesker as a playwright who was not afraid to plunder aspects of his own personality to depict powerful portrayals of women confronting domestic and societal challenges. That the writing of the one-woman plays also took place during the eleven years of Margaret Thatcher's governments may or may not be coincidental.

In his radio interview, Wesker assured Anthony Clare that 'I won't go gently into that good night'. Although Parkinson's disease finally deprived him of the ability to write letters, there is still plenty of correspondence that has made its way to Texas in which he continues to convey his support for his friends, harangues his critics and puts his latest preoccupations into outlines for future plays.

NOTES

1. Intriguingly, the only documents that are not included in the archives are the diaries themselves, which are sealed and not to be opened, until after the deaths of his two remaining children.
2. Michael Kustow, Director of the ICA and the first Commissioning Arts Editor at Channel 4.
3. He wrote a sequel to the play, *Letter to Myself* (2004), at the request of youth theatre actor Isabel Rabey, where 13-year-old Marike, upon reading her mother's letter, decides to write a letter to her future 18-year-old self.
4. Fragments of this correspondence appear in *As Much As I Dare,* which is written partly in the vocative tense.
5. Although Wesker once inferred, in a letter to a prospective Italian director, that the play was 'inspired by a Norwegian jazz singer who suggested I write a play about her life' (AW 1994: n.pag.).

6. Dexter stayed with the Weskers for seven weeks in 1959 after being released from a six-month stint in Wormwood Scrubs for sexual offences and wrote that he would be forever grateful to them.
7. In 1987 Wesker adapted *Lady Othello* into a play that was first published in 1990 by Penguin in Volume 6 of Wesker's Plays. The play, like the film, remains unproduced.
8. The rehearsal room often being the Weskers' living room, with lunch and refreshments provided by Dusty.
9. In an obscure play called *The Surprise* by G. K. Chesterton and Dorothy L. Sayers mounted at the Toynbee Hall.

REFERENCES

Barrie, Frank (2018), In-person interview with Michael Fry, London, 28 February.

Billington, Michael (1983), 'Review of *Annie Wobbler*', *The Guardian*, 27 July.

Clare, Anthony (1982), *In the Psychiatrist's Chair* (recording), BBC Radio 4, 14 August.

Cleave, Maureen (1981), 'If it weren't for the foreigners, I should be in despair', *The Observer*, 4 October.

Coveney, Michael (1983), Review of *Annie Wobbler*, *Financial Times*, 27 July.

Drabble, Margaret (1998), 'Arnold Wesker', in R. W. Dornan (ed.), *Arnold Wesker: A Casebook*, New York: Garland, pp. 75–88.

Edgar, David (1985), *Arnold Wesker and David Edgar in Conversation*, ICA Talks, 4 June, (British Library Audio C95/181).

Hayman, Ronald (1974), *Playback 2*, London: HarperCollins.

Mayer, Anne (2018), In-person interview with Michael Fry, London, 19 November.

McAuliffe, Nichola (2018), In-person interview with Michael Fry, London, 28 September.

O'Connor, Garry (1971), 'Arnold Wesker's "The Friends"', *Theatre Quarterly*, 1:2, pp. 85–94.

Staff, Susan Morgan (2001), *Anchorage Daily News*, 8 June.

TQ Symposium (1976–77), 'Playwriting for the seventies: Old theatres, new audiences, and the politics of revolution', edited transcript of a discussion between fourteen British playwrights at Oval House, July 1976, *Theatre Quarterly*, 6:24, Winter, pp. 35–72.

Weiss, Hedy (1988), 'Real-life British voices echo through compelling letters', *Chicago Sun-Times*, 10 November.

Wesker, Arnold (1971), 'The London diaries for Stockholm', in *Six Sundays in January*, London: Cape.

——— (1979), *Wesker: The Journalists: A Triptych*, London, Jonathan Cape.

——— (1994), *As Much as I Dare*, London: Century.

——— (1997), *The Birth of Shylock and the Death of Zero Mostel*, London: Quartet.

——— (2001), *Plays: 2 One-Woman Plays*, London: Methuen.

Wesker, Arnold Papers (AW) (1954), 'Letters Funny and Strange', n.d., Austin, Texas: Harry Ransom Center, Box 188.9.

—— (1958a), Letter to Dusty Wesker, 21 May, Austin, Texas: Harry Ransom Center, Box 187.5.

—— (1958b), Letter to Dusty Wesker, 20 June, Austin, Texas: Harry Ransom Center, Box 190.4.

—— (1979), Letter to Elizabeth Spriggs, 27 August, Austin, Texas: Harry Ransom Center, Box 56.1.

—— (1982), Letter to Max Stafford-Clark, 10 March, Austin, Texas: Harry Ransom Center, Box 22.9.

—— (1983a), Programme for *Annie Wobbler*, Austin, Texas: Harry Ransom Center, Box 4.1.

—— (1983b), Letter from Lindsay Anderson, 20 May, Austin, Texas: Harry Ransom Center, Box 164.3.

—— (1984), Letter from 'Fran', 20 August, Austin, Texas: Harry Ransom Center, Box 105.11.

—— (1986), Letter to Krista Jussenhoven, 19 May, Austin, Texas: Harry Ransom Center, Box 162.2.

—— (1987a), Letter from Anne Cuneo, 9 April, Austin, Texas: Harry Ransom Center, Box 31.8.

—— (1987b), Letter to Anne Cuneo, 15 April, Austin, Texas: Harry Ransom Center, Box 31.8.

—— (1989), Letter to Claretta Carotenuto, 17 January, Austin, Texas: Harry Ransom Center, Box 102.9.

—— (1990a), Text for Young Vic 1990 programme, Austin, Texas: Harry Ransom Center, Box 102.8.

—— (1990b), Letter from Carole Denton, 17 June, Austin, Texas: Harry Ransom Center, Box 68.12.

—— (1990c), Letter to Carole Denton, 25 June, Austin, Texas: Harry Ransom Center, Box 68.12.

—— (1990d), Letter to Connie Ricono, 29 December, Austin, Texas: Harry Ransom Center, Box 163.2.

—— (1991a), Letter to Claretta Carotenuto, 28 July, Austin, Texas: Harry Ransom Center, Box 63.1.

—— (1991b), Letter from Flossie B Avon, 6 December, Austin, Texas: Harry Ransom Center, Box 165.

—— (1992a), Letter to Nuria Espert, 23 February, Austin, Texas: Harry Ransom Center, Box 185.23.

—— (1992b), Letter to Nuria Espert, 13 October, Austin, Texas: Harry Ransom Center, Box 185.23.

—— (1992c), Letter to Rosemary Squire, 19 May, Austin, Texas: Harry Ransom Center, Box 162.2.

—— (1993a), Letter to Ursula Pegler, n.d., Austin, Texas: Harry Ransom Center, Box 162.2.

—— (1993b), Letter to Brenda Bruce, 30 July, Austin, Texas: Harry Ransom Center, Box 102.9.

———— (1994), Letter to Giorgio Albertazzi, 5 January, Austin, Texas: Harry Ransom Center, Box 53.7.

———— (1997), Extract from Hugh Leonard's unpublished diary, a fellow speaker at the International Congress of Theatre Writers, Athens, 16–18 October, Austin, Texas: Harry Ransom Center, Box 114.4.

Wesker, Dusty (2018), In conversation with Michael Fry, Hove, 23 February.

Wilcher, Robert (1991), *Understanding Arnold Wesker*, Columbia: University of South Carolina Press.

FIGURE 18: The Weskers, at their Bishop's Road home, London, *c.*1971: Sebastian the dog, Tanya Jo, Lindsay (named after director Lindsay Anderson), Daniel, Dusty and Arnold.

11

The Idea of Community in the Plays of Arnold Wesker from *The Kitchen* to *Beorhtel's Hill*

Robert Wilcher

The meaning of the word 'community' is difficult to pin down, and the implications of any individual use of it will depend very much on context. At its broadest, according to the *Oxford English Dictionary*, it denotes 'A body of people or things viewed collectively.' For our purposes, two of the more precise definitions will be of particular service: 'A group of people who live in the same place, usually sharing a common cultural or ethnic identity' (2.b) and 'A group of people who share the same interests, pursuits or occupation, esp. when distinct from those of the society in which they live' (5.b). The tension between these two meanings is neatly summed up by Raymond Williams: ' "Community" can be the warmly persuasive word to describe an existing set of relations, or the warmly persuasive word to describe an alternative set of relations' (Williams 1976: 66). Other dictionary definitions specify that the 'shared interests' that hold a group together may be 'religious' or 'ideological' or 'political' and that, with the definite article, 'the community' can refer more generally to 'The civic body to which all belong; the public; society' (6). Noting the widespread tendency to consign Arnold Wesker to one defining category or another, as 'Angry Young Man' or 'socialist' or 'Jewish' or 'working-class', Reade Dornan suggests that his deepest and most abiding concerns are not with any particular group or community but with the individual 'human beings' in his plays and 'their interactions with each other' (Dornan 1984: xi). John Mander long ago recognized that Wesker's interest in those interactions was manifested in the recurring theme of 'communication', which 'is closely linked with ideas about education, about community, and about Socialism', and that the 'lack of connection, in personal and social relationships [...] makes a mockery of the very term "community" ' (Mander 1961: 201, 205).

It is significant that Wesker dramatized just such a 'lack of connection' in his first play *The Kitchen* (1959), which presented a typical day in the kitchen of a large restaurant as a stage metaphor for the failure of a shared occupation to create a community in either of the positive senses described by Williams. In an environment where 'people come and people go' and the speaking of many languages causes friction, Dimitri, a Cypriot porter, emphasizes the lack of continuity in the human relationships possible in such a workplace: 'In the end who do you know? You make a friend, you going to be all you life his friend but when you go from here – pshtt! You forget! Why you grumble about this one kitchen?' (Wesker 1990b: 47). And Peter, the German cook, applies this negative and fatalistic attitude more widely to the modern world of work: 'the kitchen don't mean nothing to you and you don't mean to the kitchen nothing. But Dimitri is right, you know – why do you grumble about this kitchen? What about the offices and the factories?' (Wesker 1990b: 48). The only character who attempts to look beyond what David Rabey calls this 'social fragmentation and its cost in human integrity' (Rabey 1986: 90) is Paul, the Jewish pastry cook, whose attempt to forge a bond of solidarity and common interest with a striking neighbour makes him realize that there is 'a big wall between me and millions of people like him' (Wesker 1990b: 51–52). The purpose of this chapter is to look at the different ways in which the idea of community is explored in Wesker's drama from the social realist plays of the late 1950s and his responses to the failure of the Centre 42 (C42) project in the 1960s to his growing interest in the experiences of Jewish communities past and present in the 1970s and early 1980s and his direct artistic engagement with a particular contemporary community in *Beorhtel's Hill* in 1989.

Positive and negative versions of community in The Trilogy

Wesker's one dramatization of a vibrant community united by place and class and politics occurs in the first act of his second play, *Chicken Soup with Barley* (1958). The year is 1936 and the setting is the East End of London. As Keith Gore has pointed out, the Weskers were not the only family of poor Jewish immigrants to have made their homes there:

> The sense of community which undoubtedly existed was based on many factors, but to be poor and Jewish and immigrant, at a time when the threat presented by Nazi Germany was for many a matter of very recent experience, is an essential part of the background which forms the reality of *Chicken Soup*.
>
> (Gore 1998: 20)

But although it is true that 'the attachment to family inspires his vision of true community and comradeship', the ethnicity of the Kahns (who were based on his own family) is not the crucial element in Wesker's 'image of the golden age when life and dream seem one' (Morgan 1981: 39, 34). On 4 October 1936, when the dramatist was 4 years old, his whole neighbourhood came together to prevent a march by Oswald Mosley's fascists. In the opening moments of the play, Harry Kahn reports that the streets 'are packed with people'; Monty Blatt exults that 'every section of this working-class area' has responded to the call to action, including the 'dockers at Limehouse'; and Prince Silver adds to the list of supporters: 'The unions, the Co-ops, Labour Party Members and the Jewish People's Council' (Wesker 1990a: 14, 19). Brotherhood is a key concept for these Jewish members of the Communist Party, but neighbourliness bred of shared poverty reaches beyond race or religion or politics in this community. Harry's sister, Cissie, a trade union organizer, reminds them about a social at the weekend for a woman whose husband has been killed by a tram: 'She's a Catholic. The local priest is trying to raise some money to keep her going for a bit and we promised we'd support it' (Wesker 1990a: 29). When Monty looks back to the 1930s from the other side of the Second World War in Act III, he uses a telling image to sum up the experience of a community that has since fragmented:

> All the songs we sang together, and the strikes and the rallies. [...] Everyone in the East End was going somewhere. It was a slum, there was misery, but we were going somewhere. The East End was a big mother.
>
> (Wesker 1990a: 62–63)

Of course, the golden age was not an unblemished ideal, as Sarah Kahn insists in her dismissive reply to Monty: 'Ach! Horrible times! Horrible times – dirty, unclean, cheating!' But she, too, has an abiding memory of the compensations of a living community, which she later confides to her son, Ronnie. When his sister was seriously ill with diphtheria, a neighbour saved the girl's life: 'You remember Mrs Bernstein? [...] It was Mrs Bernstein's soup. Ada still has that taste in her mouth – chicken soup with barley [...] That saved her' (Wesker 1990a: 74).

Act II begins in June 1946, when the inhabitants of the East End are being dispersed and the spirit that energized their community is being dissipated. The Kahn family has been moved from its slum basement into a block of flats in Hackney; Ada, who was an enthusiastic Communist at 14, has lost her belief in 'the right to organize people'; Dave Simmonds's war service has dashed his illusions about 'the splendid and heroic working class'; only Ronnie, now an adolescent, looks forward optimistically to a future made possible by the election of a Labour government (Wesker 1990a: 41–42). By October 1947, Dave and Ada have left London for the country to pursue their own vision of socialism and Cissie, though still an active shop steward, is losing faith in the workers she represents. In the third act, set in the mid-1950s, there is nothing left of the old community – geographically, socially or politically: Monty has moved to Manchester, where he runs a small business; Cissie has been forced into retirement by her union; Ada and Dave are still in Norfolk; Ronnie is a pastry cook in Paris and Sarah, though still a member of 'the Party', is struggling with the bureaucracy of the Welfare State. Ronnie returns at the end of the play to confront his mother with his loss of political faith and literary ambition – 'You didn't tell me there were any doubts' – but her only way of defending her dogged belief in 'the idea of brotherhood' is to tell the story of Mrs Bernstein's chicken soup with barley (Wesker 1990a: 71, 75). The fragmentation of social life for the former inhabitants of the East End is captured in an incident that interrupts a family game of cards. The sounds of a domestic altercation in the playground below draw them all out onto the balcony, where Cissie comments: 'There's always something happening in these flats. Last week a woman tried to gas herself. [...] You live a whole lifetime here and not know your next-door neighbour' (Wesker 1990a: 67–68). True to her unabated concern for other people, Sarah goes to investigate the human drama being enacted in their vicinity, but returns with news of a trivial family squabble. This is the signal for the once close-knit group of comrades who united with the rest of the East End community in opposition to Mosley to make their farewells. The naturally gregarious Sarah distils her new social reality into a subdued parting remark: 'Harry and I don't see many people these days' (Wesker 1990a: 68).

In *Roots* (1959), the second play of what would come to be known as the *Trilogy*, Wesker used the domestic context of a family of agricultural labourers to dramatize an issue that he would later formulate in one of his earliest public statements: how to encourage the social class represented by the Trades Unions to 'read books from the libraries, listen to concerts on the radio, visit the theatres and in general take part in the cultural life of the community' (Wesker 1970: 16). This missionary project, however, is based upon a confusion between *the* community – that is, 'the civic body to which all belong' – and the more exclusive community that centres its 'cultural life' on books and concerts and theatres. In the play, Ronnie Kahn's girlfriend, Beatie Bryant, tries to make her rural working-class relatives engage with the culture that he has introduced her to. Frustrated by their stubborn refusal to respond to her appeals, she accuses them of having no roots – 'we don't know what we are or where we come from' – and of blindly consuming the third-rate cultural fare served up to them by 'the whole stinkin' commercial world' (Wesker 1990a: 146, 148). Critics have identified the conflict between Beatie and her family as that between the 'life-denying environment' of the agricultural workers and the 'stimulating one' of her 'off-stage life with Ronnie'; but the title of the play – *Roots* – complicates the simple story of Beatie's attempt 'to free herself and her family from the limitations of their working-class lives' (Leeming and Trussler 1971: 58; Asman 1998: 45). As John Orr observes, the Bryants do have 'roots' in a deeply conservative 'rural community', which are 'embedded in a tradition of class deference' that has never been 'directly confronted' by the 'Jewish immigrants to the East End' from whom Ronnie springs; and the play, in fact, demonstrates that 'the experience of the urban family does not so easily transfer to the experience of the rural one' (Orr 1989: 264–65). Indeed, although the dramatist stipulates that – except for Beatie – '*there is no sign of intense living from any of the characters*', the same stage direction recognizes a stoical dignity in the way the Bryants '*continue in a routine rural manner*', while the seasons come and go and '*little amazes them*', not even sickness and death (Wesker 1990a: 92). Furthermore, these isolated and impoverished country people are not without their own kind of creativity and 'brotherhood'. Beatie's sister takes a '*plaited loaf of bread*' from the oven with evident pride in her own handiwork; and her mother is equally proud of the touch of colour she has brought to her cottage garden, which is partly owing to the thoughtfulness of a neighbour, who gave her some geranium plants 'afore he died' (Wesker 1990a: 97, 110). Mrs Bryant's husband and another neighbour were quick to come to the aid of old Stan Mann when they found him collapsed at the side of the road; and she herself has fond memories of Ma Buckley, 'a sweet ole dear', who has been taken to the Mental Hospital in Norwich: 'We used to talk and do errands for each other' (Wesker 1990a: 126). Leeming and Trussler do not do justice to the integrity with which Wesker recreates the social world inhabited by Beatie's family – even if that integrity is at odds with the conscious message of his play – in the conclusion that '[r]ather than belonging to a community, the Bryants drift wherever tides beyond their control take them' (Leeming and Trussler 1971: 57).

The same critics are nearer the mark in their assessment of the third part of the *Trilogy*: 'Dave and Ada's struggle is different from Sarah's because it is a fight against, not for society' (Leeming and Trussler 1971: 74). *I'm Talking about Jerusalem* (1960) chronicles the failed experiment in William Morris socialism conducted by Sarah's daughter and son-in-law between 1946 and 1959. The young couple turn their backs on London and the dehumanizing work available in factories for a new life in East Anglia, where Dave plans to make handcrafted furniture. Sarah Kahn fears that this retreat into an 'ivory tower' will cut them off from other human beings, without whom socialism is nothing: 'Tell me Ada, how are you going to get to the village? Not even a road here there isn't' (Wesker 1990a: 164, 157). Sure enough, they make no effort to become part of the local community, and Dave eventually comes up against the 'tradition of class deference' among his rural neighbours in a confrontation with Colonel Dewhurst, the gentleman farmer who employs him until he is ready to establish his own work-shop. The colonel challenges him over two discarded rolls of linoleum that he has removed for his own use without permission:

> What did you come to the country for? It's a different way of life here, y'know. They're a slow people, the country people – slow, but sound. I know where I am with them, and they know their place with me.
>
> (Wesker 1990a: 186)

When Dave tries to explain that he merely took away what was clearly left out as 'junk', his employer retorts that he has missed 'the point' – 'We "ask", Simmonds: in my sort of society, we ask. That's all' – and gives him twenty-four hours' notice to quit his job (Wesker 1990a: 187). After nine more years struggling to make a living as an independent craftsman, Dave prepares to return to London and admits to a distraught Ronnie, 'Maybe Sarah's right, maybe you can't build on your own' (Wesker 1990a: 216). The burden of this third play is summed up by one of the early commentators: 'Socialism must be lived with other people; it is a community way of life, not a private escape' (Goodman 1961: 220).

Attempts to construct communities

In the plays that occupied him during the rest of the 1960s, Wesker widened the scope of his representation of the interactions between individual human beings to embrace particular power systems that operate within society at large: the Royal Air Force, local and national government, and the world of business. His experience as a conscript provided him with a microcosm of society that was 'more truly analogous to society in its stratified class system' than either the cosmopolitan collection of workers in *The Kitchen* or 'the restricted social world of the Bryants and Beales' (Leeming and Trussler 1971: 88; Lacey 1995: 87). In *Chips with Everything* (1962), he explores contrasting ways in which a disparate group of men are coerced and cajoled into a sense of common identity. The first is imposed by Corporal Hill, of their own social class but a willing agent of the institution in which they must learn to function as a disciplined unit. On their first morning of 'square-bashing', he makes his objective clear: 'I want everything to be done together. We're going to be the happiest family in Christendom and we're going to move together, as one, as one solitary man' (Wesker 1990c: 20). By the end of the eight weeks, at the Passout Parade, his success is endorsed by the Wing Commander (Wesker 1990c: 64). A more life-enhancing kind of communal spirit is built up in the conscripts through the experiences they share, though this may also be part of the strategy of those who exercise institutional power over them. It is expressed most eloquently by Andrew during a scene of relaxation in the hut: 'I like us all being together here. In a way you know I don't mind it, anything. Old Corp and his mouth organ – all of us, just as we are, I like us' (Wesker 1990c: 44). And it is enacted in the teamwork involved in stealing coke from the regimental store and the collective care lavished on Smiler, when he returns exhausted from an attempt to run away from the bullying of the corporals. Wesker specifies that the latter action should be done *'lovingly and with a sort of ritual'* (Wesker 1990c: 66). Such rituals, 'with their potential for generating a sense of community with other finite and vulnerable creatures', have been explored as a significant feature of Wesker's drama (Adler 1979: 436).

By the time *Chips with Everything* was produced in April 1962, Wesker's energies had been diverted to the C42 project, at the heart of which was the need, articulated by Raymond Williams, for left-wing artists to 'have relation to a community rather than to a market or a patron' (Wesker 1970: 46). Two subsequent stage plays reflected his travails as its artistic director, which must also have informed his artistic collaboration with the residents of Basildon twenty years later. The action of *Their Very Own and Golden City* (1965) traces the political and economic difficulties that beset Andy Cobham's attempt to realize William Blake's vision of building 'Jerusalem in England's green and pleasant land'. In 1926, he dreams of '[t]he chance to change the pattern of living for all time' by creating 'Cities of light and shade [...] Cities full of sound for the blind and colour for the deaf' (Wesker 1990b: 130, 160). The encouraging prospect held out to him by his trade union mentor – 'Perhaps the war will clear a path for you – you and your cities' – fails to materialize when the Labour Party's promises about 'postwar slum clearances' take precedence over utopian dreams of people 'owning all their own houses' and workers 'owning their own factories' (Wesker 1990b: 154, 161). Determined to bypass cautious councils and party politics, he decides to involve the future inhabitants of the cities directly in financing them – 'a real community project, a real one!' (Wesker 1990b: 167). But when the Trades Union Congress votes down his resolution to fund the establishment of factories owned by the workers in 1948, he has to accept industry financed by private capital and backed by a Conservative government. By the end of the play, set in 1985 *'or thereabouts'*, he acknowledges the limited nature of his success: 'After all, the Golden City is built; there were compromises but it's built, a hint, if nothing else, of what might be' (Wesker 1990b: 195). Left alone, however, he confesses the ultimate failure of his dream: 'Patchwork! Bits and pieces of patchwork. Six cities, twelve cities, what difference. Oases in the desert, that the sun dries up' (Wesker 1990b: 196). This work born of failure and disillusionment is, in fact, Wesker's most ambitious attempt as a dramatist to impart his

ideas about the conditions in which human beings might flourish both as individuals and as parts of a community.

The prolonged action of *Their Very Own and Golden City* had been necessary
to show how Andy's revolutionary vision that '[s]ix Golden Cities could lay the
foundations of a new way of life for all society' was watered down by compromise
in post-war Britain (Wesker 1990b: 170). The other play in which Wesker took
stock of the failure of C42, *The Friends* (1970), narrowed the dramatic focus to one
room and the passing of a single night. Gathered at the bedside of the dying Esther
are her partners in an interior design business – most of them from the 'same art
college, same warm northern city, same kind of labouring fathers and tight-lipped
mothers' – who were drawn together in their youth by the ideal of brightening
the homes of their working-class community (Wesker 1990c: 95–96). Unable to
sell their products to 'Roland's religious floor-scrubbing mum' or 'Tessa's brick-
laying brothers', they have lost interest in the shops and the business is about to go
bankrupt (Wesker 1990c: 95–96). Having lost its communal purpose, the group is
disintegrating into a collection of disillusioned and self-pitying individuals. Against
this loss of connection with each other and the society they inhabit, Esther recalls
the civilizing artefacts and activities that have brightened *her* life. After she dies
at the end of Act I, as the members of the group struggle with their private grief,
Simone – an outsider from a more privileged background – speaks as the true dis-
ciple of Esther's vision of a cultural community with roots that go much deeper
than those of Beatie's agricultural family. She recognizes that '[t]he past is too rich
with human suffering and achievement to be dismissed' and champions the value
of 'liberty and love and the sharing between all men of the good things this good
earth and man's ingenuity can give' (Wesker 1990c: 124–25). In the plays of the
following decade, Wesker was to explore further the idea of community embodied
in her impassioned plea to restore contact with the accumulated riches of the past.

Reconnecting with the past

Wesker began *The Old Ones* (1972) as a formal experiment in which 'a series of
scenes' were linked by nothing more than 'the fact that some of the characters
were related or were friends' (Wesker 1973–74: 96). John Dexter, however, who
directed the first production, felt that something more was needed – 'a framework
to contain the whole piece' – and Wesker hit upon the idea of turning the final
scene, which was to have been simply a Friday night family supper, into a celebration of the Jewish festival of Succoth (Wesker 1973–74: 93). This required the
gradual construction throughout the play of a symbolic tent partly roofed with
branches and had the effect of transforming a portrait gallery of 'old people' who

'incidentally [...] happen to be Jews' into the first of Wesker's plays 'to concern itself in any way with the Jewish religion' (Wesker 1973–74: 94–95).

The tent or 'Succah' is being built on the balcony of Sarah's council flat by her daughter Rosa and her nephew Rudi. As members of the younger generation in a secular Jewish family, they know nothing about the festival and Rosa reads aloud from a book about its significance and ritual practices. Sarah vaguely remembers it as being 'Joyful' and welcomes it as a way of remembering her father and pleasing her sister, Gerda, 'who likes these things' (Wesker 1990c: 137–38); and later, we see her binding sheaves of dried wheat to tie to the 'Succah'. But at the start of the long final scene, in which family and friends come together to revive the ancient feast, Gerda shows no interest and Teressa condemns what they are doing as 'sacrilegious' – 'I mean, we don't even remember'. Rudi, exasperated by his elders, asks, 'Doesn't anyone remember?' and Sarah replies, 'Who can remember! We were children!' (Wesker 1990c: 179). Rosa, however, persists with her reading of instructions and distributes branches, which they wave in a procession led by Rudi before sitting down to a festive meal. In the context of the play, the words of a medieval moralist resonate more than any other passage from Rosa's book: 'traditions which have their roots in the past must not be dismissed as obsolete but must be revived by the language and minds of new generations' (Wesker 1990c: 181–82). Rosa, taken aback, comments, 'That's me! *I'm* supposed to tell you what to do?' (Wesker 1990c: 182, original emphasis). Robert Gross observes that her attempt to revive the ancient ritual, 'though not ultimately successful', brings isolated individuals together and presents them with 'pieces of [the] past that have otherwise been forgotten', so that she becomes 'a collector of fragments for the community' (Gross 1998: 241). After the shared meal, always a potent symbol for Wesker, laughter, dancing and singing bring the play to a positive conclusion that justifies David Rabey's summary of its partial answer to the modern problems of disintegration, loneliness, and alienation:

> *The Old Ones* offers a notably and fruitfully complex series of dramatic images of ageing and the active exercise of informed *distinction* – considering and choosing what should be discarded, retained and developed from the past – to demonstrate and recreate active spirits of family and community.
>
> (Rabey 2016: 126)

The Wedding Feast (1974), which relocates a story by Dostoevsky to rural Norfolk, introduces into Wesker's drama for the first time the destructive power of the group that becomes a mob. Brought up as 'a young communist' in London's East End during the 1930s, Louis Litvanov – 'son of an impoverished Jewish cobbler and grandson of an impoverished Jewish cobbler' – has risen to be the owner of a shoe factory (Wesker 1990d: 113). In spite of his wealth and social position, he has never abandoned his political ideals and clings to the illusion that he is part of the community from which he draws his employees. When he stumbles by chance into the wedding party of two of them, however, latent antagonism is released by the consumption of alcohol and the men and women for whom he will always be 'the master' unite to assault and humiliate him in a 'game' that gets out of hand (Wesker 1990d: 165–66). There is no open antisemitism in this overflow of antipathy and violence, which has its origins in class resentment, but in *The Merchant* (1976), later renamed *Shylock*, Wesker confronted the issue of ethnic and religious intolerance head-on.

Spurred on by recent productions of *The Merchant of Venice* and by Shakespeare's apparent ignorance of the historical realities of the famous Ghetto, Wesker sought to recreate the true nature of the Jewish community in sixteenth-century Venice. Tubal describes the economic oppression of the 'fourteen hundred souls', whose close sense of shared identity is generated by the conditions in which they live, confined within the walls of the Ghetto during the hours of darkness, 'trapped in an oppressive circus with three water wells and a proclivity for fires' and subjected to various financial penalties (Wesker 1990d: 213). Emissaries from Portugal bring news of a recent spate of persecutions and a request for safe harbour in the Ghetto for the stream of refugees on their way to Solonika. At the end of the play, Shylock will himself feel the force of anti-Semitic hatred when he is punished for the bond he made with his Christian friend, Antonio, in mockery of what they both regard as 'barbaric laws' (Wesker 1990d: 213).

The play contrasts two communities in the city. The larger – embodying Williams's 'existing set of relations' – is dominated by 'the ancient trading families' on whom the city's 'glory' is founded (Wesker 1990d: 216). The other – embodying 'an alternative set of relations' – is composed of Tubal's fourteen hundred souls. The scion of one of the twelve families that 'claim the greatest nobility because they go back before 762, or is it 726?' is more certain that 'the *accumulated* knowledge of superiority *gives* one superiority' than he is of his own history (Wesker 1990d: 216–17, 225). In conversation with Shylock, another young Venetian disdainfully assumes cultural advantage over the inhabitants of the Ghetto: 'It must be very difficult for your tribe to produce much of art or thought, as civilized nations do who have roots in territory' (Wesker 1990d: 223). One of Wesker's purposes in reworking the story material of *The Merchant of Venice* in a more accurate historical context is to give the lie to this misconception. His Shylock is a leader in his community, a collector of books and manuscripts and patron to scholars, writers and architects, and he takes great pride in the rich cultural life of the Ghetto. In a rousing climax to Act I, he lectures the young Venetians in Antonio's house on the transmission of classical learning by Cassiodorus – 'the last and lovely link between Imperial Rome and Gothic Italy' (Wesker 1990d: 227). As the invention of the printing press brings him to an ecstatic climax – 'Suddenly – everybody can possess a book' – the curfew bells ring and the old Jew has to don his yellow hat and return to the Ghetto for the night (Wesker 1990d: 229). But not before he has delivered Wesker's most inspiring descant on the theme sounded in a minor key by Simone and Rosa: that civilization itself is nothing less than a community of human knowledge and imagination that transcends any particular time or place or social formation. The cruellest aspect of the judgement passed on Shylock for plotting 'against the life of a citizen of Venice' is the confiscation of his library along with his other 'goods' (Wesker 1990d: 257). When the Doge explains that the 'people of Venice would not understand it if the law exacted no punishment at all for such a bond', the old man replies with weary resignation, 'The law must be observed. We have need of law, what need do we have of books?' (Wesker 1990d: 257, 258).

Lessons of history

During the 1980s, Wesker dramatized three historical instances of the victimization of individuals or minorities as a result of the control of society by powerful religious and political institutions. *Caritas* (1981) was based on the fate of Christine Carpenter, immured as an anchoress in 1329 and denied release by a bishop on the grounds that 'our Church', in which the community of Christendom has invested 'power' and 'responsibility', must be 'obeyed, respected and strong' (Wesker 1990e: 109). *Blood Libel* (1991) closely followed a twelfth-century account of the murder of 12-year-old William of Norwich – later sainted by the Church – in what was believed at the time to be a ritual killing by local Jews. Dornan remarks on the story's 'deep foreboding about the sort of group hysteria that ultimately destroys outsiders in the community' (Dornan 1994: 83). The third play, *Badenheim 1939*, is an allegory adapted from a novel by Aharon Appelfeld, in which the Jewish inhabitants of a spa town in Austria ignore the signs of the coming holocaust and look forward to being transferred to Poland, 'where the dawn and a new life will await us', blindly hoping for the best and unable to imagine the worst even as the train that pulls into the station proves to consist not of '*carriages*' but of '[*f*]*reight wagons*' (Wesker 1994: 82, 92).

Towards the end of the decade, however, Wesker found himself involved in what he described as 'perhaps my most optimistic play since *Roots*', which took its title – *Beorhtel's Hill* – from the name of a former Anglo-Saxon settlement on the site of Basildon (Wesker cited in Homden 1989). The recently appointed director of the new Towngate Theatre, Anamaria Wills, was looking for a project that would 'create a real relationship with the community of Basildon' (Towngate programme:

n.pag.). She contacted the Colway Theatre Trust, which had been set up by Ann Jellicoe in 1979 'to help communities create a work of art' (Jellicoe 1987: 46). Jellicoe, whose first 'community play' had been produced in Lyme Regis in 1978, had soon discovered that a line had to be drawn 'between the needs of community and the needs of art' (Jellicoe 1987: xviii). She therefore insisted that although professional actors are not required because there is 'so much amateur talent' in local drama groups and schools, 'a professional writer, director and designer are vital' in order to 'ensure very high standards which in turn inspire confidence and commitment' (Jellicoe 1987: 8, 9). The values embedded in the Colway Trust clearly chime with those that Wesker had promoted in C42, with the additional belief that '[e]veryone can enjoy art, its demands, disciplines, rewards all the more vividly if they create, or help to create it' (Jellicoe 1987: 47). It was no surprise, then, that the Trust recommended him to Wills, especially since Wesker had grown up in London's East End, where many of the first residents of Basildon New Town had come from in the post-war rehousing programme. At first, however, Wesker was reluctant to commit himself to working with amateur actors in a kind of promenade performance that did not appeal to him (in the event, the audience sat or stood around a vast empty area, but did not promenade), and he also pointed out that he had already written his play 'about new towns' in *Their Very Own and Golden City* (Wesker cited in Homden 1989: n.pag.). But when Wills took him to the building site of the new Towngate and let him stand on the concrete slab that would be the stage, he gazed at the shell of the auditorium and exclaimed, 'This is the theatre I've always dreamed of' (AW 1989b). From that moment, the man who had wanted to locate the first C42 community hub in a New Town and had helped to mount six local artistic festivals between 1961 and 1962 was 'hooked'.

When Wesker gave an initial reading of his script to the inhabitants of Basildon who would later perform it, he explained that his brief had been to devise 'any imaginative assembly of whatever the material confronting me might suggest' (AW 1989a: n.pag.). That material consisted of books about the history of the New Town, manuscripts submitted by the people of Basildon and its surrounding areas, tape recordings of old people made by the local historical society and his own interviews with the 'young and old'. What 'slowly took shape' was 'a series of very strong visual images', 'a history which threw up issues which echoed again and again through the years' and 'voices which commented on it all'. Although edited by his own 'particular ear for rhythm', 80 per cent of the dialogue in *Beorhtel's Hill* was taken directly from what members of the community had 'written or uttered' (AW 1989a: n.pag.). It is evident that the project he had undertaken had much in common with the artistic vision he had set out in 1968: the 'arrangement of fragments is the artist's purpose in life', and the work of art 'must contain as many fragments as possible in order to confront a community constantly not only with what is happening to it now, but *why* it is happening and what happened before and what can happen later' (Wesker 1970: 106, 122, original emphasis).

Among the 'voices' heard in the play, one of the most prominent is that of Brenda, whose diary entries stretch from 17 August 1964, when she recorded being offered 'a new house in a new town called Basildon', to 19 August 1968, when the Links, an area of unspoiled woodland that she values for not being 'neat and clinical', was being bulldozed to make way for a new housing estate (Wesker 1994: 98, 101). Brenda, a married woman with small children, supplies an insight into the personal experience of being transplanted from an existing community in which she 'lived round the corner' from her mother into one that has neither 'continuity' nor 'character' (Wesker 1994: 116, 137). By Christmas 1967, she still feels like 'one stranger among many in a strange land' (Wesker 1994: 127). Her comment on the loss of the Links is typical of the self-reflective honesty with which she faces the challenges of her new life: 'I shouldn't mind, really, after all I have a house, so why do I begrudge others the same opportunity? I shouldn't mind, but I do' (Wesker 1994: 139). The other voice heard regularly throughout the play – constructed rather than transcribed – is that of the Narrator. Announcing himself as 'the community drunk', he supplies a commentary on the longer time span of the story of Basildon (Wesker 1994: 97). His cynicism is functional, as both a counterpoint to the authentic voice of Brenda and an antidote to mindless idealism about the New Town project. The very first voices we hear, to be set against those of Brenda and the Narrator, belong to the Chorus. These fifteen robed and cowled figures are described in the text as '*scene-changers, the sound-makers and controllers of light, the controllers of the traffic, of characters and crowds, the pointers of their destiny*' (Wesker 1994: 97). They appear at intervals to create the effects of thunder and lightning, carry a dead soldier from the stage, chant the slogans of the Labour government elected in 1945 and they offer a less engaged view than those of Brenda and the Narrator in articulating patterns discernible in the lives of individuals and communities: 'All things tire of themselves: the demagogue of his tongue, the revolutionary of his fervour, the singer of his song, the sower of his seed'; 'Though the sower flags/The flower blooms/What tires of itself – revives!/Be glad. Be comforted' (Wesker 1994: 97, 123). Derived from the drama of ancient Greece, which evolved from festivals celebrating communal life and values, the incongruity of a Chorus in Basildon's Towngate Theatre provides a running gag for the Narrator from his first bewildered reaction: – 'Who are *they*?' – to the line that concludes the play: 'Who *are* they? If only I knew who they were' (Wesker 1994: 98, 145).

In addition to the voices of Brenda, the Narrator and the Chorus, which run right through the play, many others are woven into the tapestry of Basildon's history: those of the contemporary crowds rushing through the streets – 'Depressing!

Bloody depressing town. Nothing ever happens [...] Wonderful town! Great little town! [...] They took my mum and dad from the slums and gave them a palace' (Wesker 1994: 102–04); those of the early Plotlanders, families from the East End, each with tales to tell, who purchased freehold land near such villages as Dunton, Pitsea and Basildon in the years before and after the First World War and constructed weekend bungalows out of fish boxes; those of soldiers returning from the Second World War. In the second half of the play, new characters make themselves heard. The descendants of early Plotlanders dispute with Housing Committees over the implementation of the New Towns Act of 1946, which paved the way for the Basildon Corporation and the compulsory purchase of freeholds. The contradictory responses of the first residents – 'There was a lot of mud and a lot of trudging [...] We had our own bathroom for the first time in our lives [...] It's a town waiting, this place. Bloody standing still and waiting [...] It's given me work, shops, clinics' – are followed by the voices of Asian refugees from Idi Amin's Uganda and those of town councillors raised in conflict over the prime minister's request that each local authority 'take in at least five families' (Wesker 1994: 137–38, 141).

Wesker fashioned the 'strong visual images' provoked by the material he had assembled into spectacular theatrical episodes that facilitated the incorporation of many non-speaking members of the large cast of 120 local performers. They included a moving tableau of the early Plotlanders during their weekend breaks away from the city – preparing food, darning socks, churning butter, reading comics, playing games; the erection of a plotland bungalow; a 'ballet' of street games; the replacement of plotland bungalows with *huge models of the four most recognizable buildings of Basildon*' and, as a grand finale, the appearance of the people of Basildon from every part of the theatre *with hundreds of flowers from their gardens*' until the floor is covered with vibrant colour (Wesker 1994: 106, 118, 135, 145). At various points in the unfolding story, a group of children, dressed in the costumes of each decade from 1914–18 to the present, rushes across the stage in pursuit of the end of a rainbow. Five strong at first, they are joined by a new group of 'kids' each time they reappear, so that by the end there are thirty of them. The production had begun with a spotlight on a single red rose in an art nouveau vase; it ends with the 5TH KID who *runs and runs and runs to find the end of his rainbow*', being given a red rose by the Narrator. As the last glow of light is narrowed onto this rose held triumphantly aloft, it *opens into bloom*' (Wesker 1994: 100, 144, 145).

Ann Jellicoe believed that community plays should avoid contentious political issues, because the Colway Trust was 'trying to help build communities, not divide them', and that 'co-operating with other people is in itself a political and humanising experience' (Jellicoe 1987: 27). Wesker had himself argued that 'one of the effects of art is to give people the feeling that they are part of a whole group, which is humanity, and to tell them that they are not alone' (Wesker 1967: 88). But if the artist also had a duty to 'confront a community' with the facts and consequences of its history, then there would inevitably be some hard lessons to learn. And indeed one of the 'issues' that his various sources 'threw up' time and again was 'the ongoing struggle to absorb strangers into this community' (Dornan 1994: 81). The Narrator first hints at this recurrent theme when Riley, an old man who accosts passers-by with his nightmare about life in Margaret Thatcher's Britain, is dismissed by two present-day housewives as a 'Silly ole bugger':

> They came as strangers to this town, from prefabs that lasted twenty years beyond their allotted time, with their broods, their steely eyes and high hopes, strangers in a rural midst. And once they were grateful for the warmth and friendliness of silly ole buggers from the old days. But now? Ah … now …
>
> (Wesker 1994: 101, 102)

The Narrator also looks forward to future conflict at the end of a sequence of 'stories' by the early Plotlanders, in which they revel in the small properties they own: 'Property! Mark that. An Englishman's home is his castle. Property! Freehold! Strangers in their midst' (Wesker 1994: 111). Later he asks whether those who settled among 'villagers who had lived there for centuries' were made welcome. Two Plotlanders reply:

NELL: Some eyed us strangely, but yes, we were made very welcome. Everyone got to know everyone else: neighbours, shopkeepers, delivery men.

IVY: When we all fell ill once, the grocer missed us. Brought us a selection from his shop.

> (Wesker 1994: 116)

When the bitter conflict between town planners and freeholders breaks out, the Narrator quotes the words of a militant defender of his property and then turns to confront the audience of fellow Basildon residents:

> 'We have done this', he said, 'in order to build our own home and free ourselves from the burden of rent and the fear of ejection.' Very moving! But thousands were homeless! So, planned town or chaotic development? Beorhtel's Hill or Basildon? And where do *we* stand, dearly beloved? With the silly ole buggers and their romantic memories, their sacrifice? With the homeless of East London? Chaotic development *could* mean character, variety. Planned development *could* mean dull monotony. Think about it – dearly beloved.
>
> (Wesker 1994: 134–35, original emphasis)

Just before Mr and Mrs Patel, refugees from Uganda, describe their plight, Brenda speaks of the dilemma they pose for the common humanity of the New Town dwellers: 'How difficult it is to welcome the stranger into your midst, but welcome them we must or die' (Wesker 1994: 139). After the local councillors have rejected a motion to house five Asian families, the Narrator is pleased for once to report a satisfactory solution to this particular community problem:

> But the Basildon corporation moved quietly in the background. The bloody old Corporation! [...] Gave two fingers to the council and allocated five of their own homes to the Asians. Got it right for Basildon. Saved them; atoned for them.
> (Wesker 1994: 144)

This leads into the upbeat closing emphasis on the hope of a better life that is reborn with each new generation.

Ann Jellicoe describes the 'overwhelming experience' of the finale to *The Reckoning* (1978), her own first community play – 'a mixture of us and them and then and now, of pride for what they did and in what we are achieving, of celebration' – and concludes that this is what 'makes these community plays both triumphantly theatrical and triumphantly community art' (Jellicoe 1987: 6). Perhaps it was in his involvement with the creative residents of Basildon New Town that Wesker found both his most challenging dramatic vehicle for a theme that runs through much of his work – the clash between social reality and the dream of a better world – and also a way of putting into practice C42's objective of forging a vital relationship between the artist and the community he serves.

REFERENCES

Adler, Thomas P. (1979), '*The Wesker Trilogy* revisited: Games to compensate for the inadequacy of words', *Quarterly Journal of Speech*, 65, pp. 429–38.

Asman, Kevin G. (1998), 'The failure and promise of "socialism as personal contact" in Arnold Wesker's *Roots*', in R. W. Dornan (ed.), *Arnold Wesker: A Casebook*, New York and London: Garland Publishing, pp. 34–48.

Dornan, Reade W. (1994), *Arnold Wesker Revisited*, Twayne's English Authors Series, New York: Twayne Publishers.

Goodman, Henry (1961), 'The new dramatists, 2: Arnold Wesker', *Drama Survey*, 1:2, pp. 215–22.

Gore, Keith (1998), 'The *Trilogy*, Forty Years On', in R. W. Dornan (ed.), *Arnold Wesker: A Casebook*, New York and London: Garland Publishing, pp. 15–33.

Gross, Robert (1998), 'Wisdom in Fragments: *The Old Ones*', R.W. Dornan (ed.), *Arnold Wesker: A Casebook*, New York and London: Garland Publishing, pp. 233–52.

Homden, Carol (1989), 'Strangers in their Midst', *Art East*, June, n. pag.

Jellicoe, Ann (1987), *Community Plays: How to Put Them On*, London: Methuen.

Lacey, Stephen (1995), *British Realist Theatre: The New Wave in Its Context 1956–65*, London: Routledge.

Leeming, Glenda, and Trussler, Simon (1971), *The Plays of Arnold Wesker: An Assessment*, London: Victor Gollancz.

Mander, John (1961), *The Writer and Commitment*, London: Secker and Warburg.

Morgan, Margery M. (1981), 'Arnold Wesker: The Celebratory Instinct', in H. Bock and A. Wertheim (eds), *Essays on Contemporary British Drama*, rev. ed., Munich: Max Hueber, pp. 31–45.

Orr, John (1989), *Tragic Drama and Modern Society: A Sociology of Dramatic Form from 1880 to the Present*, 2nd ed., Houndmills, Basingstoke: Macmillan.

Rabey, David Ian (1986), *British and Irish Political Drama in the Twentieth Century*, Houndmills, Basingstoke: Macmillan.

—— (2016), *Theatre, Time and Temporality: Melting Clocks and Snapped Elastics*, Bristol: Intellect.

Wesker, Arnold (1965), 'Let battle commence' (1958), in C. Marowitz, T. Milne and O. Hale (eds), *The Encore Reader*, London: Methuen, pp. 96–103.

—— (1967), 'An interview given to Simon Trussler', in C. Marowitz and S. Trussler (eds), *Theatre at Work: Playwrights and Productions in the Modern British Theatre*, New York: Hill and Wang, pp. 78–95.

—— (1970), *Fears of Fragmentation*, London: Jonathan Cape.

—— (1973–4), 'Arnold Wesker and John Dexter talking to Ronald Hayman', *Transatlantic Review*, 48, Winter, pp. 89–99.

—— (1990a), *Arnold Wesker: Volume 1*, London: Penguin.

—— (1990b), *Arnold Wesker: Volume 2*, London: Penguin.

—— (1990c), *Arnold Wesker: Volume 3*, London: Penguin.

—— (1990d), *Arnold Wesker: Volume 4*, London: Penguin.

—— (1990e), *Arnold Wesker: Volume 6*, London: Penguin.

—— (1994), *Arnold Wesker: Volume 7*, London: Penguin.

Wesker, Arnold Papers (AW) (1989a), Author's notes for cast of *Beorhtel's Hill*, in Towngate Theatre Programme, n. pag, Austin, Texas: Harry Ransom Center, Box 14.11.

—— (1989b), 'Theatre director's letter' by Anamaria Wills, in Towngate Theatre Programme for *Beorhtel's Hill*, n.pag, Austin, Texas: Harry Ransom Center, Box 14.11.

Williams, Raymond (1976), *Keywords: A Vocabulary of Culture and Society*, London: Fontana.

Contributors

LAWRENCE BLACK is Professor of Modern History at the University of York, UK. He has written and edited six books on post-1945 British political and cultural history, most recently *Reassessing 1970s Britain* (Manchester University Press, 2015) with Pat Thane and Hugh Pemberton. His research has been published in *Historical Research*, *Journal of British Studies*, *International Labor and Working-Class History*, *Historical Journal* and *History Workshop Journal*. He is currently chair of the editorial board of *Twentieth Century British History*. In the United States, he has been a Fulbright Visiting Professor at Westminster College, a Fellow at the Center for European Studies at Harvard and a Visiting Professor at Duke University and American University, DC; in the United Kingdom, he lectured at Durham University and Bristol University.

* * *

EDWARD BONDT is widely regarded as the United Kingdom's greatest living playwright and has been influential on subsequent generations of dramatists, including Sarah Kane, Mark Ravenhill and Simon Stephens. His plays include *The Pope's Wedding* (Royal Court Theatre, 1962), *Saved* (Royal Court, 1965), *Early Morning* (Royal Court, 1968), *Lear* (Royal Court, 1971), *The Sea* (Royal Court, 1973), *The Fool* (Royal Court, 1975), *The Woman* (National Theatre, 1978), *Restoration* (Royal Court, 1981) and *The War Plays* (RSC at the Barbican Pit, 1985).

* * *

JOHN BULL is Emeritus Professor of Film and Theatre at the University of Reading, and from 2012 to 2020 he was Visiting Professor of Drama at the University of Lincoln. He has published widely on modern and contemporary theatre, including *New British Political Dramatists* (1984) and *Stage Right: Crisis and Recovery in Contemporary British Mainstream Theatre* (1994). He is the editor of the three-volume series *British and Irish Playwrights Since World War II* (2000–5) and co-series editor of the three-volume series *From Fringe to Mainstream: British Theatre Companies* (2016–17) and is responsible for the first volume covering the years 1965–79.

* * *

HARRY DERBYSHIRE teaches Drama and English Literature at the University of Greenwich. He has published on Harold Pinter as celebrity, Pinter and style, Pinter and London and the reception of Pinter's *Moonlight* (1993); in other articles, he has considered theatre and human rights and the work of Edward Bond, Caryl Churchill and Roy Williams.

* * *

ANNE ETIENNE lectures in Modern and Contemporary Drama in the School of English, University College Cork. She has published widely on theatre censorship and is the main author of *Theatre Censorship: From Walpole to Wilson* (Oxford University Press, 2007). She has translated Arnold Wesker's *Shylock* (1976) and co-edited a special issue of *Coup de théâtre* (2014) on this play, and written Wesker's profile for the volume *British and Irish Playwrights since World War II*. Her research on contemporary Irish drama focuses on the work of Corcadorca Theatre Company, as illustrated in her co-edited volume *Populating the Stage: Contemporary Irish Theatre* (Palgrave, 2017).

* * *

MICHAEL FRY has had senior lecturing and management posts across universities and conservatoires in the United Kingdom and the United States. He currently teaches acting and directing at the Central School of Speech and Drama, Drama Studio London and is on the higher education faculty at Shakespeare's Globe. He has been artistic director of three UK theatre companies, and his plays and adaptations have been performed across five continents. His recent production work includes Anton Chekhov's *Three Sisters* at the Clarence Brown Theatre, Tennessee. His recent chapters include 'Theatre de Complicite' in *British Theatre Companies* (Bloomsbury, 2015) and 'Researching the Method' in *Journal of Adaptation in Film and Performance* (2008).

* * *

PAMELA HOWARD, OBE, is a Director and Scenographer working primarily in opera and contemporary music theatre. She is the author of *What Is Scenography?* (3rd edn. Routledge, 2019). She holds the International Chair in Drama at Royal Welsh College of Music and Drama and is Visiting Professor at Arts University Bournemouth and Professor Emeritus at the University of the Arts London.

* * *

JAMES MACDONALD is a British theatre and film director. He was associate and deputy director of the Royal Court from 1992 to 2006. He is best known for his work with contemporary writers such as Caryl Churchill, Martin Crimp and Sarah Kane. Since leaving the Royal Court in 2007, Macdonald has worked extensively in New York and in most of the major theatres across London and the West End.

* * *

CHRIS MEGSON is Reader in Drama and Theatre and Director of the Centre for Contemporary British Theatre at Royal Holloway College, University of London.

His research focuses on post-war and contemporary British playwriting, documentary and verbatim theatre and theatre and religion. His publications include *Get Real: Documentary Theatre Past and Present* (co-edited with Alison Forsyth; Palgrave Macmillan, 2009) and *Decades of Modern British Playwriting: The 1970s – Voices, Documents, New Interpretations* (Methuen Drama, 2012), and, more recently, he has authored numerous essays on twenty-first century playwriting and religion.

* * *

GRAHAM SAUNDERS is Allardyce Nicoll Professor of Drama in the Department of Theatre and Drama Arts at the University of Birmingham. He is the author of *Love Me or Kill Me: Sarah Kane and the Theatre of Extremes* (Manchester: MUP, 2002), *About Kane: The Playwright and the Work* (London: Faber 2009), *Patrick Marber's Closer* (Continuum, 2008) and *British Theatre Companies 1980–1994* (Methuen, 2015). He is the co-editor of *Cool Britannia: Political Theatre in the 1990s* (Palgrave, 2008) and *Sarah Kane in Context* (MUP, 2010). His latest monograph, *Elizabethan and Jacobean Reappropriation in Contemporary British Drama: 'Upstart Crows'*, was published by Palgrave in 2017. He is currently one of the co-investigators on a three-year AHRC-funded project *Harold Pinter: Histories and Legacies*. He is also a series co-editor for Routledge's *Modern and Contemporary Dramatists: Stage and Screen*.

* * *

SUE VICE is Professor of English Literature at the University of Sheffield, where she teaches contemporary literature, film and Holocaust studies. Her most recent publications include the monograph *Textual Deceptions: False Memoirs and Literary Hoaxes in the Contemporary Era* (Edinburgh University Press, 2014) and the co-authored study *Barry Hines: 'Kes', 'Threads' and Beyond*, with David Forrest (Manchester University Press, 2017). She is currently working on a book about rescue and resistance in Claude Lanzmann's *Shoah* outtakes.

* * *

ROBERT WILCHER lectured in Sierra Leone before joining the staff of the English Department at the University of Birmingham in 1972. He retired as Reader in Early Modern Studies in 2007 and is an Honorary Fellow of the Shakespeare Institute. His publications include *Andrew Marvell* (Cambridge University Press, 1985), *Understanding Arnold Wesker* (University of South Carolina Press, 1991), *The Writing of Royalism 1628–1660* (Cambridge University Press, 2001), *The Discontented Cavalier: The Work of Sir John Suckling in Its Social, Religious, Political, and Literary Contexts* (University of Delaware Press, 2007) and *Henry Vaughan and the Usk Valley*, co-edited with Elizabeth Siberry (Logaston Press, 2016). He has published articles and chapters on Shakespeare, Milton, Quarles, Marvell, Vaughan, *Eikon Basilike*, Lucy Hutchinson, Abraham Cowley, along with other modern playwrights, such as Beckett, Wesker, Stoppard and Rudkin. He is the co-editor of *The Works of Henry Vaughan*, 3 vols. (Oxford University Press, 2018).

Index

The letter *f* following an entry denotes a page that includes a figure.